UNDERSTANDING
AND
INFLUENCING
HUMAN BEHAVIOR

UNDERSTANDING AND INFLUENCING HUMAN BEHAVIOR

G. HUGH RUSSELL, Ph. D.
Professor of Management
Georgia State University

KENNETH BLACK, JR., Ph. D.
Dean, College of Business Administration
Georgia State University

Prentice-Hall, Inc., Englewood Cliffs, N.J. 07632

Library of Congress Cataloging in Publication Data

Russell, George Hugh
    Understanding and influencing human behavior.

    Includes bibliographical references and index.
    1. Psychology, Industrial. 2. Socialization.
3. Human behavior. I. Black, Kenneth, joint
author. II. Title.
HF5548.8.R87   158.7   80-26218
ISBN 0-13-936674-1

Prentice-Hall Series in Security and Insurance
Kenneth Black, Jr., *Consulting Editor*

Editorial/production supervision and interior design by Natalie Krivanek
Cover design by Jerry Pfeifer
Manufacturing buyer: Gordon Osbourne

Printed in the United States of America

10 9 8 7 6 5 4 3 2 1

PRENTICE-HALL INTERNATIONAL, INC., *London*
PRENTICE-HALL OF AUSTRALIA PTY. LIMITED, *Sydney*
PRENTICE-HALL OF CANADA, LTD., *Toronto*
PRENTICE-HALL OF INDIA PRIVATE LIMITED, *New Delhi*
PRENTICE-HALL OF JAPAN, INC., *Tokyo*
PRENTICE-HALL OF SOUTHEAST ASIA PTE. LTD., *Singapore*
WHITEHALL BOOKS LIMITED, *Wellington, New Zealand*

CONTENTS

2

UNDERSTANDING OUR MANY SELVES AND THEIR INFLUENCE   20

3

SOCIALIZATION AND PERSONAL IDENTITY   41

4

SOCIALIZATION AND INDIVIDUAL FREEDOM

5

SELF-MOTIVATION

6

THE FREEDOM AND COMPLEXITY OF CHOICE

135

PREFACE

Ours is the Age of Anxiety. Or is it the Age of Uncertainty? It is definitely the Age of Rapid Change. It is the Atomic Age. It is the Age of the Counterculture, the Third World, and the Computer. It is an age when basic morals seem to be changing, the world is running out of energy, and business and government leaders score low on a scale of trust. New words such as stagflation and unisex remind us of the socioeconomic evolution which seems to keep us slightly off balance. And yet we hear that "People are people." "Things are pretty much the same." "History repeats itself."

Not many of us attend summit conferences, lead revolutions, or form worldwide business conglomerates. Most of us get up in the morning and fill our day with the details of child rearing, manufacturing, servicing, selling, governing, teaching, performing, creating, and playing. We get through the day with some mixture of success and failure, joy and sadness, growth and decay. We look forward to the same old thing and know there will also be surprises. Sameness and change. Security and insecurity. Gains and losses.

But a basic drive is the desire to "get ahead—to be a little better off this year than last." Inflation is disheartening because it seems as if we may be slipping back. How can we plan to make the best use of our money and time? Which investments will be best? Should I change jobs now? How can I get a raise? What can I do to increase sales, profits, production? What will motivate my customers to buy more, my students to learn, my children to behave, my spouse to pay attention to me, my subordinates to make fewer mistakes, my boss to recognize my worth? How can I predict what people will do so that I have a little more control over my life? If only I could get others to change, my life would be better. What can I do that will work?

We don't have the answers.

We do assume that the more accurate knowledge we have about people and the situations in which they live and work, the more precisely we can predict their behavior if we attempt certain methods of influence. We assume that the truth is more helpful than myth or vague generalizations. We believe the Scientific Method is a system of thought which generates reliable knowledge. Knowing ourselves, and the impact our self-image has on inspiring or depressing us, helps us reach the upper limits of our potential or mires us in the self-fulfilling prophecy of a loser. Our genes give us a start, but the largely invisible but powerful influence of our family, society, and culture molds our personality and infuses us with those values which inspire personal decisions and aspirations. Conforming to society's dictates while preserving a realm of personal freedom is a continuing struggle that deserves our best planning. Motivating ourselves to reach for responsible achievement is a complicated process. Using our creative talents and understanding the importance of meaning in our lives helps us develop those methods of influencing others most likely to be effective.

But knowledge of human behavior is power, and with power comes the ethical urgency of personal responsibility for our actions. We look up to the truly professional person because we feel trust, security, and courage that he or she will consider *our* needs to be paramount, and will do what is best for *us*. We can become a professional human being as we allow ourselves to be guided by ethical considerations and achieve greater sensitivity to the needs of others. Communication is that process that leads us to a fuller understanding of ourselves as well as those with whom we work and live. Whether we use this deeper understanding for mutual gain or individual exploitation is a choice we must make. It is not always an easy choice. It may not be a popular choice. We believe it can be a more responsible choice if we elect to be continuing students in the science of human behavior.

The authors would like to express their appreciation to Esther E. Russell for her careful and sensitive review of this manuscript, materially contributing to its quality and effectiveness. In addition, the authors would like to acknowledge the significant contributions of Victor A. Bary, Robert W. Cooper, Bobbi DeMarco, Dorothy Farley, Debra Fixter, Lee Pedrick, Rosemary Selby, Lynn Shafer, and Katheryn Woodley, all of the American College. Their very careful review of an earlier text, *Human Behavior In Business*, provided a major source of new insights in the preparation of this volume. Similarly, Professor Russel Fershleiser of the College of Insurance reviewed the entire manuscript and made many valuable suggestions and comments. Also, William H. Rabel and Margaret M. Walsh of the Life Office Management Association made a number of comments that were helpful.

G. HUGH RUSSELL
KENNETH BLACK, JR.

1

METHODS
OF UNDERSTANDING

*If any man can convince me and bring home to me that
I do not think or act aright, gladly will I change; for
I search after truth, by which man never yet was harmed.*

MARCUS AURELIUS*

*I speak truth, not so much as I would, but as much as
I dare; and I dare a little the more, as I grow older.*

MONTAIGNE**

Human kind cannot bear very much reality.

T. S. ELIOT***

The scene is solemn. The setting formal. Human lives are involved. The outcome may affect many people for years to come. The witness is asked to stand, to place the left hand on the Bible, and to raise the right hand.

"Do you solemnly swear to tell the truth, the whole truth, and nothing but the truth, so help you, God?"
"I do."

Meditations, VI, 3.
**Of Repentance*, Chapter 2.
***Murder in the Cathedral.* Copyright 1935 by Harcourt Brace Jovanovich, Inc.; renewed 1963 by T.S. Eliot.

1

The truth is important to us, whether we testify under oath in a court of law or exchange information in daily conversations. We need accurate information to solve our problems daily, whether in management, marriage, sales and marketing, child rearing, or research. If, under oath, we willingly and knowingly tell an untruth, it's perjury. If it is discovered, we could lose our freedom for a time, as well as suffer embarrassment or loss of our good reputation. If we don't realize we are swearing falsely and tell only part of the truth—or little truth at all—that's human nature, and we get off scot-free. Free of penalty in the courtroom, perhaps, but hardly free of the consequences. Innocent men and women have been convicted because of false testimony, whether given willingly or unknowingly. Usually, both the defendant and the plaintiff hire specialists to search out the relevant facts of the case. These facts may bolster or contradict the testimony given. Based on the "truth," the judge and jury make a judgment which influences the future behavior of those involved.

Outside the courtroom we all testify every day, to ourselves and others. We may not have taken a formal oath, but it is generally understood that we are telling the truth. We take for granted that most of what we read or hear is the truth. Our political, social, and business organizations could not function without the general assumption that most people tell the truth about their activities and intentions most of the time. We rely on the general accuracy of published airline schedules and telephone directories. When someone tells us the time of day, we behave as if it were accurate, at least within a minute or two. The voting record of our elected officials may be reported in the newspapers and certainly in the Congressional Record. We pay insurance premiums, believing in the truthfulness of the printed insurance policy; we trust the banks to return our money on request; we believe our payments to the pension fund will be returned to us as income for retirement. We don't bother to weigh the butter we buy to make sure it has the full pound the package says it does, and we assume we receive a full gallon of gasoline if the meter indicates it. Our socioeconomic systems, in government and private enterprise, work most of the time because most of the information exchanged is accurate.

Most of the time we tell the truth and receive truth from others. But *most* of the time is sometimes not good enough. Not good enough at all! An untruth can cause heartache, political upheaval, miscarriages of justice, loss of profit, bankruptcy, lost opportunities, and even premature death. Of course, an untruth may benefit some at the expense of others. People do tell lies to escape punishment or gain special advantage. Printed information may be deliberately false to mislead and deceive. Some may lie and obstruct justice to gain or retain positions of leadership, where their actions can affect millions. When we discover these distortions of the truth, we are dismayed and may wonder, "Who can you trust anymore?"; but most of us continue to function as cooperative members of our society. We depend upon regulatory bodies to check the fairness of weights and measures, the purity of foods and drugs, the solvency of financial institutions, the accuracy of advertising, the legality of employment practices, and the safety of the work place. Our lives may depend upon the truthfulness of the information we receive. Certainly our success in human relationships depends heavily upon our ability to distinguish truths from untruths. Each person's distinct personality and life style has been shaped by countless experiences and lessons, which were first learned in the family, then in the classroom, and later from continued experience and from self-education (such as reading on many subjects, including human behavior). How truthful has this influential information been? Can we depend upon the accuracy of information in current books on methods of successful management, selling, interpersonal relationships, marriage, and child rearing? Individually, we cannot possibly check on the accuracy of the information being offered as a helpful guide to better living. In a sense, the regulatory body doing this checking for us is the vast group of men and women actively researching and writing in the behavioral sciences. These psychologists, sociologists, anthropologists, physiologists, economists, and philosophers, each studying some small bit of the problem, collectively contribute to a continuously changing body of knowledge.

The accuracy of knowledge about human behavior is being checked and improved by scientists working under the assumptions and guidelines known as the scientific method. The history of science shows that current research often disproves previous work. What seemed true in 1950 can turn out to be partly false thirty years later. Just when we thought we understood something, new research shows us we didn't understand after all. Knowledge is increasing in both volume and accuracy, and so is our potential ability to understand ourselves, others, and the situations in which we find ourselves.

THE MYTH AND SCIENCE
OF HUMAN BEHAVIOR

How often do we falsely "testify," believing we are telling the truth? We may repeat something we have been told, not realizing it was untrue. Gossip is a good example. We hear, then pass on, some bit of intimate information about a neighbor or colleague without even thinking we should check it for accuracy. Or, we read a book or article and confidently say, "I read something the other day and here are the facts. . . ." There is something about the printed word, or the spoken report on television, that "rings true." Oh, yes, we are occasionally skeptical of what we read or hear, but then again we may not be.

Myths and superstitions play an important part in our lives. Myths, fables, and fairy tales can make entertaining reading; in the form of allegories, they are not literally true, but they may contain a truth or a moral. It is when we mistake a myth for reality that we create trouble for ourselves!

Myths and Superstitions Influence Our Lives

Most of us "know" that the number 13 is not really unlucky, but we feel a little more comfortable with a hotel room on the fourteenth floor. When we punch the button for our floor, we may not even realize that the numbers go from twelve to fourteen. There's no thirteenth floor? No, the only thing missing is a button marked "13." Similarly, we "know" that walking under a ladder isn't bad luck, but we walk around it just to be sure. In this case it may be not only superstition but good sense, especially if the worker standing on the ladder has a loose grip on the hammer or paintbrush. Breaking a mirror, having a black cat cross your path, and opening an umbrella inside the house are considered superstitious omens of bad luck. There are many examples of such superstitions. When we fear that talking about bad luck might make it happen, sometimes we knock on wood. It is not uncommon for someone to avoid talking about their recent successes for fear it will change the good luck to bad. "Bad luck comes in threes," so the saying goes. Throwing pennies in a fountain to improve luck is another one. Childhood games may be unconsciously continued by the adult who slightly adjusts the stride to avoid stepping on a crack. After all, who really wants to "break your mother's back"? And still another example: at a party we enjoy opening fortune cookies and reading our fortunes to each other. Laughter. But a moment of uneasiness follows if the fortune cookie's message can be associated with some of our own doubts or fears. The traveler uneasy about flying may feel a little better after purchasing flight insurance. On the way to the gate is a weighing machine which also tells a fortune. With the coin in the slot, the traveler reads the message, "A recent investment will soon pay off in rich dividends."

To many of us, myths and superstitions are things that other people believe. But if you or I believe certain myths and superstitions, we are likely to see them as reality and "good, hard common sense." We are influenced by our beliefs, whether or not these beliefs can be supported by any objective reality. Sometimes these believed myths can be called prejudices. Without supporting knowledge, or before knowledge is available, we form firm beliefs which alter our perception and influence our behavior. With our minds firmly made up, our ability to see the person or situation realistically may be quite limited. We tend to notice those events which support our prejudices and to ignore those which do not.

These are some of the myths we will be examining in this book:

> Women are not capable of being effective managers. Neither men nor women want to work for a female manager.
>
> Girls are more social than boys, more suggestible than boys, and have lower self-esteem. Boys are more analytic and have higher achievement motivation.
>
> You can do anything you think you can do and want to do badly enough.
>
> We know something is true if we have seen it with our own eyes.
>
> Business is business. You have to keep feelings out of it if you want to make sound, objective decisions.
>
> If kids go wrong, it's the parents who really are to blame.
>
> You can't teach an old dog new tricks. Older employees just won't change.
>
> If you're managing people and you want something done right, you have to do it yourself.
>
> You can eliminate confusion in communication if you write out the procedures. That way, everyone who reads it will get the same message.
>
> If two scientists report contradictory research findings, one of them has to be wrong.

These will not seem to be myths if your personal experience tells you they are truths. Experience *is* a teacher. We learn much by doing or seeing something ourselves. Some would contend that we cannot really know something unless we have experienced it. But there is danger in confusing our personal experience with a general principle which has wide application.

Anecdotal Evidence Lends False Credence to Myths and Superstitions

An anecdote is a story we tell concerning an experience we've had or we've heard from someone else. By telling the story we hope to prove a point. Here's one:

> I tell you I don't *ever* want to work for a female manager again. Why, this woman replaced my department manager and it was a disaster. She came in there and made life miserable for all of us. I think she was trying too hard. Trying to act like a man. Tellin' us what to do and givin' us orders right and left. I'm a man and I just don't like a woman tellin' me what to do. And the women didn't like her either. She checked up on us every day, and in less than two weeks she had fired three people. Sure, they were slow gettin' their work done, but they had been here for years!

The only time I ever saw her smile was when I asked for a transfer. I tell you, women are not capable of being effective managers. Neither men nor women want to work for a female manager.

From this one experience, our transferred employee has formed a generalization covering all female managers. Extensive research evidence to the contrary probably will be denied or ridiculed. "You can't tell me—I worked for one!" he might argue.

Anecdotes are often interesting, and they do *illustrate* a point or feeling. But as individual experiences, they do not *prove* a point or establish a principle. We often recognize that anecdotal evidence is on the way when we hear the beginning words, "The reason I know it's the truth is that I was in a situation once where . . ." Having a bad experience with our car may be enough evidence for us to convince others not only to avoid that model, but anything made by the same manufacturer. Unfortunately, we often judge people the same way. Hearing one bit of unfavorable information about an employee may be enough "evidence" to convince us to look elsewhere for someone to promote. If the situation were reversed and we knew that one bit of unfavorable information kept us from being considered for promotion, we would want to say, "Hey. Give me another chance. And besides, that information is out of context. Let me explain. . . ." Aristotle has been quoted as saying, "One swallow does not make a spring." In the same sense, anecdotal evidence does not create useful principles of human behavior. Instead, scientific principles are based on many observations.

The Nature of Scientific Knowledge

To the extent that we allow our biases and prejudices to distort our observation of reality, we are not scientific. If we observe only a limited number of cases and from these form general principles, we are not scientific. Scientific knowledge is that which is gained by following an objective, logical, and systematic method of analyzing problems or situations. The scientist forms conclusions about human behavior based on *large numbers of observations made under controlled and repeatable conditions.* As we increase the number of observations of any particular type of human behavior, the probability increases that our observed sample will accurately reflect the true underlying pattern of that behavior in the general population. These conclusions are checked by other scientists, following the same methods, to test the validity of the conclusions. Of course, the scientist doesn't stop being a real person with all the doubts, fears, aspirations, joys, disappointments, and successes which characterize most of us. But the scientist does use methods of observation which minimize bias and lead to the development of knowledge higher in reliability and validity than that obtained from casual, personal experiences.

While the process seems slow, behavioral scientists have been building up a structure of generalizations about human behavior which can be helpful in guiding our daily activities. Each time new generalizations are established, we increase our potential for new levels of success in selling, managing, motivating, communicating, growing, and living with satisfaction. A person is not a scientist because of a Ph.D. degree or because of employment in a laboratory. A scientist is one who uses the scientific method: a disciplined way of thinking is followed, and facts are gathered with integrity. A scientist reports all the relevant facts; the non-scientist lets wishes, fears, and hopes influence the facts reported. What is clear is that any person who wishes to be well informed and to base decisions and predictions on evidence rather than hunch can do so. Anyone can improve his or her accuracy in observing human behavior, in the depth of understanding of individuals or groups, and in the effectiveness of planning for the future. The method of observation and understanding is the critical issue.

THE SCIENTIFIC METHOD

The basic aim of any science is to develop theory. Theories are carefully worded statements specifying relations among variables that explain and predict what will happen. Theories of human behavior are being revised constantly to provide accurate statements about how and why people do what they do. The variables being studied are all those qualitative and quantitative measures of motivation, communication, socialization, beliefs and moral standards, and much more that reveal the ever changing nature of individuals. The scientific study of human behavior hopes to replace myth with truth. To do this requires that an exacting method be used.

The scientific method applicable to any field of knowledge can be described in a few simple steps, but the impact of using this method is far reaching. The science of human behavior is organized around principles obtained by:

1. Defining clearly a question or problem so that we know what we are trying to solve.
2. Obtaining all relevant facts relating to the problem and suggesting possible answers (hypotheses).
3. Checking each hypothesis by testing to see if it is a solution.
4. Repeating the entire process to be more certain of the results.

If the experiment or series of observations support the hypothesis each time it is repeated, we feel increasingly confident that the knowledge is reliable. If repeated studies do not support the hypothesis, then a new or revised hypothetical solution is stated and carefully tested. The process is an ongoing one.

Following the steps of the scientific method can help us be more honest with ourselves and others. We can find more constructive means of resolving the differences which inevitably arise when people live or work together. The scientific method can help us move away from superstition and toward reality, from costly trial and error toward efforts which are more often right the first time. Lack of sound information results in mis-information. If we are uninformed on the current knowledge about motivation or other subjects of human behavior, some of our beliefs may be erroneous; we would then have to operate in a person-to-person situation with misinformation or incomplete facts.

What is important to understand is that, even in the most careful and exhaustive research on human behavior or individual differences, our conclusions will be statements of *probability* and not statements of *certainty*. Past experiences in research aimed at finding differences between successful and unsuccessful people show trends and tendencies but show few, if any, absolute differences. For example, we may find that the average age of successful salespersons is 34 years old and that of un-successful salespersons is 31 years old. But the range of ages for both groups may be large. It could be that even with the difference in averages, one of the most successful may be 26 years old and some of the failures over 40. There is some probability that an older salesperson will be more successful than a younger one, although that probability may be small. It would be easy to jump to the conclusion that we should hire only those over age 34. If we did, we would still hire some who would not succeed, and we also would not hire some who would have succeeded. How can the scientific approach be of much help to us in this practical personnel-selection problem? Let's look at what we learn and how we gain by using the language of probability as a factor in decision making.

Individual Differences and Probability

The concept of probability is difficult to explain and may not interest us until we find out how much better off we can be by understanding and using it. Probability deals with the relative frequency of occurrence of an event: how often something occurs as a ratio of the total number of trials or observations. Coin tossing is a good example. We know that a coin tossed in the air will land either showing heads or tails. Since we assume there are only two equal possibilities, we say that the probability in any given toss of a head (or a tail) is 50/50, or 50 percent. That's the theoretical probability.

Calculating the probabilities of obtaining heads in coin tossing is simple. Calculating the probabilities which lead to useful generalizations about people, and differences between people, is far more complex and difficult. For one thing, a coin toss has only two possibilities. People behave in many different ways, depending upon their age, sex, education, race, religion, background, marital status, social class; human beings react strongly to their environment, and these differences produce even more variation in observed behavior. To understand the probabilities that people will react in a certain way given certain circumstances, they must be observed in action over long periods. The observed frequency with which people do things becomes our estimate of the probabilities that they will do those things about as often in the future, if all other conditions remain the same. If, over a period of several months, a salesperson sells something to about one-fourth of all the people approached, the observed frequency is one sale out of every four attempts, or 25 percent. Our best estimate for future sales is that the person has a 25 percent chance (or probability) of making a sale to the next person approached. Experience and training along with inspired sales management may operate to increase the probability to 30 or 40 percent. This is progress!

Males and Females Are Different. When we investigate how men and women differ in their ability to assume management positions, our measurements and research will not tell us that all men are better than all women, or vice versa. But our research will yield probabilities which can help us predict which men and which women should be considered for management responsibilities. We may find that men average higher on some tests of management talent, but we must know the probabilities involved.

What are the differences between men and women? Especially since 1966 with the founding of the National Organization for Women (NOW) and other feminist groups concerned with women's rights, this question is receiving considerable popular attention. There is a body of scientific research attempting to measure the physical, hormonal, emotional, attitudinal, and intellectual differences of the sexes from infancy through old age. Differences are found, argued about, and sometimes ignored or exaggerated, depending upon the predispositions of the individual doing the analyzing. The implications of showing basic differences or similarities in the capacity of women to function in previously male-dominated occupations are widespread. Some would argue, "Women just don't make good managers. They let their emotions get in the way. And besides, men don't like to work for a woman. Even women don't like to work for a woman." We may suspect that this argument would come mostly from men, but there are women who feel the same way. On the other hand, there is increasing evidence that some women function extremely well as engineers, attorneys, managers, military officers, judges, etc. Some women can, and some women can't. But some men can do well in those occupations and some cannot. What are the differences? What are the facts? How can we know what to believe when even scientific studies sometimes contradict each other? It would be helpful in developing a greater understanding of human behavior to look at how behavioral science attempts to define differences between men and women and how we should interpret the research findings when they are published. The interpretations will be in terms of various statements of probability.

Men Are Taller Than Women?   How do men and women differ? Let's start with an easy example. Men are taller than women. Right? On the *average,* that is right. But not all men are taller than all women.

It is obvious that many women are taller than many men. Hence, our generalization that men are taller than women is too easy, too simple, and too inaccurate.

While the differences between averages is important in understanding how men and women differ, the way in which individuals deviate from these averages is just as important. These deviations from the average are described by behavioral scientists in terms of statistical measures called *standard deviations.* As a convenience in describing just how individuals range away from the average, the standard deviation is utilized. For most human measurements, such as weight, height, intelligence, creativity, and many other mental and emotional qualities, there is a characteristic way in which people are distributed around the average. About 68 percent are within plus or minus one standard deviation, about 95 percent are within plus or minus two standard deviations, and 99 percent will fall within three standard deviations away from the mean.[1] In other words, about 68 percent of all men are within 2.7 inches of the average height of 69.2 inches, 95 percent fall within 5.4 inches of the average, and 99 percent will be between 61.1 inches and 77.3 inches. The distribution of women's heights away from their average follows the same principle. About 68 percent of all women are within 2.6 inches of the average height of 64.6 inches, and 99 percent are within the height range of 56.8 and 72.4 inches.

Men Are More Aggressive?   In scientific research concerning male-female differences, it is important to separate scientific fact from fancy concerning the behavioral attributes of structural sex differences. Consider the proposition that males are more aggressive than females. If we are considering only averages, this statement has some support in fact. But our speech habits may obscure the issue. What if we were to say, instead, that more males than females are aggressive?[2] Two different ways of saying it, but what a difference it makes in our thinking:

[1] Theoretically, the measurements would be distributed equally and symmetrically on either side of the mean or average. Actual physical or mental measurements of a group will vary somewhat from this theoretical model.

[2] Jessie Bernard, *Women, Wives, Mothers: Values and Options.* Chicago: Aldine, 1975.

1. Males are more aggressive than females.
2. More males than females are aggressive.

Statement 2 suggests that aggressiveness in a group of males may average higher than in a group of females; but, as with height measurements, there are some females who are more aggressive than some males.

We must acknowledge that we are talking about *groups,* not individuals. We are talking about *averages,* not *individual* measures. The average girl reared in the average family in the United States probably will be more passive and less aggressive than the average boy reared in the average family. What are the probabilities that an individual young woman will be aggressive enough to succeed in a management training program and have a successful career as an executive?

Valid and Reliable Measures

To begin to answer this question, we need a reliable and valid measure of aggressiveness and an adequate criterion of success in management. There are psychological tests which purport to measure aggressiveness. The *reliability* of a test is the consistency with which the test measures something. If we give the test to a person, and then if we repeat it, we might expect the test scores to be the same. This almost never happens. Of course, if the person remembered all the answers and repeated the answers from memory the second time, the scores could be identical. In practice, the reliability of a measure of a personality trait such as aggressiveness is examined in other ways. Two separate but similar forms of the same test are prepared and given to the same person. The reliability of the test is indicated by how similar are the scores on the two equivalent (nearly equivalent) forms of the test. Or, one test containing a number of items can be split in two, and then the reliability is the similarity between the scores on the split halves of the test. Perfect reliability in a psychological test is an ideal which is never attained. What this tells us is that a psychological test used to explore differences between the sexes may be something less than a consistent or reliable measure of the trait.

The *validity* of a test is an indication of how well the test measures what it is intended to measure. A test could be high in reliability but not be a valid measure of the trait in question. To see if a test is a valid measure of aggressiveness, we need some other measure of aggressiveness for comparison. We might ask trained judges of human behavior to observe a group of individuals and record examples of aggressive behavior. Those individuals who are observed to engage in aggressive behavior often can be compared to those who engage in aggressive behavior rarely or not at all. We then can give our test of aggressiveness to the "aggressive group" to see if they score higher on the psychological test of aggression than the "nonaggressive group." The more the test score corresponds with actual observed aggressive behavior, the more valid the test. Again, perfect validity of a psychological test is an ideal which is never realized in practice. Tests can be higher or lower in validity.

With our less-than-ideal test, we give it to *comparable* groups of men and women. But look at the additional complication. How can groups truly be comparable? We can try by attempting to obtain groups of men and women who are similar in age, education, social background, race, religion, marital status, and all the other possible characteristics of individuals. Remember, our aim is to compare the groups on the basis of their sex and nothing else.

To continue with our example, we may proceed to administer the test of aggressiveness to our two groups which are as comparable as we are able to find. We would not be too surprised to find that the average score of the male group would be higher than the female group. But we would certainly find, also, that some of the women score higher in aggressiveness than the average score for the group of men. And some of the men would score lower than the average score for the group of women. How does this help answer the question of whether men are more aggressive than women? As before, we more accurately reflect the situation if we say that more men than women are aggressive, rather than to say that men are more aggressive than women.

In scientific research we may find significant differences in averages between the behavior of males and females, but in dealing with a particular individual these group averages are of limited value. Every individual is an individual, and we cannot make the uncritical assumption that such group differences give us certain or definite information about any particular individual.

Scientific Knowledge Based on Probabilities

The body of scientific knowledge of human behavior and individual differences consists of a great many generalizations about groups of people. These generalizations are based on the use of psychological tests and other observations of less-than-perfect reliability and validity with groups not perfectly representative of the entire population. We can say many things about human behavior as long as we remember that we are dealing with *statements of probability* and not total *certainty*.

The next time you hear someone declare with certainty, "Women don't make good managers. They're just not aggressive enough," you might want to ask, "How can you be so sure?"

It would be cumbersome to use the word probability every time we make statements about some phase of human behavior. But it is important to remember that scientific findings on subjects such as the self-image, the socialization of the individual, conflict and conflict-resolution, motivation, and communication are probabilities, and we should react to them as such.

PREDICTING HUMAN BEHAVIOR

The person who thinks ahead and makes plans for the immediate or long-range future is making predictions based on assumptions. Each sentence you utter is based on countless predictions about how your words will be interpreted and reacted to by your listener. You dress a certain way because of predictions of the weather, your future comfort, the reaction of friends, the desire to please, and so forth. Now, most of these predictions are made and acted on without much conscious thought. You assume (predict) that you can leave home in the morning at the usual time and arrive at work on time. You have made predictions about the car starting, the bus arriving, the traffic being normal, no breakdowns occurring, and so forth. But it begins raining and all schedules are delayed. Your predictions did not work out because your assumptions were wrong.

The famed Murphy's Law states, in part, that if anything can go wrong, it will! That also is a prediction. Predictions are important in planning a successful life. But the importance of predictions is their accuracy. What are the chances that a prediction will be true? What are the probabilities? In determining the probabilities involved in human behavior, the behavioral sciences play an important role. Generally, the more we understand those factors or variables which influence behavior, the more accurate will be our predictions. The story of science involves careful efforts to obtain reliable knowledge about a subject which will allow the user of that knowledge to make predictions with higher and higher probabilities of accuracy. This is also the purpose of this book.

Predictions Based on Past Experience

We use the past to predict the future. This is not a bad idea if all of the relevant conditions of the past continue to exist in the future. Let's say I find myself in the hospital with pneumonia, and my physician walks into my room. After some exchange of questions and answers, I learn that I have a 95 percent chance of completely recovering without any complications and that I should be out of the hospital in less than a week. I feel reassured by this until later, when I begin to ponder the odds. My immediate assumption was that I was in the 95 percent group and not the 5 percent group with "complications," whatever that means!

The physician gave me those "odds" because, on the basis of past experience, 95 out of every 100 similar patients recovered without complications. What the physician didn't know, and what was bothering me, was which group *I* was in. But there is no way either my physician or I can know for certain what my chances are.

Chance, or probability, is a *group index,* not an *individual certainty.* Insurance companies can predict with high accuracy what percentage of 40-year-old women will live for 10 years more, or even 30 years more. But no one can know for sure how long a particular 40-year-old woman will live. Past frequency of occurrence of specific events is our basis for predicting future occurrence of the same type of events.

Improving Predictions of Behavior

In a lifetime any one individual is limited in the number of observations which can be made in a particular situation. For an example of observation and prediction which may have serious consequences, consider this situation: as a new branch manager, you have been concerned about recruiting people who can really sell. After two failures, you stumbled across a man recently retired from the Marine Corps. He was still in his forties, was attractive in appearance, and forceful in presenting his experience in commanding troops as a reason to hire him for the sales position. Since you had no other candidates at the time, and your regional manager was calling you weekly to find out when you were going to start building a sales team, you decided to take a chance. It took him less than a month to become familiar with the catalogue, and then he began selling! He seemed fearless in calling on new accounts, worked long hours, and began making your life much easier. Your confidence in your selection ability skyrocketed!

From that point, your recruiting had a new direction. One young sales candidate from the employment agency had what looked like a good sales record, but, when you asked him about previous military experience, he not only said, "No," but talked angrily about war and his disgust with the military mind. You immediately dropped him from consideration. Others you interviewed looked attractive enough in person and in their sales experience but had either limited or no military service. After much more searching, your next three hires were all retired military men, and one was a former Marine officer. A year later when all three recently hired salesmen failed, you felt you were back where you started.

What went wrong? There's no simple answer. The whole field of personnel selection is based on extensive research involving thousands of salespersons and a great many selection procedures. What scientific research emphasizes is that one example of a success, or a failure, is a precarious basis for predictions. But, it remains tempting to base judgments of people on one or two observations of their behavior. One friendly clerk gives you a good impression of the store. One cranky clerk may be enough to keep you away forever. One selfish act may lead to the conclusion that the person is always selfish. One careless driver on your trip through a strange town creates the impression that "Drivers in that town are reckless."

As long as our personal predictions are based on our limited personal experience, those predictions are likely to be low in accuracy. If we can borrow from the millions of observations from all of the behavioral sciences, we may find useful hints which can help us make more realistic predictions. In this way, we may more readily achieve success in marriage, friendships, management relationships, sales efforts, and all other activities in which we want to improve our achievements.

DIFFERENT KINDS OF UNDERSTANDING

An assumption of the behavioral sciences is that increasing our understanding of ourselves and others improves our ability to predict the future of our interactions. With greater understanding of our talents, aptitudes, and potentialities, we can plan our future with greater certainty of achieving individual self-fulfillment. Knowing ourselves gives us courage to try new activities and possibilities. The more we understand those with whom we live and work, the greater confidence we can feel in deciding whom we can or cannot trust. Friendship comes through a growing mutual understanding between people. Thinking that we understand someone may give us the feeling of security that we can count on them to be consistent. The consistency we see in others gives them a "personality" we identify and talk about when we describe them to others.

False Consistency

Our understanding of ourselves and others is faulty if we ascribe a consistency to patterns of behavior which is not warranted. Human beings are complex, complicated, and variable! It is perplexing and often uncomfortable to pay attention to all the differences and variations which exist in ourselves and others. Our tendency is to simplify. We label someone as "A good ol' boy" and tend to see only the good in him. Or we think of another person as "logical" and expect that everything done will be logical. Such simplistic thinking is common but not appropriate. It occurs because most of us are more comfortable with consistency than with inconsistency. Our tendency, then, may be to see consistency where it does not exist.

When we gain some degree of understanding of another person, we notice certain patterns in the things done or said: "I've got your number," we may think to ourselves. We believe, "It's a safe bet" that those patterns will be repeated. When it happens that our safe bet is wrong, we may think, "Why, I can't believe she did that," or "Well, that's not like him at all!" Recognizing patterns in behavior is useful. It is a generalization which helps us to understand. A deeper level of understanding is reached when we use generalizations *and* acknowledge and use observed exceptions to the patterns. Assuming a false consistency in human behavior prevents a more realistic understanding of it.[3]

Wouldn't it be nice to *really* understand how a person close to you thinks and feels? Not always. Understanding that your spouse doesn't love you any more may lead to predictions you would rather not accept. Overhearing a conversation about yourself may give you some understandings which hurt. Other understandings can be anxiety arousing. Learning that the birth control pill you took for ten years is now suspected of increasing the incidence of cancer can be frightening. Realizing that the high-cholesterol diet you've followed all your life may have caused irreversible damage to your heart and arteries is not a happy kind of understanding.

The science of human behavior increases our understanding, improves our predictions, and adds to the influence we have over future behavior; but we may not always like what that understanding does to us. We may choose to "forget" some information we've recently received. We may put aside an article or book before finishing it because we suspect we may read something we don't want to know. In fact, probably our most common reaction to bad news is to groan, "Oh, no." We may say "I can't believe it," not really because we lack the ability to comprehend, but because we would rather not understand it. But not understanding a fact does not change that fact.

Multiple Meanings of Understanding

The process of understanding is complicated. The word itself has multiple meanings. Reading the several definitions in *Webster's Third New International Dictionary,* unabridged, illustrates the shades of meaning conveyed by the word and also points to major areas of concern to us later in this book.

To understand means to grasp the *meaning* of what is being conveyed by the words or signs being used. Most words and signs have multiple meanings to the various people who receive them. Or use them. One of the

---

[3] Daryl J. Bem and Andrea Allen, "On Predicting Some of the People Some of the Time: The Search for Cross-situational Consistencies in Behavior," *Psychological Review,* 6 (1974).

meanings of the word *convey*, as in *convey meaning*, is to impart or communicate information either directly by clear statement or indirectly by suggestion, implication, gesture, attitude, behavior, or appearance. But two people are involved in this process. The sender of the message intends one meaning by the word thought of and spoken, but does the listener *interpret* that word with the same meaning? (We examine this problem in detail in Chapter 8.) The sender acts as if the intended meaning were conveyed, and the receiver acts as if the interpreted word were conveyed. For example, I tell you that I need some information from you "right away," and I intend the meaning, "Stop what you are doing instantly and get it!"

You hear that I want some information "right away," and you interpret the meaning, "As soon as I finish what I'm doing now, I'll obtain the information." Do we both understand the same thing? Obviously, not! The words "right away" conveyed information, but the meaning varied because of some differences between us. How can we be more sure that both of us understand the same message? Most of the following chapters will contain suggestions for reaching that level of understanding.

Another meaning of *understanding* is to grasp the *reason* or *logic* of a statement or situation. We may easily understand that a manager failed because of a lack of training or insufficient capital. But someone else's behavior may be hard to understand because we don't see any reason for it or because it doesn't make any sense to us. Do you understand why a book on human behavior is divided into chapters, even though behavior occurs only in whole? Does it seem reasonable to you?

To understand can also mean being able to *hear clearly*, or being able to make out the words. There may be so much noise around us that we cannot understand each other. Or if you are a Northerner, you may not understand a Southerner because of the accent. In each case, the word-sounds are there but are not understandable.

Understanding also means having a thorough or *technical familiarity* with the subject and developing expertness in the practice of using that understanding to become more competent in whatever we choose to do. To thoroughly "understand" any human being, we would need technical expertise in psychology, sociology, anthropology, physics, chemistry, biology, neurology, medicine, philosophy, theology, and much more. When you say that you "understand" your customers, employees, friends, etc., what is that level of understanding?

There is another sense in which we understand. When we know something or *accept it without its being mentioned*, we may think of it as being understood. It is understood that employees in an organization will follow established procedures unless permission is granted to do otherwise. Obviously, not all employees have the same understanding in this sense, either. We may *infer that something is true*, even though we don't have certain knowledge that it is so. Hearing a rumor about labor troubles is enough for a person to say, "I understand that there's going to be a strike next month." Or in still another way, we may *clarify certain conditions* by asking, "Am I to understand that you are disregarding the conditions of this contract?"

Knowledge is Power

This idea that knowledge gives power to its possessor has been stressed over the centuries by writers in the fields of science, politics, economics, religion, and all human endeavors. The doubling and redoubling of scientific knowledge available to humankind has accelerated our capacity to hurt and to heal, to destroy and build, to lengthen or shorten our life. We can use an increased understanding of human behavior for self-enhancing or self-defeating purposes. The better we understand our friends, family, business colleagues, and others, the more able we are to cooperate with them and confirm their sense of worth and dignity. Unfortunately, we can also use understanding to manipulate and hurt others. Ethical considerations and moral behavior are also part of our study of human behavior, *necessarily*.

SUMMARY

Sometimes the truth hurts. Rationally, we might agree that it is better to know the truth about people and situations, especially where the outcome is important. Emotionally, we may choose to believe in part of the truth as a means of protecting ourselves from being hurt. It is very human to both want and resist truth. The scientific method is a way of overcoming the all-too-human tendency to accept that truth which comforts us and to ignore or reject that which disturbs us.

The aim of science is to develop theory. Theories specify relations among variables with the purpose of explaining and predicting human behavior. The practical problems of selling, managing, marriage, child rearing, and getting along with people are often stated in terms of, "What will, or will not work?" The contributions of science are determining the probabilities that certain actions will be followed by certain consequences. While our personal needs may demand statements of *certainty* about what will motivate others, our predictions and ultimate control will depend upon statements of *probability* about how people might behave in certain situations.

QUESTIONS FOR REVIEW
AND DISCUSSION:

1.   Probabilities derived from research on human behavior in groups have limited value in guiding individuals in making decisions. Explain.

2.   How can the results of research help you to make important personal decisions in your life?

3.   In the personnel selection process, why doesn't a successful person with a specific employment background provide solid evidence that we should hire others with the exact same background experience?

4.   The words we use may not have the same meaning for others. What are the implications of this for the student of human behavior?

2

UNDERSTANDING OUR MANY SELVES AND THEIR INFLUENCE

Know thyself. *

                                                    SOCRATES*

This above all: to thine own self be true,
And it must follow, as the night the day,
Thou canst not then be false to any man. **

                                                    SHAKESPEARE**

The folly of that impossible precept, "Know thyself";
till it be translated into this partially possible one,
"Know what thou canst work at." ***

                                                    THOMAS CARLYLE***

Socrates was a shrewd observer of humankind. He saw that we had the capacity and the need to examine our own mind. He was a philosopher and a teacher. His technique of teaching is still used and is known as the "Socratic method." He asked questions. He asked what others meant when they used the words *truth, morality, patriotism.* "What do you mean by your*self*," he would ask. Now, 2,400 years later, this question is

Juvenal (Satire XI).
**Hamlet*, Act I, Scene 3.
***Sarton Resartus*, bk iii, Chapter 7.

still popular. What is the self? What is the self-image, and how does it influence our lives?[1]

As the title of this chapter suggests, we each have many selves. And each of these selves influences our behavior and that of others with whom we work, live, or play. The selves we are largely determine what we will do, whom we will love, when we will fail or succeed, how well we live, and when we will die. The human being is a self-examining animal, and the outcome of this self-examination helps determine the future.

THE SELF-IMAGE

How important is the self-image? It could be a matter of life or death! The image we have of ourselves influences what we think we are able to do. The salesperson who believes the sale will be made is more likely to be successful. The volunteer fund raiser who believes the quota will not be met will probably demonstrate a self-fulfilling prophesy. The recent heart-attack victim whose self-image is "I'm as good as ever" will probably over-exert and have another heart attack; this time it may be fatal.[2]

The image we have of ourselves *does influence* what we are able or willing to do, but it *does not determine* what we are able to do. How often have you said, "I can't see myself doing that," and not even tried? Or, after some thought, said to yourself, "I think I can see myself doing that," and then went on to exceed even your own expectations. When Roger Bannister first ran the mile in a fraction of a second under the "impossible four-minute barrier," a sports writer said that he had "opened the way" for other milers. The world record for the mile run, which had been on a plateau for nine years prior to Bannister's feat, was broken again less than a month later by John Landy, and since then the mile time has steadily dropped as dozens of athletes have run it in less than four minutes. Undoubtedly, Bannister's successors were better able to "see themselves" running faster than previously they had thought possible. But "seeing yourself" running the mile in less than four minutes is not the same as being *able* to run the mile in that time. Because someone has an

[1] For a recent statement on the importance of the self in the sciences of human behavior, see: Brewster M. Smith, "Perspectives on Self-hood," *American Psychologist,* vol. 33, 12(1978).

[2] The expectancy that a certain effort will result in a desired performance is a central concept in what is known as the Expectancy Theory of Motivation. For a comprehensive treatment of this theory, see: E.E. Lawler, *Motivation in Work Organizations.* (Monterey, Calif.: Brooks/Cole, 1973.) The extent to which individuals may attribute characteristics or causal relations to various objects as explanations for their appearance or behavior is considered in the Attribution Theory of Motivation. A discussion of this may be found in: B. Weiner, *Theories of Motivation: From Mechanism to Cognition.* (Chicago: Markham, 1972.)

image of being able to do something does not always mean it is possible.

A popular myth about self-image must be questioned: "You can do anything you really believe you can do and want to do badly enough." It is a myth because we do have physical and mental limits to our capabilities. Of course, we see these human limits extended with every meeting of the Olympic Games. And scientific breakthroughs in knowledge regularly occur through the increasing mental achievements of researchers. But the "Power of Positive Thinking" approach can lead to dangerous over-generalizations as well as to inspiring thoughts.

"Have faith in yourself and you will succeed" cries the promoter of all good things. "Dare to be great" was a theme attractive enough to persuade thousands of people to give up millions of dollars to a promoter who appealed to the emotions of the general public. The desire to believe in and to aspire to unreachable goals is very human, but it also can be very destructive. Consider the following true incident:

> Mary was a girl of average intelligence and the daughter of a physician and her Ph.D. husband. Mary's grade average of C in high school was an indication to her mother that Mary was just not trying. Her mother had talked about college since before Mary entered kindergarten. "You can do it," she would say each time Mary brought home a poor report card. And Mary believed her mother. Mary's reaction to her mother's beliefs was that her mother was right: she could do it if she tried hard enough. But try as hard as she could, Mary ended her high school career with a mediocre record. She felt guilt and remorse that she somehow didn't have the will power or self-discipline to get higher grades. She felt she was letting her parents down. Mary wanted to stay at home and continue working as a waitress, as she had been doing part-time, but her mother had convinced her that she should go to the best college that would accept her. Mary saw herself as an underachiever. She believed that all she needed to do was to live up to her own potential. Mary believed her mother, and she managed to believe that she should go to college, that she would do well in college and would even continue on to a graduate degree as her mother had done. She entered her freshman year with a new determination that she would live up to her mother's expectations. She believed she could do it. It was only a matter of will. A question of motivation. She tried. And she failed. She had no inner resources to accept this failure. . .there was nothing left, nothing to believe in! And she attempted suicide.

Suicide is one of the leading causes of death among teenagers. There are many different reasons for this ultimate act of self-destructiveness. Failure to live up to one's own expectations or the expectations of significant others is only one of many reasons why a teenager attempts suicide. But believing that one can accomplish something is far different from being able to do it. Unfortunately, the "positive mental attitude" which gives us the belief that "I can do it" may lead to a tragic result, as illustrated by the story of Mary and her mother.

On the other hand, believing that you cannot do something leads to a set of circumstances which dictates that you will do far less than you are capable of doing.[3] Do you remember when you were in a classroom—or a seminar or educational conference—and you wanted to ask a question? Did you decide not to ask the question for fear that others would think it was a stupid question or that they might laugh and make fun of you? Have you ever decided that a suggestion you wanted to make in a committee meeting probably wasn't worth mentioning, and, therefore, you failed to bring it up? And did you ever have the experience of hearing someone else bring up the same question or suggestion and seeing them praised for asking such a penetrating question or giving such a brilliant suggestion? And did you feel like kicking yourself? Well, join the crowd. Most of us have had that experience, not once but many times. Our self-image kept us from making a contribution. Our self-image kept us from making the most of our abilities. Kept us from learning, from exploring, from trying. Kept us from growing.

The Impact of the Self-Image

What an important concept. It inspires us to reach record heights. It moves us to utter despair. It influences what we are able to do, but it does not *determine* what we are able to do. What is this image we form of ourselves? What are its characteristics? How does it limit? How does it inspire? How can it be changed? How is it damaged? How can we control it and use it to our best advantage? How can we control our self-image rather than permit our self-image to control us?

Our assumption, in this book, is that you will come closer to becoming that individual you are capable of being if you know who you are, what your major talents are, what your self-enhancing and self-defeating attitudes are, and what work atmosphere allows you to do your best.

Do you know who you are? Do you wonder about your *self*? You probably have often said, "I know my own mind. I know what I want." But you have also said, "I'm beside myself!" Or, "I don't know how I feel about that." "I could kick myself!" "I don't know what's gotten into me." "I respect myself." "I care about myself." "I'm self-assertive, self-critical, sometimes self-doubting, but I'm self-sufficient and self-disciplined, too." You may be self-made and self-possessed; you may question yourself and believe in yourself at the same time.

[3] One theory of motivation suggests that a strong human need is to maintain a sense of *consistency* between what we think we can do and what we observe ourselves doing. For a discussion of the Consistency Theory of Motivation, see: Robert C. Beck, *Motivation: Theories and Principles*, (Englewood Cliffs, N.J.: Prentice-Hall, 1978), chap. 10.

Well, how many of you are there? While we may think of ourselves as one person, we are, more accurately, a committee. We are a number of selves. And how these selves agree or disagree with each other becomes the story of human behavior in organizations.

The Known and Unknown Self

There are some things we know about ourself and many things we don't know. Some parts of our self are conscious and some are unconscious, or beyond our awareness.[4] Freud used an iceberg as an analogy to help explain why we are often confused about who we really are. He said that like the iceberg we see only the tip of our own personality. Some small part of us is above the surface and visible. That is our conscious self. A larger part is hidden from our awareness. There is much that is subconscious, or below the ordinary level of awareness. But the iceberg is a whole entity. It is one piece of ice. Our personality also is unitary. It is whole. We are aware of part of it, and part of it we—consciously—know little about. What are the implications of this fact?

Imagine yourself as an iceberg. Figure 2-1 suggests that one-eighth of the entire being (iceberg) is above the surface. One-eighth of your personality is visible to you and is obvious. But seven-eighths of your psychic being is below the surface. It is unconscious. It is there but is not readily observable.

For example, you know why you bought your last car. But do you, really? Motivational researchers who use projective tests, in-depth interviews, and other research methods report that some men buy large, high-horsepowered cars because of an unconscious sense of sexual inadequacy. Because of a sense of frustration or insufficiency, some men overcompensate by buying an automobile which gives them a feeling of power, speed,

figure 2-1

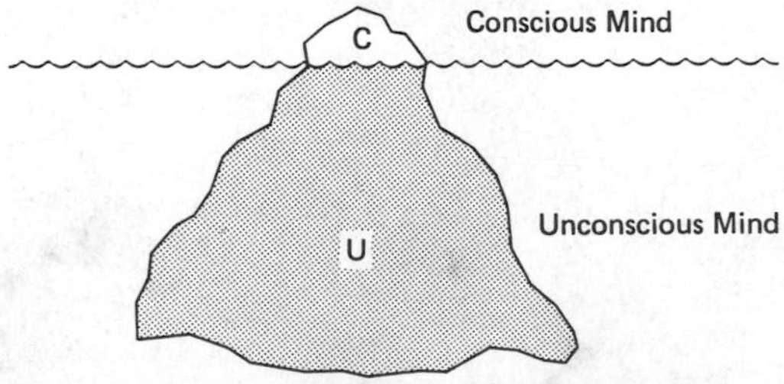

4 The "Johari Window," a model originated by Joseph Luft and Harry Ingram, can be used as a group exercise to help individuals disclose more of their known self to others and to obtain feedback from others to increase self-awareness. The reader is referred to: Joseph Luft, *Group Processes: An Introduction to Group Dynamics*, 2nd Edition. (Palo Alto: National Press Books, 1970).

and status security. Note that we are talking about *some* men, not *all* men. But even so, those who design advertisements for this year's models project the potential owner as being in charge, powerful, the owner of a castle or an estate, or as one so attractive that beautiful women are irresistibly drawn to him. Now, as an average male, do you consciously think of your own sexual adequacy when you approach the Cadillac or Lincoln dealer and look over the new line? Probably not. But you may be motivated by the unconscious appeal of the advertising, nonetheless.

Psychologists and psychiatrists know that their patients are often unaware of their motivations, needs, and aspirations. An overprotective mother may have unconscious feelings of hostility toward her children, but she may go to great length to demonstrate her concern for their welfare. She exaggerates her concern and protection for her children as one way of convincing herself that she not only has no negative feelings for them but actually has only the most positive, loving, and protective desires for their comfort.

A large amount of clinical observation and research evidence suggests that much of our behavior is determined by motives which are only partly conscious. The National Safety Council suggests that many automobile "crashes" are actually suicide attempts. Many single-car crashes involve individuals who consciously or unconsciously have a need to injure or kill themselves. Strange as it seems, the basic human need for self-preservation can be negated by a desire to no longer live. Our behavior is determined not only by needs and desires of which we are aware but also by motives of which we are either dimly or totally unaware.

Figure 2-2 helps illustrate some of the complications of trying to understand how two people manage to communicate with each other, consciously and unconsciously, self to self. Person A, an automobile salesman, consciously wants to communicate to Person B, a potential customer. A consciously tells B that owning the new model, "Le Master," will be a good investment because of the high trade-in value in the next few years. B hears this argument and feels good about it. A consciously emphasizes that "Le Master" is owned by young men who are rising in

figure 2-2

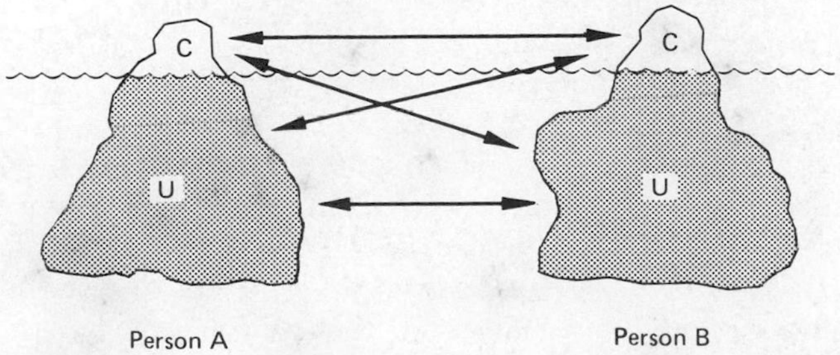

Person A Person B

the executive ranks. B consciously hears these words, but unconsciously fantasizes that owning "Le Master" will give him prestige ordinarily reserved for young executives. A is not aware that he has affected a haughty air in his description of "Le Master"; in fact, he has closed the door of the model and moved away out of an unconscious suspicion that B cannot really afford the car and so there is no point in continuing the sales talk.

B unconsciously detects this subtle rejection and responds, unconsciously, with the feeling that, "I'm as good as anybody, and I want to own a car that young executives drive." Without realizing it, B expresses stronger interest in "Le Master," which A consciously detects. A returns to the model and suggests that B come to his office and discuss financing.

Both A and B have engaged in conscious and unconscious communications and have mixed conscious and unconscious communication. Both A and B are interacting with a conscious and an unconscious self in the sales transaction. While this example illustrates these two parts of the self, we need to examine even more complicated aspects of the self-concept.

OUR MANY SELVES

A long-running television game show is called "To Tell The Truth." Three contestants answer questions from a panel, which tries to determine who is the "real" celebrity. The big moment comes when the master of ceremonies asks, "Will the real Mr. _____ please stand up." There is always some coy hesitation before the real person reveals his or her identity by standing. Frequently, a phrase from a TV show or commercial enters our language and becomes part of us. "Will the real 'person' please stand up," may become part of a conversation when an individual's multiple motives or social roles are being discussed. "Are you for us, or against us?" may be asked with humor or with anger. "What do you stand for, anyway?" may be hurled as a challenge in business, political, or marital debates. "Who are you really?" may be asked when duplicity is suspected.

"Will the real 'you' please stand up?"

"Will you reveal what you *really* believe?"

"Will you tell us what you *really* feel?"

"What are you *really* going to do?"

Reality is not a simple subject. Combine the concept of reality with the concept of self and we have an even greater complication. T. S. Eliot reminded us that "Humankind cannot bear very much reality." Well, let's see. "How do you like my new suit?" you ask your friend. "Do you really want to know?" he answers. Well! Now you're on your guard. Why is this "friend" asking me if I really want to know? "Of course, I want your honest opinion," you hear yourself saying. But, wait a minute. Do you *really* want to know what others think of you? And if you do *really* want to know what others think of you and they tell you, is what they say *really* what they mean? And, anyway, do the opinions of others define the self we are?

What is real is what is actual or true, not what we think is true. The real self can be thought of as the total iceberg (Figure 2-1). We are who we are as a result of an inheritance, a lifetime of experiences, a set of values and attitudes, and an exposure to multiple situations and opportunities. It is not hard to imagine that each adult reading this book has had millions of experiences, large and small, in his or her lifetime.

For the newborn infant, life begins as an explosion of sights, sounds, tastes, pressures, temperatures, feelings, pains, comforts, smells, and movements. The infant's internal chemical, neurological, hormonal, digestive, and homeostatic condition is affected by being breast or bottle fed. The infant is affected by all its early parental treatment. It responds to being handled with care or indifference, to being fed on demand or by schedules, and to being kept in a nursery or in the parents' room. Ashley Montagu, the anthropologist, maintains that this first series of experiences largely determines the infant's later capacity for love and a humanistic life. Every minute of our life is filled with experiences, some of which we are aware and some of which are unconscious.

The 40-year-old person reading this book has lived approximately 21 million of these minutes so far. These many experiences during our waking and sleeping states contribute to the self we are. Many of these experiences were beyond our conscious awareness at the time, and of course many of those early conscious experiences have long-since been "forgotten." There is some question as to how much of our lifetime of experiences are actually lost to our memory. Under hypnosis, individuals can recall childhood experiences which would otherwise be beyond conscious recollection.

Our perception of our selves is not the same as the real selves. But we often behave as if our perceptions were reality itself. Take any three eye-witnesses to an automobile crash and we are likely to hear three different testimonies. Three sober citizens witness a crash and see it from their different perspectives. By the time the investigating officer arrives, the three witnesses report versions which have changed during the elapsed time. When these three go home to their families, the version repeated there will change again. Two weeks later, or perhaps a year later, when called upon to testify in court, it will not be surprising to hear new variations on the original themes. Confront any of these three with the possibility that their own version may be slightly distorted, and you can expect to hear, "But I saw it with my own eyes!"

Perceptions may not be reality, but we behave as if they were. You perceive that buying the new car "Le Master" will make you the envy of the neighborhood and a hero in your own household. But the actual reactions may be very different: Your neighbor berates you for buying a gas guzzler during an oil-shortage crisis, and your righteous teenager picks up the theme, accusing you of being decadent. Your spouse complains that the big new car is hard to park. You discover that the servicing and repair costs are running twice as much as on your previous model. In a similar way, our perceptions of our selves may differ from what we would like to be, what we disclose to others, and how others see us.

Table 2-1 illustrates some of the complexities of the concept of self. It outlines six major ways of defining the self we are.

Real Self

Admittedly difficult to define, this self is the total of all we have experienced as well as our potential for continued growth. It is the self we are now, whether we are conscious of our whole being or not. It is made up of the self we have been in the past. The successes and failures, the joys and despairs, past injuries, recognitions, awards, losses, loves, and rejections. It is untapped talents and unforeseen needs latent within us, which push for satisfaction. It is the person we could be if only . . . if only we could be exposed to the right combinations of people, materials, money, and opportunity. We are unaware of much of this real self. As with the iceberg, much of our physical and psychic being is beyond our level of awareness. Part of that unconscious reservoir of experiences, memories, knowledge, and creative impulse is available on instant demand or recall. This portion of our unconscious available in the form of recall or recognition has been called the preconscious. For example, the manager faced with a conflict between an older and younger subordinate, both of whom are earning the same salary, can think back to see if any past event or experience contains hints on how to handle the present problem. The salesperson trying to answer an objection from a prospective customer may be able to delve into the unconscious storehouse of past selling experiences to select from previously successful responses. The young parent faced with absolute defiance from a 4-year-old child may try a strategy used by his or her grandparents years ago; the parent's behavior will be determined by remembered ideas and by other attitudes deeply buried in the unconscious. Research articles on the creative person frequently state that the highly creative person is "in tune" with his or her unconscious, having a greater capacity to retrieve information from the unconscious storage area. The individual who is able to cope with and reduce anxiety

table 2-1 **THE MANY SELVES WE ARE**

1	2	3	4	5	6
Real Self	**Perceived Self**	**Idealized Self**	**Disclosed Self**	**Disclosure Perceived by Others**	**Self as Believed by Others**
a. Self you are now	a. Self you think you are	a. Self you would like to be	a. Self you tend to disclose to others	a. Self others consciously see you disclosing	a. Self others consciously see you as being
b. Self you were	b. Self you think others see you as being	b. Self you would like others to see you as being	b. Self you unintentionally disclose to others (unconscious disclosure)	b. Self others see you unintentionally disclosing	b. Self others unconsciously see you as being
c. Self you can be		c. Self you think others would like you to be		c. Self others unconsciously see you as disclosing	c. Your total self as believed by others
		d. Self others would like you to be			

The self we are at any one moment depends on who the "others" are and what the situation is.

is more able to draw from an unconscious source than the individual overwhelmed by anxiety. In Chapters 5 and 6 we will examine ways in which we can increase our creativity and diminish our anxiety so that much more of our Real Self is available for productive problem solving.

Perceived Self

The self that we are consciously aware of is known as the *perceived self*. This self is always less than the *real self* simply because we are only aware of that tip of the self above the surface. But our perceived self varies depending upon the others around us at any given time. You see yourself one way while playing golf with your regular foursome. You see yourself in another way while holding your child on your lap. Another self you are aware of goes to work in the morning, acts like the proper boss in delegating work to your subordinates, and accepts directions from your immediate superior. Your consciously perceived self feels nervous just before giving a speech. You see yourself as being inadequate in accepting the chairmanship of the community fund-raising drive; but—as you see how readily friends and acquaintances accept your invitation to serve on various teams and committees—you begin to see yourself as being more successful than previous chairpersons. You may see yourself as being well informed on the important statistics of the American and National baseball leagues, but as inept in discussing the merits of an opera star. Your *perceived self* depends upon whether you are male or female, black or white, Protestant, Catholic, or Jewish, employed or unemployed, rich or poor, and so on.

This image you have of yourself has a long history. You build this image over a period of years, and it is formed mainly because of the way people have responded to you in the past. If your parents did not love you as a child, or if you grew up without parents, as an adult you may have a feeling of low self-regard, a feeling that no one could possibly be interested in you.

You do certain things and avoid some because of others' reactions to your behavior. Generally, you behave in a way which gives you pleasure or satisfaction and avoid behaving in a way which decreases your satisfaction. You thus establish a kind of equilibrium in your behavior. You behave within certain rather well-established limits. It is our behavior within these limits that we think of as "ourselves." This is what people refer to when they speak of our "personality." You behave the way you do because you think it is consistent with the picture you have of yourself and with the picture you want others to have of you.

By the time you are an adult, you have achieved a self-image which is relatively stable and consistent. People who know you can rather easily predict your behavior, and you know pretty much what you will or will not do. As you grow older, you are likely to become less adventuresome and less prone to behave in a way which is grossly inconsistent with your self-image. The common expression "I just can't see myself doing that" reflects this tendency to restrict our behavior in accordance with the picture we have of ourselves.

Whatever your self-image happens to be, one thing is clear: you are the most important person in your life. If someone has taken a photograph of you in a group and shows you a copy, your gaze centers immediately on the picture of yourself. You may look casually at the other people in the photo, but when you locate your image, your attention is riveted to this spot. This does not mean that you do not have genuine feelings of regard and interest in others. It does suggest that you spend more time thinking, being concerned about, protecting, and satisfying yourself than you do about any other person. This does not diminish the stature of being human, but it emphasizes the natural and inevitable self-centeredness of our existence.

Idealized Self

A third definition of self centers around the ideals we have developed over the years. We would like to have an image of our self which is better than, or at least different from, what we now have. For a variety of reasons, we would like to see ourselves as being more charming, generous, thrifty, persuasive, loving, intelligent, and so forth. This *idealized self* we would like to be may not be the same as that self which we would like others to see us as being (compare 3a and 3b in Table 2-1). We may wish that we could feel supremely confident and sure of ourselves but want others to see us as being humble and open to suggestions. Still another different *idealized self* is that which we think others *want* us to be (3c, Table 2-1). Our belief that our parents want us to be cautious, conservative, and quiet-spoken may encourage us to act that way in their presence. But what if the self-image they envision for us actually includes taking the initiative more often, trying new things, and being more assertive (3d, Table 2-1)? The idealized images we have of ourselves may often conflict with each other.

The self we would like to be depends somewhat upon the person or persons to whom we are reacting at the moment. In the presence of our boss, we may think of our *idealized self* as being assertive, objective, cool under pressure, unemotional, and utterly self-confident. With our spouse, we may find these same qualities creating friction, so deference, dependence, and emotional involvement may be uppermost in our idealized concept of self. As a parent our *idealized self* may be still different. Do we have the self-image of the perfect parent, or do we see ourselves as a failure? We ask ourselves questions and agonize or exult over the answers. For example, what kind of parent are you? Are you spending enough time with your children? Are you doing everything for them you should? Do you like one more than the others? If so, how do you feel about that? Do you pretend you like them equally, do you admit one is your favorite? Do you think, ideally, you should be more religious so you can set a better example for them? Should you stop smoking or drinking in order to be closer to your idealized image of yourself as a parent?

What happens now if there is a difference between the self you perceive yourself to be and the self you would like to be? The possible reactions can range from feelings of guilt to active efforts to organize your time so that you can more often do those things which are consistent with your idealized self.

The self you would like others to see you as being will likewise vary depending upon who those others are. How many people are influential in your life? Two? Five? Fifty? To some extent, your desire to please each of these significant people tends to shape that image you know of as your self.

Here, too, is a potential conflict. The self *you* would like others to see you as being may not be the same as the self *you think* those others would like you to be. What you want and what you think others want for you can motivate you in conflicting directions. Perhaps you would like your manager at work to think of you as a daring and enterprising salesperson ready to try new techniques that will produce a breakthrough in market penetration. But you also believe your manager would like you to pay attention, listen to directions, and do the standard things which have been successful in the past. The difference in these two self-images may lead to feelings of resentment. But suppose that what your manager really wants is to see you generally follow standard procedures. However, he or she probably would also like to think you are occasionally ready to try some imaginative sales approaches (3d, Table 2-1). The salesperson you would like to be, the one you would like your manager to think you are, the salesperson you think your manager would like you to be, and the one your manager actually wants you to be can represent four different self-images. A significant lack of agreement among these four views of your self as a salesperson can create problems of communication, coordination, and goal achievement in your work situation. Do you think your situation would improve if these four idealized selves were more similar? Would it help your manager to know your aspirations for changing your self-image? Would you be better off knowing what your manager wants you to do or be? We will have to postpone answers to these questions until we examine additional dimensions of the selves we are.

Disclosed Self

A fourth definition of self is that which we disclose to others. Just as we are aware of only part of our *real self*, so we probably will disclose only part of the self we are aware of. You know a great many things about yourself which you decide, for one reason or another, to keep to yourself. There are memories, feelings, judgments, and so forth that you may choose not to disclose or share with others. The psychologist, Sidney Jourard, has done extensive research on the readiness to disclose, relating it to one measure of mental health. He also suggests that physical ailments and disabilities may be related to low levels of self-disclosure, particularly among men. His research and that of others indicates that men typically reveal less about their personal lives than women. This lower level of self-disclosure may be associated with a greater tendency toward tension, suicide, cardiovascular disorders, and of course, loneliness.

We *intentionally* disclose selected aspects of our multiple selves to those with whom we work, play, and live. The details disclosed will vary depending upon how close we feel to the person, how much trust we feel, and on our judgment as to the appropriateness of the disclosure. Erving Goffman discusses this disclosure of self in terms of presenting a "line" and maintaining "face." The line a person presents is a combination of verbal and nonverbal expressions which discloses the views of self and judgments made of others. Maintaining "face" is defined as "the positive social value a person effectively claims for himself by the line others assume he has taken during a particular contact."[5] A person maintains face when the line being presented conveys an image which is internally consistent and which also is supported by the judgments and reactions of others. If you are presenting a line (for example, "I'm current") which includes the notion that you always keep current on the information in your field, and if someone then asks you to comment on a widely publicized controversy in your field that you have never even heard of, a loss of face results. But seeing your discomfort at losing face may make the other person feel uncomfortable, too. The other person may try to help you regain face by saying, "Gosh, as hard as I try to keep up with every little detail in my field, I am sometimes surprised, too." Because your line has not been fully supported by the reaction of the other person, you may decide to revise what you disclose in the future.

Sometimes we disclose information about ourselves without realizing it. We *unintentionally* reveal something we thought we were keeping to

[5] Erving Goffman, "On Face-Work: An Analysis of Ritual Elements in Social Interaction," *Psychiatry*, vol. 18, 3, (1955). For an extensive analysis of the concept of self and its relation to society, see: Erving Goffman, *Frame Analysis: An Essay on the Organization of Experience.* (Cambridge, Mass.: Harvard University Press, 1975).

ourselves. Imagine that you are being interviewed, along with others, for consideration as the next regional sales manager. It means a real promotion for you. Your line includes statements of confidence in your own ability, and you try to act calm and composed. But while you may not realize it, your hands are shaking, and you look strained. The person interviewing you perceives this disclosure of nervousness although you may have tried to conceal it. What are the consequences of a conflict between what you intended to disclose and what others perceive you as disclosing? Quite possibly a lowering of trust in the relationship.

We unintentionally disclose information about our selves for at least two reasons: (1) we want to conceal something, but don't quite succeed; or (2) we disclose some aspect of ourselves of which we are not even aware. In either case, others may perceive aspects of our self which influence their behavior and their responses to us, but we are unaware of why. In effect, we are unaware of part of the reality which surrounds and affects us.

Disclosure Perceived by Others

A fifth dimension of our selves is defined in terms of how others perceive us. Their perceptions and interpretations of our selves are based not on a certain knowledge of our *real self* or our *perceived self*—and not even on our *idealized* or *disclosed self*—but on information they receive from us. As in the discussion of understanding in Chapter 1, what we intentionally or unintentionally disclose in conversations is not the same as the information received by others. What I say and what you hear are likely to be different in significant ways. Others base their perceptions on the information they receive, not that which was sent. Others form some opinion of us depending upon what they perceive us disclosing intentionally and unintentionally, and they also form their opinion based on information they unconsciously receive and interpret. But what others perceive us as disclosing is not the same as the image they really have of us. Again we are referring to the *real self,* but this time as believed by others.

Self as Believed by Others

The sixth dimension of our selves is that total of all perceptions, beliefs, memories, and experiences others have accumulated about us. This is what others believe we are. And it is the basis of decisions and actions by others concerning us. As with our own self-images, what others believe about us is only partly conscious. Others react to us based on conscious beliefs but also on many unconscious beliefs, needs, and tendencies. This *real self* as perceived by others probably contains many misconceptions and gaps. It certainly would not correspond to the *real self* we began discussing in the first definition. But out of that collection of conscious and unconscious thoughts and impulses, others love us, reject us, support and injure us, hire or fire us, and generally make up the social environment which influences our own lives.

RESPONDING TO THE IMAGE
OTHERS HAVE OF US

Much of our behavior is strongly influenced by our intense desire to look favorable in the eyes of others. This can be both a negative and a positive kind of influence. If someone important to us has an uncomplimentary image of us, we may decide to prove that he or she is wrong by outdoing ourselves in achievement. Or we may react by saying to ourselves, "Well, I have the bad reputation; I might as well live up to it."

The father who cannot trust his child and conveys this feeling to the child probably will encourage rebellion and untrustworthy behavior. The manager who thinks of employees as being lazy and ungrateful may encourage those very attitudes if his or her opinion is recognized by the employees. Some outstanding managers seem to have the ability to appreciate more in their employees than they appreciate in themselves. This is not a false optimism. The manager simply holds the highest possible image of the employees. When this impression is conveyed to them, they quite often outdo themselves to live up to that expectation.

The expectations we have help determine how we perceive a person or situation. If we expect a business associate to turn down a suggestion we want to make, we are more likely to "see" reactions in his voice or behavior which seem disapproving of us. However, expecting that our suggestion will be liked may alter perceptions so that we overlook the person's actual lack of interest and assume that our suggestions will be supported. In other words, what we expect to see frequently determines what we do see. Even a highly experienced scientist recognizes this tendency and strictly follows the scientific method so that the scientist's perceptions are more in accord with reality.

The fear of something happening to our self-image not only affects how close we get to people but also determines how effective we are in influencing their behavior. Every time a salesperson talks to a prospect, there is the possibility of failure or success. When failure or frustration is experienced, it is possible for self-doubt to creep into the salesperson's mind. If we attempt to be friendly toward our neighbor, there is always a possibility that we will be told to mind our own business. If other people like us and respond to us favorably, we congratulate ourselves on being nice people. But if people respond to us unfavorably, or if we are hurt by others, we are likely to feel unsure of ourselves and wonder what kind of person we are.

Being well regarded by others is one of our most basic needs. We tend to live in a way that insures we will continue to be well regarded. The only way we know to do this is by living up to the picture of ourselves which we believe will most result in pleasing others. Having established this self-image through a process of receiving praise and punishment, none of us is too willing to change the way we behave. We have established an equilibrium in our behavior, and we don't want to "rock the boat." Thus, we develop a strong need to preserve our image, both outwardly and inwardly.

We need to avoid having our favorable "self-picture" disturbed. If we happen to stumble and fall while going up some steps, one of the first things we do is look around to see who saw us get into such an embarrassing position. We are concerned about how other people see us. We want to be sure that they get an "accurate" picture of us. What we usually mean by "accurate" is that we hope others see all our good points and overlook our weaknesses.

When someone criticizes us, the favorable picture that we have of ourselves and that we hope the person has of us is threatened. It is difficult to accept criticism because we would like to view ourselves as being above criticism or reproach. It is difficult because it means that someone else doesn't have quite the same high regard for us that we have. It hurts to be criticized. We may vigorously deny that we refuse to accept criticism, and we may protest that we really want people to tell us what they think of us, but it is still painful to have anyone disturb our self-image. How do you feel if you happen to overhear a conversation between two of your friends as they are discussing you? If you hear some unflattering things, you are likely to feel pretty deflated.

There is a way to avoid being hurt by other people and to avoid the incidents in life which threaten to alter or diminish the favorable picture we have of ourselves. We are not likely to be hurt or to have to change our self-image if we don't let ourselves get too "close" or too "involved" with others. We can hold people at arm's length, emotionally, and avoid being disturbed if they happen to do something which bothers us. We can avoid damage to our self-image if we keep people from getting to know us too well. Of course, we have to pay a price for this, because in addition to taking less risk of being hurt, there is much less chance of being loved.

We resort to a good bit of artificial behavior to keep people from getting too close to us or seeing through our defenses. But maintaining this distance from other people is expensive because it also keeps us from being known, appreciated, and even loved by them. This can become a kind of vicious circle. The fear of damage to our self-image can keep us from getting close to others, and failure to get close can result in frustration and loneliness, which in turn threaten us with the self-image of failure and prompt us to maintain even greater emotional distance.

If, however, we have the courage to expose our self-image to possible change and can move toward a challenge, we may find ourselves building a better and sounder self-image, one which simply needs less defending.

OVERCOMING THE TYRANNY
OF THE SELF-IMAGE

In a very real sense, we are tyrannized by the view we have of ourselves. Our behavior seems largely controlled by the scope and depth of our self-image. When we change our self-image, a wider range of behavior may open up, leading to greater self-fulfillment. But, again, risk is involved in the attempt to change and enlarge this view of the self. It takes strength and courage to experiment with a new and healthier self-picture.

The young child is often molded and perhaps oppressed by the reactions of important adults. The child learns to suppress spontaneous expressions of physical and emotional behavior because these often lead to rejection or disapproval from parents. He or she learns that sometimes it is not safe to "be myself" if one wants to keep the love or good will of one's parents. If this thinking continues into later life, it is easy to see why many adults are convinced that if people really knew them well they wouldn't like them. An adult may continue to have this childlike view of self even though it is no longer appropriate. The child, after all, is controlled and confined by the parents. Lacking mature decision-making powers and unable to leave the family, the child can do little but bow to the weight of parental approval or disapproval. Because the child is not yet able to make fine discriminations as to which feelings or behavior are permitted and which will be punished, the child is likely to overreact by suppressing spontaneous feelings. The child becomes guarded and fearful, censoring what is said to avoid disapproval. Some censorship is necessary to live in society; overcensorship can create problems later as an adult.

Adults can make fine distinctions between situations . . . if they will. They have the potential for avoiding inappropriate overgeneralizations . . . if they choose. If we are laughed at because of a question we have asked during a seminar, we can make the decision that those who laughed were inappropriate in their behavior, and we will be neither embarrassed nor deterred in asking further questions. But the "child-thinking adult" may assume that because others laughed he or she, therefore, is stupid (negative self-image) and that the others are right in their implied judgment. In a number of ways we can alter our thinking so that the image we have of ourselves can grow and expand to permit behavior which is healthy and satisfying instead of self-defeating.

The person in the seminar may not like being laughed at—and probably would prefer to avoid it—but he or she may also value learning something. And a question is one of the best ways of doing this. Using the ability to weigh values the person decides that it is appropriate to ask questions and inappropriate to laugh at someone's efforts to gain knowledge. Armed with this perspective, the person can say (or think) that those who laughed must have a problem! But the most important consequence of thinking as an adult instead of as a child is that self-improving behavior (asking the question) continues and self-defeating behavior (withdrawing in embarrassment and no longer speaking up) is resisted.

There are other ways of thinking to help overcome the tyranny of a too-narrow self-image. Is there anyone reading this book who has not done something foolish or made some kind of mistake? It is understandable to regret the mistake; it is inappropriate to let one mistake become the total measure of our worth. Having one accident does not mean that you are a poor driver. Preparing one unpalatable meal does not mean you are a poor cook. One mistake, one indiscretion, one foolish statement, does not mean that a person is an indiscreet fool. Tragically, many do feel that one mistake brands the man. From Shakespeare's *Julius Caesar* we read: "The evil that men do lives after them, the good is oft interred with their bones."

We can protect our self-image if at the time we make a mistake we remember our past successes. Life is a succession of events; the long-range view is important. In the same way it is appropriate to remember past mistakes at the time of a great success to help minimize delusions of grandeur.

The concept of seeking a larger perspective helps maintain a healthy, growing self-image. People who fail in business need not picture themselves as failures. Other facets of life are important, too. One may fail in business but be a success as a father, mother, husband, wife, friend, or companion. Implicit in this concept is the larger concept of the worth and dignity of any person just because he or she exists! The ultimate aim of each of these suggested ways of thinking about the self is the ability to like ourselves as the persons we are. And in an overall sense, this is one of the aims of this book.[6]

[6] The interested reader may want to explore research evidence on the relationship between self-esteem and work productivity: Edwin A. Locke, "The Nature and Causes of Job-Satisfaction," *Handbook of Industrial and Organizational Psychology*, Marvin D. Dunnette, ed. (Skokie, Ill.: Rand McNally, 1976), chap. 30.

Learning to like ourselves may sound, for some, like self-adulation or false pride. But Hillel, an early Hebrew sage, said, "If I am not for myself, who will be for me? If I am only for myself, what am I? If not now, when?" And from quite a different source comes a similar idea in the form of a prayer used by Alcoholics Anonymous: "God grant me the serenity to accept the things I cannot change, the courage to change those I can, and the wisdom to know the difference."

Self-acceptance is an important aim of the growing individual. It is the very essence of the scientific method discussed earlier: the acceptance of things as they are! It is the beginning for the person who wishes to improve. Self-acceptance does not mean complacency or relinquishing the desire to change. Self-acceptance means gaining the very perspective and foundation that allow for growth. The rational, mature human being begins each day by confronting the self one really is and accepting that self for what it is. Freed from the tyranny of having to deceive oneself, the self-accepting adult takes the next step toward becoming a full and whole human being. One seeks to expand one's value not only to others but, more importantly, to oneself!

SUMMARY

The image we have of ourselves does *influence* what we are able or willing to do, but it does not *determine* what we are able to do. What we see ourselves as being able to do may or may not be realistic, but our behavior is based largely on this image of ourselves. We have many selves, and each of them plays a part in influencing how we behave. Our *real* self is something of which we are only partially aware. The *whole* self has many components. There is the self we would like to be, the self we disclose to others, the self others perceive us as being, and the self others believe we are. All of these selves interact to produce our patterns of beliefs and actions. We respond both to the person we think we are and the person others think we are.

We begin our understanding of the uniqueness of individuals when we discover how our self-images influence our own behavior. We increase our ability to understand others when we know ourselves more fully. Knowing ourselves includes admitting that we often do things to avoid seeing ourselves as we are, thus helping to overcome the self-defeating tyranny of the self-image.

Much of what people do is aimed at pleasing others and being well regarded by them. A natural consequence of this strong need to please others is the tendency to cover up our *real* selves and present a *front* to others which we hope they will like. We try to avoid being hurt by not showing anyone who we really are. This avoidance of open, genuine contact may eliminate some pain, but it also inhibits the growth of the individual toward becoming a more loving and loved human being. We can learn to change our behavior and self-image so that we can more often achieve success in life.

QUESTIONS FOR REVIEW AND DISCUSSION

1.   The self-image limits but does not determine our behavior. Explain.

2.   Believing that you can do something may be self-defeating. Discuss.

3.   Self-disclosure may help us live healthier lives. How?

4.   Our self-image may tyrannize us. Think of an example from your own life and explain it.

5.   Self-acceptance may be the beginning of real change toward becoming a more mature adult. Discuss.

3

SOCIALIZATION AND PERSONAL IDENTITY

Man is a social animal.

SPINOZA*

'Tis education forms the common mind:
Just as the twig is bent the tree's inclined.

ALEXANDER POPE**

Accidents will occur in the best-regulated families.

CHARLES DICKENS***

You, as a unique individual, are a constantly changing blend of in-herited potentialities and of the socializing effects of your environment. The process by which you learn to behave as the individual you are, in a complex social environment, is called *socialization*. The mental and physical characteristics which were yours at birth have been shaped by the sociocultural events in your past and are being influenced by your present social and work situation. You are a product of your society, strongly

*Ethics, Part IV, Prop XXXV
**Moral Essays (1720-1735), Epistle I
***David Copperfield (New York: E.P. Dutton & Co., Inc., 1953).

influenced by your family and even by events taking place before you were conceived.

BECOMING AN INDIVIDUAL IS A SOCIAL EVENT

The way in which each of us becomes the unique individual we are is *shaped* by the influence our society has on us; this influence begins at least nine months before birth. The mother and father of the new human being came together for a variety of religious, economic, educational, legal, racial, moral or immoral, expedient or casual *social* reasons. The moment of conception is a social as well as genetic event that modifies the fetal environment. The hormonal levels of the mother during the first few months of pregnancy contribute to the feminization or masculinization of the child. Cigarette smoking, certain drugs, alcohol, and the pregnant mother's diet can affect the fetus. Emotional strain in the mother may affect the movements of the fetus in the uterus. The psychological state of the mother may result in her overexertion and possibly a miscarriage or in a deliberately induced abortion—an early end to the infant's social life.

Whether the birth is planned to take place in the home or hospital is a decision tinged by society's norms and the parents' values. There is a body of medical and psychological opinion that suggests that the amount of love felt and transmitted to the newborn has a strong bearing on the child's ability to receive and give love later in adult life. These, and other socially determined events, begin the process of influencing the way in which each individual grows into a person different from any other.

Other socially determined situations and conditions—and the responsibilities associated with them—further influence the personality and health of each individual. For example, a deficiency of protein in the baby's diet, especially in the first 18 months, may cause some degree of mental retardation. This is more likely to be the case in poverty-stricken families. Based on this relatively recent knowledge of protein deficiency and mental retardation, does society have any responsibility to provide an adequate diet to all infants? Certainly society will be called upon to provide help, perhaps lifelong care, for these early victims of an unfortunate interaction between the parents and their social environment. The race, educational level, ethnic background, and many other social influences operate to maintain some parents at a poverty level. The answers to these problems involve legal, economic, religious, emotional, and humanistic issues.

Every individual begins life with certain physical, emotional, and intellectual characteristics; a certain heredity. But the infant at birth is extremely adaptable and responsive to the cultural and social environment. Which is more important: heredity or environment? This is a continuing debate among genetic and social scientists. Both factors contribute to the uniqueness of each of us. We often hear someone called a "born leader" or a "born salesperson." Most social scientists would agree that one is not born with a certain level of excellence in any vocational field, but instead one learns from society those skills necessary to excel in sales, management, teaching, sciences, and so forth. But certain intellectual and physical characteristics are inherited which allow an individual to make superior use of specific training in a field of endeavor.

SOCIETY AND THE CULTURAL BACKGROUND

A *society* is an enduring and cooperative social group whose members have developed organized patterns of relationships through interaction with one another. *Culture* refers specifically to the values, ideas, and meanings we give to human social interaction. Society refers to a structure, an organization, a series of interactions. Culture refers to the meanings of these interactions and how they are expressed by the material possessions or artifacts of the group. Some of the groupings and characteristics of our society are presented in Figure 3-1.

In it, a dozen aspects of our society are shown as being intertwined. Each has an impact on the other. Your immediate family (nuclear family) comprises part of a social class that altogether has a certain amount of economic and social power. You are a member of a sex group that is a major factor in your psychological development and the socioeconomic opportunities available to you. Your recreational and leisure-time activities are an important part of your life, as are your racial and ethnic identity. The education you are able to obtain, and the governmental and legal interventions in your life, further contribute to your uniqueness. All of these social influences in your life are tempered by and sometimes conflict with your religious affiliation. These factors, and others too, make up our society.

The largely unseen but powerful influence of our culture helps determine how our *self* is formed and how we will react to our present and future circumstances. Culture and society are simply two different ways of looking at the individual engaged in social activities. The culture helps shape the way our society is organized and functions, and the societal interactions and transactions modify that cultural heritage, which is passed on to future generations. These two concepts of society and culture cannot be separated, and the term *sociocultural* is sometimes used to reflect this

figure 3-1   Society influences the individual

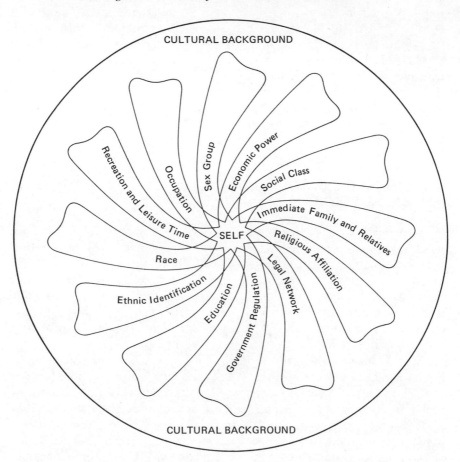

fact. Much of this sociocultural influence on the development of the self we are is obvious; but even more of this influence is subtle, unconscious, and invisible. Whether we see and understand these forces or not, their influence largely determines how we and the significant others we relate to will behave.

Our behavior, motivational patterns, modes of communication, and systems of religious, political, economic, and social beliefs are inexorably modified and guided by the sociocultural forces which surround us. We can become more responsible and self-determining individuals to the extent that we can make these unseen forces more visible. Becoming more aware of the sociocultural pressures on us may allow us to plan a life of self-fulfillment rather than becoming trapped in a self-defeating pattern.

If a traveler has a map of the territory, and can interpret the many symbols and signs posted along the way, the destination may be reached quickly and efficiently. But without the map, and an inability to read posted directions, the trip becomes an experience of frustration and despair. Let's look at the sociocultural map of the territory in which we live. Let's memorize some signs, symbols, and standard procedures. Let's try to understand how we have been shaped and molded so far and how we are pushed, pulled, twisted, and bent even now as we try to "get along" with ourselves and each other.

Culture Is Invisible

Does the fish know it is in the water? Probably not. Does the fish know that the worm is connected to a hook at the end of a line held by a human hand? Well, maybe some do. Or at least some may be wary of unusual conditions—a fishing line, the shadow of a boat— intruding on the environment. Does the human know it lives in a cultural sea? Does it see the connection between pollution of air and water and the hastening of human demise? Well, maybe some do. Does the mother see the connection between her permissive, indulgent treatment of her favorite child and the stormy, rebellious behavior of her teenager ten years later? Do city administrators grasp the connection between increased oppression of disadvantaged groups in the inner city and the subsequent riots and burnings? Can we understand why low-income families are less likely to come in for free flu shots than higher-income families? Does the salesperson see the connection between various words used in the sales presentation and the immediate increase in defensiveness of the prospect? Does the manager understand why air conditioning the cafeteria is followed by decreased morale and a strike by the workers in the hot assembly-line area? Some explanations for these and other types of human interaction—both successes and failures—may be found in an examination of the concept of culture and its role in our society.

What is culture? The word *culture* has acquired a number of different meanings and is consequently a confusing word. Culture is popularly thought of as a special training or refining of the mind or manners and an acquiring of certain tastes. Used in this sense, we might say an individual is "cultured." Another meaning of the word has to do with a way of life for a group of people. Culture in this sense includes the human behavior patterns that are learned and the human values and attitudes that are transmitted from one person to another. It is in the latter sense that culture will be discussed here.

Culture is a collection of ideas. Culture is the pattern of ideas and habits in our minds which gives us the solution to many of our problems.

Culture is that part of a person's surroundings, or environment, which is socially created. Culture is made up of all the achievements of all the people who have ever lived within a certain area, to the extent that these achievements have been remembered or recorded or somehow communicated to people who are now living.

One tiny facet of our Western culture is the idea of "ladies first," or allowing women to pass through doors or to do certain things before men, although this is changing with the movement of women toward a more equal position with men. In another culture, the wife may walk a few paces behind her husband. Material facets of our culture include underground sewers and charity hospitals; chlorinated water and monitoring devices for air pollution; bath houses, spas, fashion shows, and drag races; Saturday football, hot dogs, ice cream and cold beer; soap operas, civic clubs, volunteerism, and progressive income tax; short-shorts, mid-calf-length skirts, the turtle neck, and Levi's—the list could go on forever. Like a jewel with a nearly infinite number of facets or surfaces, our culture is a compound or collection of material things, ideas about material things, and ideas about ideas.

Cultural Traits.

The basic unit of a culture is called a *cultural trait*. It is a bit of behavior or a pattern of responses which is characteristic of the culture. It is these behavioral traits which distinguish one culture from another. For example, eating takes place in every culture, but the variations in eating behavior help define a culture and help differentiate it from another.

Consider how many ways of eating there are. You can eat alone, with a friend, with the family, or in some other group; you can eat on paper plates or china with silver; you can eat standing up, sitting down, or on the run; you can have instant breakfast, instant soup, quickly heated TV dinners, or a six-course feast; you can eat health foods, junk foods, grits, or grouper; you can chew each bite forty times or swallow an oyster whole; you can smack your lips and belch your pleasure or keep your mouth closed while you chew and pretend that you didn't hear someone's stomach growl; you can eat silently and mechanically or with much conversation, gusto, and ritual; you can open your lunch box and share food with each person in your work team, or you can sit alone at your desk and finish dictating a report. You can accept an invitation to dinner and arrive exactly on time at 7:30 P.M.—and be praised by your host for punctuality; or you can be thought hopelessly gauche by another host who certainly didn't expect you any sooner than a half-hour after the specified time. The cultural traits we acquire in life help determine our individuality. Understanding others is easier as we become aware of those cultural traits we have learned.

Culture as a Motivational Influence

The influence of culture is of tremendous importance in motivating us to act socially. Culture is all around us and moves us in obvious and mysterious ways. Culture is as ever-present as the air we breathe. Air is vitally important to us even though we cannot see it. We cannot actually see the wind blow, but we can see the effect of the force of the wind. When the wind blows hard, we automatically lean in the direction of the wind to maintain our balance. The wind moves us, or "motivates" us, to react in certain ways. We grip a package tighter, squint to keep dust out of our eyes, hold down skirts, or lower an umbrella.

In the same way, our culture exerts pressures upon us, and we almost automatically move in response to these pressures. If we could somehow develop a conscious, objective view of cultural pressures, we could be more aware of their influence. It is impossible to have a complete understanding of one's own culture; too much of it is unconscious. But the more we can learn about the seen and unseen things which influence us individually and as group members, the more we can predict and influence not only our own behavior but that of others as well.

As just one example of how culture motivates us, consider the dimension of time. In one family—an important purveyor of culture to us—the parents may strongly emphasize the importance of doing things quickly, getting work done "on time," no matter what it takes, and the virtue of being first in line or the first one done. Another family may stress doing a job well, no matter how long it takes; "take your time and do it right," may be the admonition. Two children, one from each of these two families, will be motivated differently when presented with a timed test of intelligence or when answering test questions during a one-hour exam period. The cultural traits we acquire, which help make up the real live person we are, act as a largely unseen but powerfully effective source of motivation in every area of our life.

Culture Can Be Thought of as a Balance Wheel

Culture allows a large group of individuals to coexist with a *minimum* amount of disruptive variation: it provides a balance. We can expect, for example, that as we drive down the street, most drivers will stop for red lights and stop signs and, in the American culture, will drive on the right-hand side of the street. The fact that cultural patterns exist allows us to do a much better job of *predicting* human behavior. Individuals who come from a common cultural background are likely to have similar responses to their problems. Culture provides many ready-made solutions to many of our problems. This is a tremendous advantage since it eliminates much trial-and-error experimentation to find our own individual solution to problems of daily living. Culture, then, makes our society more *consistent,* more *predictable,* and more *economical* in the sense of conserving human time and energy.

The All-American Culture

There is not much in our American way of life that is exclusively or originally "American." Much of what we do and much of what we are have been borrowed from other cultures and other times. The following description helps us understand this process of cultures contributing to one another, sometimes referred to as *cultural diffusion:*

> Our solid American citizen awakens in a bed built on a pattern which originated in the Near East, but which was modified in Northern Europe before it was transmitted to America. He throws back the covers made from cotton, domesticated in India, or linen domesticated in the Near East, or wool from sheep, also domesticated in the Near East, or silk, the use of which was discovered in China. All of these materials have been spun and woven by processes invented in the Near East. He slips into his moccasins, invented by the Indians of the Eastern woodlands, and goes to the bathroom, whose fixtures are a mixture of European and American inventions, both of recent date. He takes off his pajamas, a garment invented in India, and washes with soap, invented by the ancient Gauls. He then shaves, a masochistic rite which seems to have been derived from either Sumer or ancient Egypt.
>
> Returning to the bedroom, he removes his clothes from a chair of southern European style and proceeds to dress. He puts on garments whose form originally derived from the skin clothing of the nomads of the Asiatic steppes, puts on shoes made from skins tanned by a process invented in ancient Egypt, and cut to a pattern derived from the classical civilization of the Mediterranean, and ties around his neck a strip of bright-colored cloth which is a vestigial survival of the shoulder shawls worn by the seventeenth-century Croatians. Before going out for breakfast, he glances through the window, made of glass invented in Egypt, and if it is raining, puts on overshoes made of rubber, discovered by the Central American Indians, and takes an umbrella, invented in southeastern Asia. Upon his head he puts a hat made of felt, a material invented in the Asiatic steppes.
>
> On his way to breakfast he stops to buy a paper, paying for it with coins, an ancient Lydian invention. At the restaurant a whole new series of borrowed elements confronts him. His plate is made of a form of pottery invented in China. His knife is of steel, an alloy first made in southern India, his fork a medieval Italian invention, and his spoon a derivative of a Roman original. He begins breakfast with an orange, from the eastern Mediterranean, a cantaloupe from Persia, or perhaps a piece of African watermelon. With this he has coffee, an Abyssinian plant, with cream and sugar. Both the domestication of cows and the idea of milking them originated in the Near East, while sugar was first made in India. After his fruit and first coffee, he goes on to waffles, cakes made by a Scandinavian technique from wheat domesticated in Asia Minor. Over these

he pours maple syrup, invented by the Indians of the Eastern woodlands. As a side dish he may have the eggs of a species of bird domesticated in Indo-China or thin strips of the flesh of an animal domesticated in Eastern Asia which have been salted and smoked by a process developed in northern Europe.

When our friend has finished eating, he settles back to smoke, an American Indian habit, consuming a plant domesticated in Brazil in either a pipe, derived from the Indians of Virginia, or a cigarette derived from Mexico. If he is hardy enough, he may even attempt a cigar, transmitted to us from the Antilles by way of Spain. While smoking he reads the news of the day, imprinted in characters invented by the ancient Semites upon a material invented in China by a process invented in Germany. As he absorbs the accounts of foreign troubles, he will, if he is a good conservative citizen, thank a Hebrew deity in an Indo-European language that he is 100 percent American.[1]

When we listen to a politician tell us that, if elected, he or she will do everything to maintain "the American way of life," what is meant? The American way includes our total society and culture. Because the phrase includes so much, it has relatively little meaning. One of the most outstanding characteristics of our nation is the amazing diversity of its people. America constitutes not one culture, but many. Rather than talk about "the American way of life," it is more accurate to speak of the American *ways* of life. As a nation we are tied together by a common language and form of government. But regional differences in customs, values, opinions, and attitudes vary so much that we can understand the American way of life only by studying its variability. Within any one region there are likely to be a number of racial and ethnic groups. These various subgroups have their own characteristic ways of thinking and acting. We can think of these groups as cultures within a culture, and refer to them as *subcultures*. A subculture is not completely different from its surrounding environment; a subculture includes some of the dominant features of the larger culture, but it also contains certain different features.

The United States is a mixture of cultures represented by people, or their ancestors, who have been reared in different countries and whose behavior is influenced by their earlier experiences. Immigrant groups come from different continents, bringing with them distinctive cultural practices and beliefs. With the passage of time there has been a certain mixture of customs and values, with some groups tending to retain their original culture more completely than others. The culture of the United States is generally made up of many subcultures, each with distinct mannerisms and often a different language or a unique vocabulary. Large cities often have a "Chinatown," or a Polish, German, or Italian

---

[1] From Ralph Linton, *The Study of Man* (New York: D. Appleton-Century Co., Inc., 1936). Reprinted by permission of Prentice-Hall, Inc.

neighborhood, as well as areas known for their exclusive racial or religious identification. These specific areas of cultural identity are subcultures within the larger culture of the United States, but the primary identification and affiliation of people in these subcultures may be with their original cultural heritage, with marginal or even nonexistent recognition of what might be called the general "American" culture. Where there are social, legal, or economic pressures requiring a group to maintain an isolated or segregated existence, it becomes a *ghetto*, creating long-range consequences for both the subculture and the larger culture, of which it is physically, if not spiritually, a part.

Each of us as an individual is a *product* of the total American culture (or foreign national culture, if foreign born) plus several smaller cultures. Each of the cultural influences has shaped our thinking, our response to events, our beliefs, attitudes, prejudices, preferences, and perceptions. The businessperson who was reared in an upper-class home in Utah, in the Mormon church, and is currently the president of a leading civic club in Los Angeles will not hear the same things said by a financial adviser as will the businessperson who was once a member of a street gang, was educated in a trade school for "exceptional" children, and who now manages a women's ready-to-wear shop and is the vice-president of the same civic club in Los Angeles.

These two people are different personalities partly because of their different cultural backgrounds. They may wear almost identical clothing, support the same candidate for mayor, and both appear on a list of prospects obtained by the financial adviser from the same client. But their different cultural backgrounds have given them a different slant on life and a different way of reacting to motivational appeals. The person who is aware of variations within our own overall culture and who realizes the motivational impact of these variations on individual behavior will have a communication and understanding advantage over a colleague who does not.

Ethnocentrism as a Cultural Value

Inevitably, when groups differ, or when people from different subcultures come into contact, conflict arises. One characteristic of people within a certain cultural group is that they usually feel superior to those from other groups. This emotional attitude that one's own race, nation, city, religion, political affiliation, or culture is superior to all others is called *ethnocentrism*. An ethnic group possesses common characteristics, values, attitudes, and behavior patterns and tends to see itself as being better than other groups.

Ethnocentrism appears to be characteristic of most cultures in the world. This attitude is a measure of the loyalty necessary for the self-identification and persistence of the groups. Group members resist, both consciously and unconsciously, any threat to the stability of the group. This need to resist influence from the outside may be in the form of attack on outside groups, isolation from different groups, or pressure applied to inside members to avoid criticism of the group itself. An example of this is the appearance of bumper stickers with the slogan, "America—love it or leave it." Although our Constitution guarantees the individual's right to be openly critical of our government, overzealous ethnocentric citizens may decide that anyone who does not fully support all domestic and foreign policies here should live elsewhere.

Ethnocentrism can have the function, then, of maintaining the *security* of the group, and at the same time it can enforce a rigid *conformity* which retards or prevents needed changes and improvements. One difficulty in being highly ethnocentric is that it is not an objective point of view. To feel that one's own particular likes and affiliations are superior to others' may prevent a full appreciation of others' talents, resources, and differences. It increases the difficulty of understanding and cooperating with them. When we believe our own culture to be the best and fail to learn from other cultures and subcultures, much can be lost.

What does the concept of ethnocentrism say to the individual who lives in the world of business and depends on working effectively with people to provide financial security? The self-centeredness of ethnocentrism not only diminishes objectivity in seeing and understanding others, it also becomes a barrier to communication. Furthermore, it interferes with the coordination of efforts of fellow workers. Ethnocentrism spawns prejudice, suspicion, antagonism, hatred, ill will, and blindness to the ideas and the multiple contributions made by people of varying backgrounds. For example, financial consultants, whether they be in life insurance, mutual funds, securities, real estate, or are trust officers, attorneys, and so forth, find that their clientele consists of people from every ethnic group, some whom they like and others whom they dislike. These likes and dislikes are probably the result of early social conditioning, but the sentiments remain to bias the perception. These likes and dislikes are bound to influence the results of coordinative efforts, in spite of the conscious wishes of the participants.

If our early cultural conditioning leads to preconceived notions of superiority and inferiority, the probability increases that we will engage in behavioral patterns which are essentially self-defeating. Individuals who defeat themselves through prejudiced perceptions of those on whom their success depends—and who are unaware of the self-defeating nature of their perceptions—are doomed to repeat a pattern of diminished accomplishment and lessened satisfaction. Persons who become aware of how their *perceptions are determined by their culture* and *who practice the art of scientific thinking,* rather than falling victim to the scourge of "tribal superstition," achieve a partial or full measure of human freedom. This achievement is dependent upon their ability to confront reality. When they confront reality, they stand a chance of becoming real, genuine, self-determining, free individuals.

Our culture, then, is the most pervasive influence in the way we live, think, and feel. It is an influence inside us and around us. We reveal this in the cultural traits we acquire. Cultural values, when shared by the majority of the members of a society, help provide consistency and predictability in our lives. But at the same time, acquiring cultural values and traits tends to produce ethnocentrism, a self-centered view of situations, which may reduce cooperation with other societies based on different cultures. We acquire this cultural mantle through our memberships in various groups making up our society. The first group which begins this process of orientation and indoctrination is our family.

SOCIALIZATION THROUGH THE FAMILY GROUP

One of the most important groups in your life is your family. It is important because it is the primary socializing influence in your lifetime. This first family—your mother, father, and siblings—is known as the *family of orientation.* If you have married and borne children you, your spouse, and your children belong to another family known as the *family of procreation.* This family also has an impact on you. Two families. Two different types of influence. Two sources of information to help you understand your own behavior. How have these family groups helped form your many selves? Let's look at the "American Family" as a socializing influence.

Socialization is the process by which you learn to control biological drives, learn what values and behavior are acceptable to others, and acquire that identity you call your *self.* All the influences illustrated in Figure 3-1 play a part in forming the self, but your *family of orientation* was the first and probably the most important influence. There is a growing body of evidence that the first 18 months of life in this family of orientation are of particular importance in the formation of lifelong personality patterns. At birth, the infant does not discriminate between self and the rest of its world. The emergence from the relatively constant temperature and pressure of the womb into the bright lights, strange sounds and smells, and the sudden grasping of hands constitutes the "birth trauma." From the constant nourishment through the umbilical cord, the infant must change to a feeding schedule convenient to hospital staff, whether hungry or not. The first hours, days, and months of life are times of enormous assimilation of physical and mental nourishment. At first, the infant does not know any difference between its self and the rest of its world; this differentiation has to be learned. Gradually, the distinctions are made as the infant interacts with reality and is forced to accommodate to its surroundings. Even then, this young person sees the world only from a self-centered point of view and is unaware of its own limitations in perspective. During the first year and a half of life, the infant begins to broaden its perspective and starts understanding the real differences between its own actions and the world beyond. At this early age there is increasing use of symbols: words, movements, postures, colors, textures, and time periods. With these symbolic means of communication, the infant is increasingly socialized in a manner consistent with the family's value and behavior expectancies and in turn learns to manipulate portions of its physical and social environment.

Family Socialization Involves Frustration

The infant and young child experience an enormous amount of frustration during the early process of socialization by the family. Food must be eaten at certain times and in certain precise ways. Elimination must be controlled and must be performed only in specific places. Clothes must be worn whether the child wants to or not. Even crying and yelling, which come naturally from the young child's frustration with learning, must be subdued or suppressed. Subjectively, the child reacts to the early restrictions, lessons, admonitions, punishments, confinements, and thwarted expressions with mixed feelings of anger and resentment. The adult might experience an equivalent degree of disturbance in a very oppressive workplace, or perhaps in a prison. Of course, the child may also experience much satisfaction in the early family situation. Many basic needs for nourishment, love, comfort, and security are nicely satisfied in the family. But there is an accumulated tension associated with the many frustrated impulses of the child, so that escape from the family and its influence is often a major drive by the time the child is a teenager.

Socialization may occur at the expense of self-esteem. Sometimes it's not what is thwarted so much as the *way* in which it is done. This damage to self-image can develop both in the family and in the workplace. The child in the midst of the socialization process needs to learn to get along with others and, increasingly, to take care of itself. The employee needs to "learn the ropes" and fit in with the team, even though personal needs might be unsatisfied. This process of learning can be done while leaving intact the person's sense of dignity. Or the person's self-confidence can be so damaged that depression or withdrawal may be the reaction to socialization. Generally, the use of *power over others* leads to defensiveness and resistance to the one using the power. If power succeeds in encouraging obedience, change, give in or give up, then loss of self-esteem is the likely result. Examples of using power over someone include threats of punishment or taking away something valued; giving orders, moralizing, or name-calling likewise lower feelings of dignity and worth in the victim; even giving someone suggestions or ready-made solutions to problems robs the individual of the learning experience and the good feelings associated with self-diagnosis and achievement.[2]

Picture for a moment a typical scene between a parent and child at home. The father looks up from his paper and sees his son watching television.

John, go to your room now and do your homework!

Aw, I don't want to now. I want to watch this program.

Do as I say . . . and do it now!

Why do I have to do it now?

Because, I said so . . . I'm your father.

Well, I'm not going to do it.

You better get to your room now, or I'll make you wish you had!

Oh, all right . . . Why do you have to be so mean?

Don't you talk to me like that, stupid!

Can you imagine the same sort of conversation between a manager and a subordinate?

Irene, I thought I told you to have the report ready by quitting time.

Yes sir . . . but I had three customers call in for service requests, and they said they needed the information right away.

Irene, you know that we had a group meeting just last Monday to straighten you and the other clerks out about priorities around here. These reports come first. When someone calls, tell them that we can't get the information to them right now. They can wait.

But they were so insistent, and I have a hard time saying no.

Well . . . just say, "I'll get to it first thing in the morning," and then call them back. But if you don't finish a report the same day we give it to you, you'll get yourself into trouble around here!

In both examples, the child and the employee were given necessary instructions, but the way in which it was done left a residue of bad feeling.

---

[2] For a research-based analysis of how power, use of sanctions, and lack of consideration for feelings may adversely affect the effectiveness of organizations, see: Chris Argyris, *Interpersonal Competence and Organizational Effectiveness* (Homewood, Ill.: Richard D. Irwin, 1962). The many kinds and uses of power are examined in: David C. McClelland, *Power, The Inner Experience* (New York: Irvington Publishers, Inc., 1975).

What would be better? Let's look at some assumptions and possible alternatives.

Assume the father and the manager are interested in the progress of the child or subordinate. Both feel some responsibility to socialize, teach, train, and develop their charges. Is it possible to socialize and at the same time to increase the sense of self-esteem and worth in the individuals involved? The following suggested illustrations are not meant as absolute answers to these common problems, but only as possible alternatives based on several principles. First, can we elicit the *cooperation* of the child or employee? Can we encourage their *participation* in identifying the problem and finding the solutions? Can we *reinforce the desired behavior* and help the individual feel better, more self-confident, and more self-responsible? Can we find ways of resolving differences between individual impulses or needs and the requirements of the family or organization? Let's try.

Again, picture the family scene between father and son.

John, do you have homework to do?

Yeah.

It's nearly eight o'clock, and you've agreed that you need to be in bed by ten on school nights.

I know . . . but I want to watch this program.

Can you do both?

Well, no.

What's more important to you? Watching the program or doing your homework?

Well, I want to watch the program . . . but I know I should do my homework.

How will you decide?

I'm gonna watch the program.

And what will happen if you don't finish your homework?

My teacher will probably be mad . . . but I don't care!

Tell me about your homework assignment.

Oh, I'm supposed to outline the process of photosynthesis.

Photowhatsisis? What's that all about?

Here, let me show you. You had chemistry in high school, didn't you?

Yes, but. . . .

Well, photosynthesis is the formation of carbohydrates from carbon dioxide and a source of hydrogen in chlorophyll containing cells of green plants exposed to light involving a photochemical release of oxygen through the decomposition of water followed by various enzymatic synthetic reactions that . . .

> Whoa . . . I don't follow you. But it does sound interesting. I'd like to see
> your work when you are finished. In the meantime, let me read
> something that might help me understand what you are talking about.

This illustration suggests the parent's interest in the child, in his
dilemma concerning some "wants" versus some "shoulds," and in the
child's world in general. It is not a "how-to" solution to the old problem of
making a child do his or her homework. It is, instead, an example of how
trying to understand the child's complex feelings and attitudes which surround the child's attempts to deal with socializing influences might
produce results which benefit the child. A potentially exciting learning
process may be encouraged, while preserving a close relationship between
parent and child and also preserving the child's sense of personal worth
and dignity. If the parent avoids a "power-over" approach and attempts a
"power-with" approach, a better outcome is more likely. "Power with"
means that two people can do something together better than it can be
done individually. It means combining resources for mutual benefit. It
means a parent and child can meet the challenges of socialization
together while preserving the freedom, individuality, and integrity of the
child.

Using the same principles of trying to obtain cooperation and
participation, what could the manager do with Irene?

> Irene, I see that the report isn't ready.
>
> Yes sir . . . I tried to have it ready, but three customers called for service
> requests. They said they needed the information right away and that
> took so much time I couldn't finish the report.
>
> You decided the service requests should be done before finishing the
> report?
>
> Yes sir. I know we had a meeting Monday and you said the reports
> should be finished by the end of the day even if people called in to re-
> quest information in their files. But I have a hard time saying, "No,"
> when these important businessmen call and insist on getting the infor-
> mation immediately.
>
> You understand reports are first in priority, but you feel overwhelmed
> by someone demanding immediate attention to their problems.
>
> I sure do.
>
> Irene, do you think we have a problem in the way we schedule the work
> here?
>
> Well, it's a problem for me. I don't want you mad at me for not getting
> the reports done . . . but I hate it when a customer interrupts me with a
> demand for immediate file information . . . I don't know what to do.
>
> Have you thought of any possibilities?
>
> I like the work here. I enjoy working on the reports, and I like to please
> the customers who call in. But I can't seem to handle it when there is a
> conflict.

I can understand that, Irene. Let's see if you and I can work out some different procedures that might make scheduling of work easier.

Well sir . . . I do have one suggestion. . . .

Okay. Let's talk about it.

At least, in this illustration, Irene is not being threatened by her manager. It sounds as if they both recognize the problem and are in a mood to discuss ways of resolving conflicts and improving work efficiency. Methods of making the system work may be found without intimidating Irene and making her feel defensive. Effective solutions to problems within the family or in the workplace depend upon the values and attitudes of parents and managers.

Social Values Are Learned in the Family

The socialization of the child reared in the American Family depends fundamentally upon the values, attitudes, and behavior patterns of the parents or parent-substitutes. And the parents' values and attitudes were derived from their parents in turn. The black father unable to find work, whose wife is the sole support of the family and who was recently "busted" again while watching a demonstration, will transmit a different story of the "American Dream" than the white father who is a junior partner in a law firm founded by his grandfather. The first-generation son of an immigrant Russian carpenter, who now heads his own construction firm, will tell a different story to his son than the man whose father was on welfare will tell his son. The child reared by grandparents born in the nineteenth century will learn a different culture from the child of an unwed teenage mother who rejected abortion and marriage. Lower-class families tend to have larger families, smaller incomes, more crowded living conditions, and fewer material possessions than middle- or upper-class families. The lower-class father probably holds a job requiring strict obedience to rules and procedures; he probably emphasizes rules in the home and reinforces these rules with physical punishment, more so than the middle-class father. In terms of socioeconomic and educational status, women are more likely to marry above themselves and men to marry below themselves. But overwhelmingly, the children of the poor are likely to grow up poor themselves. Socioeconomic mobility is possible and evident, but even more striking is the tendency of children to follow in their parents' footsteps in moral, sexual, and economic behavior.

The family group, as the first conveyor of norms, values, and attitudes to the child, has the enormously responsible and complicated task of conditioning and programming young people entering our society. The ideal goal is to provide a good start toward becoming a mature adult able to cope with the external world as it exists. Whether the family recognizes these responsibilities and complexities and provides that good start is another matter. If the rules of the family are compatible with society's larger network of rules, customs, and laws, the child will have an easier time adjusting. But in some ways the family may not wish the child to adjust, but rather to confront, change, or rebel against that society. The family is a subculture within a culture.

Rules for proper behavior, whether within the family or the larger society, are referred to as *norms*. Family norms are those guidelines, rules, and laws that consciously and unconsciously shape family life. Some of the rules are casual ones, but some are extremely important. The rest fall somewhere in between. The family also is part of the larger system known as society and is guided by its norms too.

Norms exist as standards of behavior, and we expect conformity to them. But it often happens that infants, children, and adults deviate from these norms. What do we do then? Well, it depends on the importance of the norm. Those norms from which we may deviate without too much fuss are referred to as *folkways*. Those norms from which deviance brings on the wrath of parental and social sanctions, we call *mores*. Going to a formal social function in a sports outfit is a violation of folkways, but getting into a fist fight and injuring someone who laughs at the violation of a folkway is a violation of mores. The difference between unimportant and important norms is generally learned within the family. How we feel about these norms—that is, our ideas about the norms as being good, right, and meaningful—constitutes the value system which is also learned from the family. *Values* are the principles or reasons which support the existence of the norms.

Let's look at some examples of child rearing to illustrate the concepts of norms, folkways, mores, and values. In some families it is the norm for everyone to help with household chores. "Be sure to make your bed before you go to school," 6-year-old Sally hears from her mother. Because her mother always has stressed the importance of having a neat and orderly household, Sally intends to make the bed, but she forgets. Making the bed would normally be considered an unimportant rule in the family, and, sure enough, Sally's mother simply reminds her to do it next time. But look at another family. Norma's mother says, "Be sure to make your bed before you go to school," and Norma also forgets. But Norma is a 6-year-old child whose mother is neurotically obsessed with neatness and order. Her mother discovers the deviation from the bed-making norm and severely beats Norma, requiring a later trip to a hospital emergency room for treatment of bruises and a concussion. A child-abuse case? "She fell down the stairs trying to rush for the school bus," her mother tells the examining physician. Norma is too terrified to say anything. Now, picture how differently Sally and Norma will respond to a demand such as "Let's be neat" when they are faced with it later in life. Unfortunately, Norma's experience is not rare. Any large metropolitan hospital will receive perhaps hundreds of child-abuse cases during the year; only some are documented and prosecuted, but every one constitutes a socializing experience for the child involved.

This comparison of norms in Sally's and Norma's families illustrates not only that what are folkways to some may be mores to others but also illustrates how values can be transmitted to the child. In each case the rule is the same: "Make your bed." But the values learned are quite different. Sally learns that neatness is desirable. Norma learns that it is urgently important. In their later life, Sally may rush around emptying ashtrays before the guests arrive. Norma may whisk away an ashtray and wash it the moment anyone puts out their cigarette, regardless of the time of day. And how will Sally and Norma teach their children the norm of neatness?

The family, as the first socializing influence in the child's life, teaches the child what is expected of him or her as a boy or a girl and later as a maturing adult. But the lessons are not always healthy. The parents with unhealthy attitudes pass these on to their children as readily as others pass on healthy attitudes. The child will learn many lessons on how to cope but may also learn self-defeating ways of living. The child who adjusts to an authoritarian father by being submissive is likely to have difficulty being assertive later with adults who are in positions of authority. The salesperson with "call reluctance" and the employee afraid to discuss a raise with the manager may be following silent and unconscious "instructions" which have been buried in the unconscious self for years.

The pleasure or pain of relating to people is learned in the family. For example, a gregarious mother and father enjoy having friends visit in their home. They talk about the expected guests with warmth and anticipation. The children hear the words and see the greetings with handshakes, touching, kissing, and hugging. Another child in a different family rarely sees strangers in the home. When a guest is anticipated, the parents anguish over whether the furniture is good enough for the snobs who are coming and whether they will make fun afterwards of the food served, the clothing worn by the hosts, and so forth. When the guests arrive, the children see the strain in their parents, and afterwards they hear sarcastic remarks about the uppity manners and undesirability of the visitors. The child who learns to value withdrawal from strangers may grow up to be an adult who has problems in public settings. For example, an adult with such a background who is asked to help in a fund-raising drive may experience intolerable conflict.

Occupational choice may be related to early family learning. The child learns to value truth, fairness, and respect of others long before these values are verbalized by the parents. The child likewise learns to value deception, exploitation, and disdain for others at a preverbal level in the family experiences. Before the age of three, the child will absorb values such as intimacy, warmth, companionship, cooperation, trust, helpfulness, and many others which encourage the person as an adult to move toward people with pleasant expectations. Such a person may find, years later, that work in one of the helping professions, such as medicine, psychology, social work, or vocational counseling, is interesting as a career. Or, the child may absorb values that stress self-sufficiency, keeping a distance from others, controlling the situation, being wary of unusual or new situations, and may prefer definite and well-structured activities. Occupations which emphasize solitary or individual achievements and demand attention to details and orderliness may be preferred. The varieties of values which may be acquired early in life are many, and so are the varieties of possible occupational pursuits. It is no accident that the personality structure of the typical police officer differs significantly from that of the accountant or musician.

Sometimes, norms and their accompanying values are taught without the use of words. A government-sponsored anti-smoking TV commercial shows a father and small son walking along a wooded path on a beautiful day, obviously enjoying each other's company. The father picks up something and throws it, and so does the son. The father walks with a certain gait, and so does the son. They both sit against a tree to rest. The father lights a cigarette and puts the package on the ground between them. The son picks it up . . . looks at it and . . . . The audience is left to imagine the boy copying his father's smoking habit. In the late 1950s a rally of the Ku Klux Klan was held in Hurt Park in Atlanta, Georgia and reported in *Life Magazine*. The pictorial report showed an adult Klansman wearing the white robe and, standing next to him, a toddler similarly outfitted in a miniature Klan outfit. What values are being absorbed by this child too young to verbalize an understanding of what is going on?

Sexual Identity as Influenced by the Family

Within his family, what self-image does a boy develop about his "boyness" and his later "maleness"? And what about a girl and her later views of "femaleness"? The middle-aged father reading this, who was born in the twenties or thirties, might offer this definition of what it is to be masculine:

> My boy learned what it is to be a "real man." I taught him that he should grow up to be strong and self-reliant. Depend on himself and not lean on anybody else. I showed him that if he wants to get anywhere, he needs to be tough, aggressive, and be in control of the situation. He can't let his feelings get in the way. He's got to be unemotional and hard. I'm glad to say that he's become a real scrapper. He competes to win . . . not to come in second. He doesn't give up. Just keeps slugging away; never

lets down; gives it all he's got. He knows his stuff with mechanical things, and is darn good in everything he's tried in athletics. I'm proud of him . . . he's a real man.

On the other hand, this boy's mother might have a different definition of what her son should be like:

> I'm proud of my son. He is just like his father in so many ways. But, I do wish he didn't have to be proving himself all the time. He always has to be the best, but he is often unaware of how others feel. There are times when I'm not sure he knows how he feels about himself. He doesn't seem to be aware of offending someone until it's too late. I don't think it's that he doesn't care about others, but he often gives that impression.

Both parents may love their son deeply, but may be showing it in different ways. Both the boy's parents are teachers of their culture; both are agents of socialization within the family. But these two teachers may also help create mental and emotional conflicts in the boy's mind; the boy's self-image may contain some inconsistencies. If the teachings from his parents are somewhat different, as the above examples would suggest, he may have to make a choice as to which leader he will follow. He may have to ally himself with one and alienate himself from the other.

Even with the consciousness-raising of the women's movement in the seventies, the female child is traditionally taught that she should be passive, quiet, clean, docile, tender, nurturing, and a "little lady," whatever that means. Even before entering school, a girl learns that the ideal grown-up woman is a mother first and foremost. If she must enter the world of work, she may plan on becoming a nurse, a secretary, or perhaps a schoolteacher. These future occupational roles are reinforced by most textbooks in the public school system, which show females in these occupations while males are depicted as engineers, managers, doctors, lawyers, construction workers, and so forth. Television advertising of children's toys shows boys operating powerful machines, such as an aircraft-carrier launching system, and girls playing with dolls, baby carriages, and homemaking equipment. The women's movement notwithstanding, such advertisements continue to reinforce society's stereotypes of the sexes. The women's movement, begun in the mid-sixties, has had some effect on raising the consciousness level of the American public and on reforming their views of acceptable male and female occupations, but the change of an entire society and its culture comes very slowly.

Every family is unique, just as every individual is unique. Families differ, and so do the messages received by the children of these families. The Self we are depends greatly on how we were socialized by our own family. We know our own family of orientation was unique, yet most of us feel we grew up in an "American Family." But what does this mean? Is there such a thing as the American Family? Or are there millions of different versions of the American Family?

Varieties of Family Structure

The Census Bureau defines a family as a group of two or more persons related by blood, marriage, or adoption and residing together. Couples living together without legal marriage are looked upon with greater public tolerance now, and they constitute a variation of what ordinarily is thought of as a family. Single-parent families are increasing in number. And unwed mothers are more and more willing to identify themselves and, in fact, some have made the news because of their insistence on receiving the same fringe-benefit considerations from employers as do the more "normal" mothers who take maternity leave. Family styles are changing.

Consider these variations in the makeup of the family and its influence on the children:

Both parents living in the home
Mother as head of household: father absent
Father as head of household: mother absent
Educational level of parents
Socioeconomic level of the household
Presence or absence of siblings
Occupation or outside interests of mother and father
One- or two-income family
Racial orientation
Religious orientation
Presence of other relatives in the home
Ethnic orientation of the family
Presence of a stepparent
Presence of a parent-figure, not a natural parent
Sex-role orientation of parents
Age of parents
Mixed racial, ethnic, and religious marriages

The reader can imagine other factors which make families different. Both parents living in the home with the children is still the most common family structure in the United States. In spite of the sensational news stories to the contrary, the concepts of family life and continuing marriage are the typical modes of family life. Everything else is an exception. But there are many exceptions. Divorces are increasing, but the institution of marriage still seems to be the preferred way in which adult males and females live together. Divorce statistics frequently are cited which claim that for every 1000 marriages there are 250 to 350 divorces. This leads one to conclude, erroneously, that one of every three marriages will end in divorce. Not so. Let's assume that in one year 1000 people marry and 333 people get a divorce. Some of those divorced this year were married last year, some the year before, and some are divorcing after several decades of marriage. To get a more accurate picture of the instability of marriage and the popularity of divorce, we would have to follow those 1000 people who married this year and see what their individual records of marriage were over the next 40 or 50 years—or as long as those newly married people lived. If we were to interview a large group of the readers of this book who are at least 55 years old, we would find that over 80 percent of them are still married to their original spouse or have been married only once. If we interview 1000 people who are married, we'll find that some married this year, some last year, and some 30 or 40 years ago. Of every 1000 people now married, only 11 or 12 will divorce this year. These figures do not suggest that there is a headlong rush toward dissolution of marriage vows by the entire population. In addition, there is a high probability that the divorced person will remarry. In fact, it is more likely for a divorced person to marry again than for a single, never-married-before person to marry. And the chance that a second marriage will end in divorce is no greater than for a first marriage. Marriages end by death twice as often as by divorce. For these and other reasons, sociologists are concluding that "more Americans are spending more years in the marital situation than ever before in our history."[3]

Even though the typical nuclear family consisting of the natural mother and father and their children is still the most common family type, the variations from this pattern are important in understanding and predicting individual behavior. The family may consist of only one parent, either through death, divorce, separation, or desertion. When this happens many different forces are brought to bear on the children. Conceivably, some unhealthy pressures may be relieved. If the natural parents were at odds in their value systems and were teaching the child contradictory lessons, the absence of one can minimize the conflicts experienced by the child. As a result of the death or absence of one parent, conflicting feelings can remain with a child unless help is given in reconciling the feelings of hurt, rejection, anger, guilt, remorse, and relief. The absence of one parent from the nuclear family can be traumatic, or it can be a freeing, growth-inducing experience. Often, in the biographies of creative people, we find that the death of a parent accelerated the growth of the child in resourcefulness. A child, suddenly deprived of a parent, may "grow up" and become a young adult through assuming family duties and responsibilities.

[3] John Scanzoni, *Sexual Bargaining* (Englewood Cliffs, N.J.: Prentice-Hall, 1972).

We cannot automatically assume that an intact nuclear family is better than a "broken home." It depends upon the individuals involved. A different set of circumstances is created when, after death or divorce, a new parent-figure appears in the family. The stepparent who replaces the mother or father in the home is usually a stranger to the child. Inevitable comparisons will be made with the natural parents. If the natural parent is dead, the child will make comparisons between a live stepparent and the memories of the dead parent. Memories have a way of changing in either a positive or negative direction. The child may develop such an unrealistically high memory-image of the natural parent that no stepparent could hope to live up to it; or the memory-image may be unrealistically negative, so that the child is unncessarily burdened with feelings of guilt, anger, etc. Then, too, the child may resent the stepparent as an intruder into the "real" family. The stepparent, in turn, may see the child as a nuisance and a competitor for the attention and affection of the spouse. The remaining natural parent may try to play the part of mediator between the warring child and stepparent. Divided loyalties and deeply conflicting emotions may affect every member of this newly structured nuclear family. But, let us also recognize that many such newly structured families are cohesive, loving, and content, perhaps more so than the nuclear family.

The *extended family* is a family unit consisting of a nuclear family and one or more relatives living together. The additional relative may be a grandparent, uncle, aunt, cousin, etc. It is the lower-socioeconomic family which is most likely to have additional relatives living in the home. The middle- and upper-income families are usually more able to provide separate living facilities for grandparents or other relatives.

These additional relatives added to the nuclear family may create complications. For example, the grandparents represent still another set of values to which the child is exposed. In addition, the child's parents are playing the role of the child to the grandparents, as well as being the parents to the young child. Such parents may experience role conflict, with all its uncertainties and confusions. The child may sense this role conflict in the parents and be confused by it. One grandparent may become the indulgent patron saint, dispensing gifts, support, and refuge for the disobedient child being chastised by the parents. The clever child may learn how to manipulate parents and grandparents to its own advantage. On the other hand, additional relatives in the family unit may bring a wider range of experience and wisdom to the growing child. And while there are additional mouths to feed and bills to pay, there are also more hands to help with the housework and child care. Many mothers are employed only because of the availability of a trusted relative to care for young children. But some relatives may not be trustworthy. Frustrated, neurotic, or mentally ill relatives are sometimes responsible for physical and sexual abuses against children, who may be too frightened to report the incidents to their own parents.

Racially or religiously mixed spouses and their children present still other variations in the American Family. Unless the in-law groups are exceptionally tolerant, the mixed couple may find themselves ostracized from both of the subcultures. The Jewish parents of a new bride or groom may have difficulty accepting the gentile in-law, remaining convinced that their offspring has repudiated all their teachings. But they will still insist on the "briss" (circumcision) and later "Bar Mitzvah." The Catholic parents may exert continuing pressure on their daughter and her Protestant husband to rear their children as Catholics. *Guess Who's Coming to Dinner* was a movie and Broadway play illustrating the anguish and hope which can arise in a racially mixed relationship or marriage. *My Fair Lady* told the story of conflicts inevitable when couples from widely varying socioeconomic classes form a relationship. These are cases of differences in religious beliefs, skin color, and social backgrounds. Values differ, and so do the expectations of the social groups surrounding the married couple. Early parental teachings are not easily forgotten or repudiated. The children of a mixed marriage may experience differing societal influences from their individual parents, influences of which the parents themselves may be unaware.

Open and Closed Family Systems

We have been examining the family in its role of socializing new members of our society. Families may be characterized as a *system* of interactions, roles, activities, and traditions. Families differ enormously in their makeup, system of values, norms, and methods of teaching. They also differ in their degree of contact with the larger society and in how accurately they interpret that society to their children. Unless the family is aware of the outside world, the child's orientation to it will be deficient. The family system of people, resources, and activities may be relatively *open* to outside influence or relatively *closed*.

The open family tends to have extensive contact with nonfamily individuals. The employed parent may have close ties with friends or business associates in which there is a sharing of troubles and successes. Business, social, or political contacts may be invited to the home for dinner or leisure activities. These outside contacts may bring with them many kinds of influences which may make a lasting impression on all members of the family. Parents of an open family may take the children to political events, cultural experiences, business meetings, and recreational settings. Such children may be aware at a very young age of intricate social customs, details about travel and about foreign countries, the varieties of cultures throughout the world, etc. An open family may invite foreign students into their home for traditional occasions of Thanksgiving, Christmas, or Hanuka celebrations. Open-family parents are more likely to seek out teachers, principals, and counselors to discuss school matters, such as unrealistic demands being made on the children, possible tutorial help for them, and so forth. Outside specialists, such as psychotherapists, music and dance instructors, sports and crafts specialists, may have intimate and extensive influence on the children of an open family. The parents of the open family may intervene readily when the children come to the attention of the law.

There is no attempt here to suggest that this open style of family living is necessarily better than a closed one. But the diversity of outside contacts for each family member and the increased familiarity with the larger society provide a very different learning experience than that of the closed family.

A closed family relies almost entirely on each other as members of an isolated group. A family may live in a closed style because of physical isolation from neighbors or business contacts. A farm family, for example, may live too far away from others to permit easy and frequent contact. Of course, with effort, an isolated farm family may follow an open style of living. A family also may be closed because of suspicion of others. A family ethnically different from their neighbors may live a closed existence not from choice but because of the cooperative rejection of their neighbors. Strong religious ties may induce a family to be self-sufficient, depending upon each other for comfort, support, and inspiration. The closed family must rely on each other for love, friendship, approval, companionship, personal and technical assistance, and other forms of help. The emotional burden on members of the closed family may be greater than with the open family. But the closed family may have some advantages. In our mobile society, families frequently move to a different community because of employment requirements, health problems, etc. The closed family, developing a high degree of internal intimacy and trust, may better withstand the strains of geographic and social mobility. However, these intense dependencies within the family may make it more difficult to cope with the external world.

CHANGING FAMILY INFLUENCE

The family as an influential group is undergoing change in its functions. As the United States shifted from an agricultural to an industrialized nation, patterns of family life also changed. Earlier, the family was much more of an economic group. On the farm, and in many of the crafts, the mother, father, and children participated in the enterprise. Parents often expected children to follow in their footsteps: the son of the farmer would take over the farm; the shopkeeper's daughter might marry and, with her husband, continue the family business; the lawyer's son would be expected to continue in the profession; the politician's daughter might marry the newly elected representative and continue as a powerful although unseen, political influence. In the early years of our country, the family was not only an economic unit but was an important source of identity. The family name was an *identity,* the *socioeconomic status* of the child, and an *ideal of values* and activities toward which the child would aspire. For example, the child may have been known in the village as "George Russell's son," and given an identity and sense of personal worth commensurate with that of the father. The child's status in the village would parallel that of the father. And the values of the father would be absorbed by the child. The family was considered the primary source of vocational training, religious indoctrination, and moral development. The family was the major source of social norms, sexual identification, work satisfaction, and recreation.

Times have changed!

The increased urbanization of the twentieth century, the techniques of mass production, two major wars and two minor ones, the advent of Social Security, and the establishment of thousands of social agencies for human aid, education, and welfare have changed standards of living and the way family members relate to each other. In the predominantly rural culture of the nineteenth century, children were an economic aid to their parents. In the modern urban culture, children are more likely to be an economic liability. More and more costly education is required to prepare children for self-sustaining vocational or professional activity. With the trend toward permissive child rearing, and with more extracurricular recreational and educational opportunities, children are less likely to help with household chores. Painting and repairing the house, housecleaning, yard work, and other maintenance activities may be done by paid professionals, while the children are taken to lessons, games, or entertainment—at least in many middle- and upper-class families.

Parents Depend on Other Institutions.

Many parents depend upon the church or synagogue, school, and commercial agencies to take on the responsibility for the moral, educational, and social development of their children. Taking the children to Sunday school may relieve some parents of the need they feel to talk to them about morality and ethics. A common view is that the public school is paid for by taxes to teach not only the three R's but also to instill proper discipline. And a charm school, or perhaps the psychiatrist, should be able to reform the little demons into genteel citizens. "What are we paying good money for?" asks the indignant parent when their child goes to the equivalent of "obedience school" and comes back still disobedient. And think about this real-life example of parental guidance. The parent gets an early morning call from the police department: "Mr. Grant? We're holding your son on a DUI charge. If you want to come down, you can arrange bail and take him home." The parent does some quick thinking and, in a burst of righteous indignation, tells the officer, "Let him stay there overnight. I think it will teach him a lesson. I'll be down in the morning." Later on, this same parent may scream in outrage when it is discovered that the child was the victim of repeated homosexual attacks during that one night in jail. "What's this country coming to?" may be the parental theme song as this family tragedy is retold to any willing listener. Paying taxes, dues, pledges, or private tuition may help parents feel less guilty about their abdication of parental responsibilities, but it will not change the course of events.

It is a fact of life that the modern American family has an important but diminished influence on its children's social awareness and sense of responsibility.

Why has the family lost some of its influence? For no one reason. But for many reasons. Many families were deeply affected by the Great Depression. The silent rage and impotence of the often unemployed father, the mixed feelings of the newly and sporadically employed mother, the fright and anxiety in the children of the depression are probably clear memories for some readers. Many younger readers will remember listening with polite indulgence as their parents talked about how hard times were back then. It will seem unreal to the reader employed since the mid-forties, who has seen a steady growth in income, the standard of living, and fringe benefits provided by both government and private enterprise. The older generation will have fears, doubts, cautions, and conservative attitudes not necessarily shared by the younger generation. The family of World War II vintage and beyond has had social and economic experiences which create a new and unique structure of influence for the new generation. During World War II women entered the employment force in positions not usually filled by women. "Rosy the Riveter" described a new female occupation as well as being a war song. Women entered the fields of mechanics, engineering, medicine, and law. In many cases they were assistants to the male professionals, but women were experiencing different economic and social opportunities and freedoms. Women entered the armed services. In large numbers, women became heads of households. The economic depression seemed ended, but new social, economic, and humanistic forces were operating to change the shape of the American family and its influence on the "war babies" now reading this book.

Mother Goes to Work

If the American family is experiencing a revolution now, the revolutionaries have almost surely been women more than men. In the twentieth century, women have experienced far more profound changes in expected sex role, economic opportunity, and personal freedom than men. Prior to 1920, women could not vote. But after the Nineteenth Amendment to the Constitution was ratified in 1920, women could vote but had few additional opportunities or freedoms. During World War II women did have unusual occupational opportunities, but after the war, men returned to the civilian work force and many women returned to traditional family interests. During the 1960s, several events led to the growth of the women's movement, which is currently influencing not only the structure and function of family life, but of corporate and government organizations throughout the nation. In 1961, President Kennedy established the President's Commission on the Status of Women. In 1963, Betty Friedan's book, *The Feminine Mystique,* was published and widely read. And in 1964 the category of "sex" was added to Title VII of the Civil Rights Act, guaranteeing women equal employment opportunity. Guaranteed opportunity and actual opportunity were not the same, however, during that period from 1964 to the present. But increasingly, women are seeking and fighting for the opportunity to function in a variety of employment situations outside the traditional category known as "homemaker."

If the mother's employment creates a two-income family, not only is more money available but the mother may become more influential in family decisions concerning the use of the total income. Children in these families may be more exposed to the cultural effect of joint-parental decision making, rather than decisions made solely by the "man of the house." Salespeople and financial advisors need to realize the growing economic power of women and their interest in shaping the financial future of the family unit.

Some employed mothers will virtually abandon their children because of the time and concentration spent on work. But others will surely bring a richer life to their children and a more realistic view of the society the children are being prepared to enter. A better atmosphere may be created for the children whose mothers are reaching higher levels of self-fulfillment.

The socializing of the child in the family unit has much in common with the proper management of human resources in organizations. In both instances, the child or employee has a system of values and needs which may both conflict with and conform to the larger needs of the family or organization. The individual must adapt to the organization, and the organization must change, adapt, or modify its structure and processes to accomodate the uniqueness and variety of its members. This dual process of socialization of the individual and humanization of the organization may lead to the fusing of the individual's values and talents with the values, needs, and goals of the larger unit. Inevitably, conflicts arise. How these conflicts are recognized and reconciled makes a difference in the healthy growth or pathological deterioration of all individuals involved. Similar factors contribute to the diminished influence of the family in the child's life and the diminished influence of organizational management on the productivity of the employee.

The Peer Groups Compete with the Family

Important as the family group is in socializing children, other groups are similarly important and may prove to be dominant in shaping the emerging personality. If these other groups such as classmates, neighborhood gangs, fellow employees, or club members happen to espouse the same values as the original family group, the original socialization becomes secure and long-lasting. When an important peer group deviates in values from the family group, trouble begins. The individual is in conflict. The family values are older, but the peer-group values may be more exciting, more fun, or more profitable. Now what? If the conflict between the two agencies of socialization becomes intense, the individual caught in the middle tries to resolve the conflict. The most common method of dealing with such conflict is to renounce one of the groups. The older the child, the weaker the family influence, and the more important other groups become.

More than twenty-five years ago, David Reisman, in the classic work *The Lonely Crowd,* concluded that the approval of a peer group was one of the most important motivating influences in determining social behavior. Sociologists since then have confirmed the importance of peer pressure. When the young child, socialized by the family group, enters school, new socializing pressures are exerted. New values are introduced in both blatant and subtle ways. And the child is a receptive pupil. Bring this child into the company of similarly socialized and thwarted children, and a gang is formed. Parents would be amazed to overhear children in the first grade compare notes on their respective families. Primary and secondary school teachers overhear and frequently are told directly intimate and sometimes humiliating details of the children's family life. The more accepting teachers may be confidants of their pupils. The less accepting teachers may reinforce the child's tendency to tell and maintain "secrets" only with his or her new peer group. The underground is formed! From the child's point of view, it becomes increasingly clear it is "us versus them." Twenty years later it is the union versus management. Or colleagues versus the boss. Or citizens versus the IRS. The peer group is "in." The parents are "out of it."

The influence of the family group is profound and pervasive. It is the young person's earliest and most intensive learning experience. Its influence continues throughout life. How can we account for the powerful and counter-familial influence of those first peer-pressure groups? How can we explain the wild and disobedient behavior of the formerly sweet and well-mannered "baby of the family"? How can a "good" boy or girl suddenly go "bad"? What happens to the precious child of the righteous and law-abiding family who participates in acts of vandalism, tries drugs and alcohol, and engages in sexual experiments even before the teen years?

Peer pressure is one among a number of factors we have looked at which may help diminish the influence of the family on the child. An additional problem in the child's life is the way in which trust is established and broken.

Trust and Trust Shattered

The word *Watergate* has entered our language as an indicator of breach of trust. "It's another Watergate" is a phrase which expresses the thought that once again, trust has been betrayed. Trusting another person gives us great comfort, but having trust violated causes despair. Trust is a concept which enters the child's life long before the word is known. Being fed, held, loved, cared for, and comforted creates within the infant the preverbal feeling of trust; it is trust in the idea that being a person is good. Needs will be met. Love will be given. Self will be valued.

The family is where trust is initially experienced and, most likely, where trust is first shattered. When the child is hungry and immediately fed, when the child is wet or cold and is comforted, the feeling of trust in others is increased. Long before the right words can be used, the child learns to trust. The child counts on basic needs being satisfied in a consistent and predictable manner. But a child's trust can be broken in seemingly insignificant situations. Here is an example of trust being shattered and the long-term consequences which may occur:

> Charles was a 48-year-old, white businessman with a problem. He was in psychotherapy to find out why he was lonely, insecure, and inept in dealing with people. His recent third divorce convinced him that he was

a real loser. He stated that he had no real friends. He was not happy in his work, yet had no idea of what else he should be doing. He was skeptical of receiving any help from the "shrink," yet here he was, seeking that very help. He told this story. "I was four. It was a Sunday. I was playing in the living room, and Dad was there, too. I was sitting in the big leather wing-back chair. It was my father's chair, and I liked to sit in it when I could. That day my dad was standing nearby lighting his pipe. I jumped up and climbed up the back of the chair and stood up on the back and yelled, 'Catch me, Daddy.' He stood there with his arms outstretched. I jumped. But he dropped his arms and backed up . . . I hit the floor. I wasn't hurt, but I didn't know what to think. Then I remember he was standing over me and pointing his finger. 'Let that be a lesson to you, son. Don't trust anybody!' Well, I ran to my room and cried. I felt awful. That night at dinner I couldn't look him in the eye. He tried to be friendly, but I remember pulling away when he put his arm around me. You know, I don't think I've been able to trust anyone since then. I just can't trust anyone. . . ."

For Charles as an adult, it required a certain amount of trust in his counselor to be able to talk about that painful experience. Recognizing the connection between a childhood experience and his later difficulties in forming trust relationships did not make it immediately easier for him to feel more trusting of acquaintances or colleagues; greater insight did give him the courage to make new efforts to reach out for relationships that might lead to mutual trust. His story may seem unusual, but similar incidents are common in the growing-up process. Encouraging the toddler to walk a few steps toward the outstretched hand of the parent can be an exciting moment for both. But if the parent moves away just as the infant almost reaches the hand and continues to say, "Come on . . . come to me . . . just a little more," the infant may plop to the floor crying. The implied promise of a hand being offered, and the disappointment of the hand being moved out of reach, can seem like a breach of trust.

As the child grows older, the influence of the family seems to grow weaker. The child learns to keep little secrets from the parents. True feelings are not always expressed. Later on, the parents may feel they can no longer communicate with their adolescent children. Is it possible children learn to distrust their parents because they catch the parents telling lies? Can you trust someone who lies to you? Of course not! Why expect the child to believe parents who do not tell the truth? Some parents reading this will undoubtedly object: "I don't lie to my children." Sometimes we may lie to our children intentionally, but more often we lie because we don't know any better. We lie because we don't know what we are talking about. We lie because we never bothered to find out the truth about the society we try to describe to our initially believing child. Lying is usually defined in terms of willful misleading. We can tell an untruth without intending to. It's still an untruth!

Here is a lie: "Now, the doctor is going to give you a shot. But it won't hurt a bit." The trusting child holds out an arm and gets hurt.

Here is another lie: "You don't have to take that from anyone. You go back out there and let him have it . . . and he won't bother you any more." The child follows instructions and gets "creamed."

Still another: "A proper diet to insure a sound body includes lots of whole milk, eggs, and butter." Medical research indicates that each of these foods is high in cholesterol and is a suspected causative factor in excessive occlusion of coronary arteries, leading to a higher risk of heart attacks.

One more: "I don't know what this younger generation is coming to, what with all the drugs being used. I don't see why they need to do it. We, certainly, don't need to depend on junk like that." This is a more subtle twist of the truth, but one the child or adolescent is increasingly aware of. Antacid carbonates, caffeine, acetylsalicylic acid, phenacetin, ethyl alcohol, and tobacco are the most common pain-relieving, mood-altering drugs, and diet pills, sleeping pills, antihistamines, and a variety of tranquilizing pills are additional drugs often used by the parent who is mystified by the drug usage of the younger generation. Of course, the effects of LSD and aspirin are profoundly different, but both are drugs taken by individuals who want to feel better. The point is, young drug users who listen to critical, condemning, and, from their point of view, hypocritical judgments from older drug users may decide to leave the hearth and seek their counsel elsewhere.

SUMMARY

What may we conclude from the complexity of family socialization patterns and the great diversity of their influences on children? Families are different and so are their children. Early learning experiences in the family are influential in determining how the adult will react to advertising, sales approaches, compensation plans in industry, political candidates, etc. If we wish to understand and thereby predict the future behavior of our spouse, colleague, subordinate, supervisor, or sales prospect, it can help to know something about their family and especially their reaction to their family influence. For some, the family is the ideal model of behavior. For others, the family represents all that is bad, distasteful, and repulsive. Some will conform, and some will rebel. Many highly creative individuals have come from broken homes with such traumatic circumstances that they learned at an early age to depend upon themselves and to strive for some form of personal expression. Or perhaps it is because of their creativity that they have developed means through which their selves are not damaged but in fact enhanced. The family is a socializing experience, and the more we know of an individual's family background and attitude about it, the more likely we are to understand the Self they are now and will probably be in the future.

QUESTIONS FOR REVIEW AND DISCUSSION:

1. Is the "Self" we are a result of our inheritance or our environment? Discuss.

2. How do the socio-cultural influences affect our daily behavior? How can we increase the real control we may have over our lives?

3. Our families may have been the most important influence in our developing years. Do our family values and mores still influence our daily lives as adults? If so, how?

4. How has the women's liberation movement changed our lives? What are the changed assumptions and changed opportunities?

4

SOCIALIZATION AND INDIVIDUAL FREEDOM

The most anguished issue for our age is surely that of the increasingly crucial struggle between man's impulse life and his capacity for intelligent and flexible self-control.

MICHAEL BELDOCH*

Your impulses have been channeled and your growth directed by an intricate network of social control. Submitting to this control was not an easy or smooth process: rebelling and acquiescing were accompanied by both pain and pleasure. The frustration of individual wants and needs can be upsetting, but social control also involves learning skills which can bring great delights. Becoming a member of a social group means giving up certain freedoms but gaining many new freedoms, too. Cooperating individuals in groups can accomplish far more than any individual alone. But as a member of a group, you may not always want to do what the group decides.

Human Behavior in Business (Englewood Cliffs, N.J.: Prentice-Hall, 1972).

THE DILEMMA OF SOCIALIZATION

The socialization of the individual involves a dilemma. It *is* important that society exercise some measures of social control over its individual members. However, this pressure to conform to the group's standards may discourage initiative, innovation, and creativity. We each have celebrated the two hundredth birthday of our nation with our own combinations of pride, prejudice, cynicism, and hope. We may see the occasion as a time for reflection or ridicule, but it is a reminder of a nation begun with a revolutionary plan to find a better balance between individual rights and the power of the state.

> We hold these truths to be self-evident, that all men are created equal, that they are endowed by their Creator with certain unalienable Rights, that among these are Life, Liberty, and the Pursuit of Happiness.—That to secure these Rights, Governments are instituted among Men, deriving their just Powers from the Consent of the Governed,—

How powerful should that government be? What are the rights of the individual? The debates on these issues were held in streets and forums 200 years ago and are still continuing. In 1789, the year of our Constitution, men desperate to avoid the tyrannies of pre-Revolutionary foreign control signed their names to a document unparalleled in the world. This blueprint for a nation was already a compromise with freedom; the Articles of Confederation ratified by the colonies in 1783 had provided for a national government too weak to deal effectively with other nations, to provide for its own funding, or to cope with the problems between the states. The Constitution of 1789 provided for a much stronger national government. The first ten amendments guaranteed individual freedoms for citizens, and those which have followed have either increased or decreased individual freedom, depending upon your point of view. Title VII of the Civil Rights Act of 1964, prohibiting discrimination in employment because of sex, race, color, religion, or national origin gives greater freedom of opportunity to many but gives less freedom of choice for employers. Our legal system is another source of social control. Its influence depends upon interpretations made in the courtrooms. Other forms of social control can be as influential, if not more so, in determining our freedoms.

Various Forms of Social Control

Consider just a few forms of social control, where the pressure to conform comes from family, friends, peers, supervisors, and various other officials:

Customs, manners, and codes of morality

Ridicule and gossip

Licensing and certifying institutions

Threats of ostracism

Status, prestige, and class memberships

Written and unwritten rules for admission to clubs, churches, and other organizations

Dress codes for men and women

Role expectations

Definitions of masculinity and femininity

Economic, political, and social power

You can probably think of many other means of control through social influence. In view of the many forms of social control of our thoughts and behavior, the idea of personal freedom must be seen as a relative matter. We can be stimulated to great heights of creativity by the approval or love of others, but such outside influence can also produce slavish conformity. Our behavior is influenced strongly by an enormously intricate network of social and cultural forces which are often invisible and subtle and, therefore, powerful and pervasive. Perhaps a greater degree of freedom is experienced by the enlightened person who most clearly recognizes the manifold pressures which shape and limit personal freedom.

You have been *shaped* by your society, *conditioned* to respond to subtle influences with predictable responses, *programmed* to feel, think, and behave within certain definite limits, and *taught* to believe that you have a mind of your own. How much is your mind your own? How free are you to make choices regarding your values, attitudes, behavior patterns, level of education, sexual mate, occupation, income, and life style? How much of your apparent freedom, in fact, is determined by our changing society? The answer is, it's hard to know! We can look at some additional social influences in our lives so that we can increase our understanding, improve our predictions, and increase our control over our lives.

There is a strong tendency for us to be

1. trapped in a status category
2. tyrannized by role expectations
3. duped by a masculine or feminine identity

Understanding how status, role expectations, and sexual identity become powerful determinants of our individual personalities may help free us to become the person we are capable of being.

Trapped in a Status Category

Status refers to the relative position or rank we hold in a group. Vance Packard's book, *The Status Seekers,* is a popular discussion of the typical American in search of status symbols and the possessions and activities which appear to give status. *Webster's Third New International Dictionary* contains this definition: ". . . . the status seekers . . . (are) continually straining to surround themselves with visible evidence of the superior rank they are claiming—Vance Packard." A person's relative status in a group has sometimes been compared to the "pecking order" found among chickens. In the barnyard, and in all higher-animal communities, there is a hierarchy. The animals arrange themselves in order of importance or power. Chickens peck each other according to rigid rules. At the top of the order is one chicken that pecks but is not pecked by any other chicken. At the other end of the scale is one pecked by any and all but who cannot peck any other chicken. Likewise, people see themselves as being above and superior to some but below and inferior to others.

The chicken is one of the oldest domesticated animals. Our observation of the chicken has added some expressive words to our vocabulary. "Dumb cluck" is a stupid or naive person, while a "cock of the walk" is one that dominates a group or situation, especially overbearingly. "Cocky" describes an arrogant, jaunty individual, while "cocksure" suggests someone with a great deal of confidence or certainty. Man and chicken are different, but there are similarities in the way they and other animals achieve rank. Some chickens and people are stronger than others, as well as being more intelligent, resourceful, wise, and experienced. Some become older, sicker, and weaker and slide down the scale of status. But humans stratify themselves according to much more complex rules and arrangements.

The Basis for Status Assignments. Everyone makes status judgments. Not everyone agrees on what constitutes a higher-status assignment because people are different. But there is a remarkable degree of consensus among the general population, and these overall judgments tend to be consistent over periods of time. Status, and the symbols of status, tend to affect each other. A person may acquire higher status by changing jobs, but a person already possessing high status may increase the status of a new job. The job of insurance agent is generally seen as one of average status.[1] When an agent goes from servicing lower-income accounts to servicing business accounts, the agent's status level is increased. If the new president of the chamber of commerce comes from a wealthy family and is a life-insurance agent, this knowledge may increase the perceived status of the occupation in the eyes of the citizens of that community.

A variety of situations, characteristics, and circumstances determine a person's status in a social group. Some of the more important are: wealth, possessions, income, occupation, race, sex, education, family

[1] Robert W. Hodge, Paul M. Siegel, and Peter H. Rossi, "Occupational Prestige in the United States, 1925–1963," *American Journal of Sociology*, (Nov. 1964), 286-302.

name and history, location of residence and place of work, appearance, mode of dress, political or social power, and age. One of the most obvious and measurable determinants of social status is occupation.

In a nationwide survey made in 1947 and again in 1961, thousands of people were asked to make judgments regarding the relative status positions of many occupations. One of the remarkable findings of these two surveys is that the rankings obtained during the different years were almost the same (ibid). Those occupations at the top include: U.S. Supreme Court justice, physician, and nuclear physicist. Occupations in the middle were: undertaker, welfare worker, and newspaper columnist. At the bottom were: garbage collector, street sweeper, and shoe shiner. These rankings are averages; there are differences among those polled, and there would be differences within each occupation if individual names of people were identified. While a U.S. representative in Congress receives a very high average ranking, certain named representatives may be seen as having low status, especially after a well-publicized scandal. A restaurant cook receives a relatively low average status ranking, but a chef in a famous dining establishment enjoys high status. The meat chef ranks higher than the poultry chef, who would be higher than the salad chef. The waitress would be ranked even lower. What happens, then, when the low-status waitress gives food orders to the high-status chef? Trouble!

William F. Whyte is known for his research in the restaurant industry—and for his solution to the chef-waitress status problem. He found that the female (low-status) waitress giving food orders to the male (high-status) chef created an interpersonal situation of stress and resentment. The solution was to introduce a simple device (a spindle) into the food-ordering process. The low-status waitress put a written food request on the spindle. Without exchange of words, the chef removed the paper from the spindle and supplied the food. Silly? Certainly. Unless you happen to be either the waitress or the chef.

Traditionally, women have been employed mostly in lower-paying jobs and have consequently had less economic power. Until recent legislation, it was difficult for women to obtain credit cards in their own name. Also, it was more difficult for them to arrange home mortgages than for men. What has changed significantly in the last decade is the greater opportunity and readiness of women to plan childless marriages, to strive for entrance into professional and managerial positions, and to choose the options of divorce or a living arrangement without marriage. Public opinion is changing regarding appropriate roles for women. The fact is, a slight majority of our total population is female. And with the consciousness-raising efforts of the women's movement and individual feminist groups, men and women are likely to alter their views that women naturally have lower status than men. Salesmen, financial advisers, loan officers, school principals, employers, and just about everyone else need to realize that women are having an increasingly important impact on our economic and social scene. The social status of women is indeed being revolutionized!

Wealth is a definite factor of status. The wealthy generally are considered to be in the upper class. Although those who are newly wealthy may aspire to upper-class status, they may not be accorded that position by those who have been wealthy for generations. The old rich look down upon the new rich. Income is a status factor. It may even be a symbol of personal adequacy for some men and increasingly so for some women. How dollar income became associated with personal adequacy is a long story, but that association is suggested in media advertisements, novels, and other popular literature.

Higher education is associated with higher status. At least, sometimes. The holder of a Ph.D. may enjoy high status among university colleagues but be disliked by blue-collar workers who laugh at the "egg head" newly hired by the company as a consultant. In one social group, the M.D. will be accorded higher status than the Ph.D., and in another group, perhaps a research academy, the M.D. will be ranked below the Ph.D. The wife of a vice-president of a corporation may be reluctant and then embarrassed to admit that she has "only" a high school diploma. The applicant for a management-trainee position may indicate on a résumé that his or her college work was taken "at the University," trying to imply that a degree was obtained, when, in fact, less than a year or two of college credits were completed. Education is important to us in determining how we rank ourselves.

Sometimes we try to equate status symbols with status itself. The middle-class executive may beg, borrow, and even steal to afford the down payment on a mansion which suggests a status position far beyond his annual income. The family finances may be placed in jeopardy by purchasing a luxury car when an economy model is barely affordable. The rising executive may purchase a Brooks Brothers suit but continue to wear short socks, not realizing that knee socks which cover the bare leg suggest a higher status. The book *Dress for Success* goes into detail on how colors, textures, styles, and tailoring determine apparent status for both males and females and perhaps can influence the outcome of a sale, promotion, or business negotiation.[2]

Being busy seems to convey higher status than having nothing to do. For the insecure person trying to prove something, keeping someone else waiting for an appointment is a stratagem meant to be a "put down." The person who can "keep someone waiting" assumes a superior status. The young professional starting a new practice may be reluctant to

---

[2] John T. Molloy, *Dress for Success* (New York: Peter H. Wyden, 1975).

acknowledge that an appointment is possible within the hour. We gauge someone's importance by how difficult they are to see or how far in advance we must schedule to see them. In many ways, status is a numbers game. How busy? How much money? How old? How many people supervised? How many rooms in the house? How many acres in the ranch? How many square feet in the office? How close is the office to the president? How many publications or patients per year? How many hours worked a day?

Status Can Be Confining. How do you feel about being labeled, categorized, rigidly stereotyped, and pigeonholed? It probably depends upon the kind of label, category, stereotype, and pigeonhole in which you are placed. But, we do these things to each other and to ourselves. We seem preoccupied with who is better, stronger, wealthier, more prestigious, more powerful, sexier, more "in," and so forth. When we describe a large group of people, all of whom have a common socioeconomic status, we use the word "class." The upper, middle, and lower classes do exist, even if it is sometimes difficult to define them. Each has different value systems, interests, goals, ways of dressing, favorite recreational activities, preferred foods, and styles of living. The class we are in, and our perceptions of our status positions in various social situations, sharply limit our behavior and determine our feelings about ourselves and others. In a real sense, we are trapped in a status category. We are trapped in a social system which dictates status and determines what we can and cannot do as members of that system.

Our general status, or class position, comes initially from our family. The 1- or 2-year-old child may not be aware of status differences in the day-care center, but, before entering the primary grades, this awareness begins growing rapidly. The upper-class first grader probably will notice that the teacher is responding differently to him or her than to the lower-class child. Whether the teacher shows favoritism to the upper-class child because of a sense of awe for the upper class or shows the reverse because of a sense of resentment depends upon the teacher's perceptions of class differences. We behave differently because of our perception of status, and the word *role* is used to describe the pattern of behavior we think is expected of us. Status is a position, a ranking; role is the part we are expected to play in that social position.

Just as a child acquires a status position from its membership in the family of orientation, so does the wife tend to acquire a status position from her husband. The movement among some women to liberate themselves from this and other dependencies is beginning to change this tendency, but, as with most social changes, it is likely to be slow. Some women elect to retain their maiden name when they marry as one means of retaining their own identity. Others aspire to employment in a business or profession in order to establish their own status position outside of their marriages. But the status of many women still is determined by the husband's status. For example, a woman is being interviewed on a talk show. The interviewer begins with the question, "Tell me something about yourself. What does your husband do?" If the male reader finds nothing strange about such a question, he might imagine the scene reversed, in which he is asked to tell something about himself by beginning with what his wife does.

The various branches of the military certainly are good examples of rank consciousness. Not only does the captain outrank the lieutenant, but one captain outranks another who has one less day of service in that rank. And at a social function of officers and wives, the captain's wife has a superior social position to the lieutenant's wife.

As a further example of being confined in a status category, we can consider the intelligence levels of high school seniors. Higher status is conferred upon the more intelligent (The star athlete may enjoy even higher status). But, status varies also with social class. Of high school seniors, the more intelligent aspire to higher status levels of occupation. But when students of similar intelligence but differing socioeconomic class are compared, research shows that the hope of entering occupational categories varies directly with the class background.[3] The socioeconomic class of the family strongly conditions the child to select an occupational level similar to the father. Family, friends, the neighborhood, and the school so influence the child that a "free choice" of occupation is limited to a relatively narrow range of jobs. Of course, there is some class mobility in that the child of a laboring-class family may enter one of the professions, but the small percentage of children doing this tends to confirm the theory of intergenerational recapitulation: "Like father, like son."

Why do we do these things to ourselves? Why do we trap ourselves in status categories and often deny our natural inclinations to be available, to be helpful, or just to have fun? Why has status seeking become such a vital and sometimes life-destroying activity? Why does the person facing financial ruin sometimes react by committing suicide? Why does the person perceiving an insult react at times by killing the offender? Why does the person who does not know the answer to a question attempt a bluff which is detected by everyone? For one reason or another, we are tyrannized by role expectations.

Tyrannized by Role Expectations

There is a good reason why we so often do what is expected of us. It creates cooperation, harmony, and predictability in a complex society of people with different needs and abilities. To be an acceptable member of

---

[3] E. K. Wilson, *Sociology: Rules, Roles, and Relationships* (Homewood, Ill.: The Dorsey Press, 1966), pp. 210-12.

any group, we must behave to some extent as we are expected to by the group. If we fail to play the predetermined role, we may be expelled from the group. If we step out of the role, or behave in unexpected ways, the group will judge that we have made a mistake, "gotten out of hand," and need to be "brought back into line." The more important our group is to us the more rigidly we play the expected role. The role we play is not only a series of activities but includes the appropriate emotional responses as well. The mother who takes excellent care of her children but who does not show the expected emotions of warmth and love, gives the impression she is not properly playing her role as a mother. The father who takes excellent care of his children but who, further, shows certain "feminine" characteristics of love and tenderness by his words, gestures, embraces, etc. likewise may give the impression that he is not properly playing his role. Of course, we are talking about American culture, in which the father often is expected to be friendly but firm, instead of showing love through embracing, especially with sons. In the same way, a manager is encouraged to show interest in his or her employees but not to let that interest become "personal." The salesperson is expected to show interest in customer needs while not appearing overly concerned with making the sale. The woman in an occupational situation is expected to maintain the "feminine" role (whatever that means), and the man in the same occupation, doing the same things, must play the "masculine" role. (More about sex differences will be discussed later in this chapter.)

When we enter a new group we frequently are unaware of what our role should be. And the members themselves may not be consciously aware of the expected role we should play. There is usually agreement, however, when the expected role is not followed. Deviating from the expected role draws attention to ourselves and generates activity on the part of the group to ease or force us back into the expected role. Many of our social standards (folkways and mores) and our role expectations are unwritten rules, but deviation from these rules is recognized and often punished as swiftly as if it were clearly written into civil law. We learn what to do in a given situation by watching other people. We learn by imitation, just as we did as children. But we may notice only part of the expected role. In small ways we may deviate although we may be unaware of it. Others will notice these slight deviations and realize that we are just "not with it."

Here is an example of such deviation from the expected pattern and the consequences that can follow:

Sam was being groomed for higher management positions. He knew it, and so did everyone else. He was not yet annointed for a specific spot but was one of the rising young executives everyone was watching. At the end of the first quarter of the fiscal year, Sam was asked to join other junior and senior officers in the boardroom, where a special lunch was being served prior to an open discussion of possibilities for the next quarter. Sam was more than pleased to be included. He was proud, almost ecstatic, and a little apprehensive. His wife had urged him to wear his best suit, a black pinstripe, and Sam had picked out a black tie with a narrow stripe to go with it. He tied a perfect Windsor knot and buttoned down the collar of his shirt that morning, all in anticipation of the formal lunch that day.

As he entered the boardroom, he felt good. He knew he was dressed well, and he could still smell the faint odor of his freshly dry-cleaned suit. What he didn't notice was that everyone else was wearing colors. A plaid here. A check there. A blue blazer and gray slacks. A beige suit with a subtle texture. Sam didn't notice, but everyone else saw that he was the only one with such a dark, formal appearance.

Sam was careful not to sit down until the president took his place. He knew this was proper. The salad was brought in and Sam began eating with an increasing glow of good feeling. He did not notice that he was the only one eating. Not everyone had been served. After a quick glance, the president also began eating as an almost automatic gesture to help "save face" for Sam. The fleeting impression in the president's mind was that Sam was a "good boy." "He's certainly trying hard," the president thought. "A little too hard. He needs a little more polish. We'll have to hold off on him for awhile. Maybe I can get someone to talk with him and. . . ."

In this example, the president was noticing slight deviations from role expectations and was making business decisions accordingly. We can argue about the appropriateness and fairness of Sam's dressing and eating habits influencing the president's decision-making process regarding managerial promotions. But the facts in this true illustration reveal that both Sam and the president were tyrannized by role expectations.

Role expectations help form and maintain prejudice. And prejudices add to the tyranny of role expectations. If whites expect blacks to be unreliable and irresponsible, whites will compare notes and support each other's biased observations. If blacks expect "Whitey" to take advantage of and exploit the economic powerlessness of black citizens, this group consensus solidifies into a prejudice. With these prejudicial attitudes, whites will see irresponsibility in blacks, whether it exists or not, and blacks will be convinced of white exploitation, whether it occurs or not. Usually, when patients are admitted to a mental hospital, there is an initial period when diagnostic tests and interviews are undertaken to plan a treatment program. If a patient is labeled "schizophrenic," the professional staff will be watching for schizophrenic behavior. As soon as the diagnosis is applied, subtle, unconscious, verbal and nonverbal responses from the professional staff begin to "confirm" the diagnosis, and the patient's "schizophrenic" behavior is duly recorded. The patient responds to these expectations by emphasizing schizophreniclike behavior. It becomes a self-fulfilling prophecy. The expectation increases the anticipated behavior.

Perhaps the greatest tyranny in our lives comes from the expectation that we behave in a "masculine" fashion if we are male and in a "feminine" way if we are female. Dr. Sidney Jourard, in his extensive research on the psychological and physical consequences of aspiring to a sex role, points out the sometimes lethal consequences of role playing in his book *The Transparent Self.*[4] The question of proper masculine and feminine roles in our culture is now undergoing extensive examination, with legal, moral, and human-potential consequences. Perhaps in attempting conformity with the vague role expectancies associated with masculinity and femininity, we are duped or misled in the most far-reaching and cruel manner.

Duped by a Masculine or Feminine Identity

Now this subject is "another can of worms." A can full of worms suggests many intertwining, almost unending things, difficult to sort out and without any clear notion of where the mess begins or ends. With sexual identity, it too is difficult to know where to begin.

Men and women are different. We know they're different, but not everyone is sure just exactly how. We tend to think of anatomical differences immediately. And, of course, the average man is taller, heavier, and stronger than the average woman. The XX chromosomes of the female and the XY chromosomes of the male predetermine certain biological differences; but "The artificiality of the concepts *masculine* and *feminine*, considered purely in biological terms, has been repeatedly noted during the past generation."[5] From clinical research, it appears that the sex role of the individual depends not only on biological criteria but also on early social and psychological factors occurring during the first two years of life. But this is a medical and biological matter that is well outside the main concern of this book.

Masculinity and Femininity. As we will examine in Chapter 8, words mean what we think they mean. We respond to the meaning words have to ourselves, not what they have to others. You and I will differ in the way we define *masculine* and *feminine*, but our attitudes and actions will be in response to whatever meaning we assign to these important words. Turning to the dictionary is not much help. We'll find that being masculine means having the qualities traditionally distinctive of or appropriate to a male. Words like strong, virile, and robust appear in the definition, but so does the word *manly*. Femininity is defined as involving "the gentler virtues," which is another way of describing being passive. If we ask a sample of men and women in our culture, we might find common

---

[4] Sidney M. Jourard, *The Transparent Self* (New York: D. Van Nostrand, 1964).

[5] Joseph Zubin and John Money, eds., *Contemporary Sexual Behavior: Critical Issues in the 1970's* (Baltimore: The Johns Hopkins University Press, 1974), pp. 212-14.

usages of certain adjectives which define masculinity: aggressive, adventuresome, bold, assertive, logical, objective, hard, unemotional, self-sufficient, tough, effective, and competent. We would find other adjectives to define femininity: passive, dependent, warm, emotional, weak, soft, intuitive, supportive, nurturing, domestic, helpless, and docile. Both men and women tend to use the same adjectives in their definitions of masculinity and femininity. We can be reasonably sure, however, that a word such as "aggressive" will have a wide range of meanings to many people.

Because of new social, legal, and economic trends, the general concepts of masculinity and femininity are being changed. If masculinity was formerly defined partly in terms of a man taking care of a woman, supporting her financially, and being the active provider—with the woman being the passive recipient—then the definition now is being changed. If femininity ever meant being shy, retiring, quiet and docile, and staying "in her place at home" to provide comfort and homemaking services and to display proper obedience to her husband, then that definition is now being changed. For a generation, Margaret Mead, and more recently, Betty Friedan, Elizabeth Janeway, Caroline Bird, Gloria Steinem, and others have been female vocalists in a choir singing a cantata with a theme glorifying individual identity rather than sexual identity. Their plea is that we not be duped by sexual-role expectations but instead be inspired by our individual talents; that we appreciate human talent wherever we find it and eliminate self-defeating competition between the sexes; and that we achieve more human freedom by recognizing our similarities instead of perpetuating the fetish of sexual superiority and inferiority.

Masculinity and femininity are incredibly difficult concepts to define, yet each of us is strongly led or, more accurately, *misled* by our perception of the proper male or female role. As Ledderer pointed out in his book, *The Ugly American,* the *un*informed American is a *mis*informed American. We can say, too, that the person uninformed about the facts and myths of sexual identity is a person who is misinformed, misled, and duped.

It appears highly probable that the prevalent misconceptions about masculinity contribute to the shortened life of many males (*and* to the female who aspires to some personality characteristics considered "masculine").

Here is an example of how one man's concept of masculinity may have contributed to his premature death.

"Myocardial infarction" was the diagnosis in Sol's medical record. He had been aware of the admitting procedures, but only dimly. Now he was focusing on his wife, Dot. "What's happening? What the hell happened! The pain! Incredible. But I feel better now. Help me up. Crank the bed up. Come on Dot!" Dot was squeezing his hand but was having trouble finding words. She tried repeating the instructions she had been given that he should lie still, but Sol would have none of it. He sat up. The nurse came in at that moment and lowered him back down with a quiet but insistent order, "Lie still. You've had some heart damage. It's important that you be as quiet as possible. The doctor will be here shortly and he'll talk to you."

For the next few weeks, Sol alternately raged, protested, sulked, and complained. "Hell, I'm as good as I ever was. Just let me out of here. All I need now is to go home and get back to work." Two months later, Sol was with the old golf foursome and insisting that he was just fine. He felt pretty tired after the first nine, but he shrugged off suggestions that he go back to the clubhouse and take it easy. "Your only trouble is that I'm one up on you," was his reply. But he did ride the cart from then on. On the seventeenth tee, Sol was dead.

His friends agreed that Sol couldn't accept any disability. It was a threat to his masculinity, they said. And they were right! Sol played the masculine role right down to the seventeenth hole. Privately, he had been enormously threatened by his convalescence. He worried that his place in the firm would be taken by one of the "young Turks" just waiting for the chance. He mentioned this one time to Dot, but not to anyone else. He didn't know what else to do but fight. He fought the pain. He fought the fear. He fought to be the man he always had been. He was thoroughly tyrannized by the masculine role he felt compelled to play. And he played it to the end!

Sol was a type "A" personality, as Dr. Meyer Friedman would define it in his book, *Type A Behavior and Your Heart.*[6] Intensely competitive, striving for achievement without ever letting up, always wanting to crowd ever more activities into an already long workday, barely able to contain the rage and impatience he often felt with the slower pace of others . . . Sol was playing out his version of the vigorous, aggressive, successful, and very "masculine" executive. He felt a sense of pride in maintaining a "killing" pace. In getting by on four hours of sleep. In being at the office before anyone else. And in being the last to leave . . . with a full briefcase of work to do that night. Chain smoking, fast talking, fast eating, and reveling in the disbelieving and slightly jealous comments of admiration from others concerning his workload. Sol had learned his sex-role lessons well, and he was rewarded well in payments of money and awe.

Of course, not every man with Sol's personality description will have a heart attack. None of the cardiologists and scientists would claim that. But with a type "A" personality added to a high-cholesterol diet, little ex-

---

[6] Meyer Friedman and Ray H. Roseman, *Type A Behavior and Your Heart* (New York: Knopf, 1974).

ercise, heavy smoking, and obesity the probabilities rise sharply. The probabilities of heart attacks go up, also, with women who fit the same profile. Some women entering a traditionally male occupation emulate those "masculine" characteristics they perceive as being associated with success. Duped by the same delusion many men are, these women engage in the self-defeating practice of "masculinizing" their personalities. The damaging stress in Sol's approach to life stems not from hard work and aspirations for excellence but from a culturally induced need to prove his masculine adequacy. The tragedy is that once sexual-role adequacy has become a concern to an individual it cannot ever really be "proved" to the person's satisfaction. The male who has experienced literal sexual impotency knows that the next sexual encounter becomes a "test case." The next sexual encounter may be motivated more by a need to prove sexual potency than by the sex drive itself. Suppose that next encounter is successful? Will the next one be? And so the next one and the one after that become matters of adequacy-testing and a source of anxiety which can spread to all areas of life.

Fears of inadequacy in playing the masculine role, which include concerns over the success of the sex act itself, are aroused easily. Likewise, a woman may experience strong doubts about her feminine adequacy, especially if she enters a traditionally male occupation.

Women as Managers? This is, indeed, a loaded question. It is a question "loaded" with emotional overtones for both men and women. It is a question "loaded" with present and future implications for our entire economic and social structure. The answers require further explorations into how men and women see themselves and each other, especially in the workplace.

Sylvia Porter, the popular financial columnist, reports on an interview with Professor Eli Ginzberg, chairman of the National Commission for Manpower Policy, in which Ginzberg stated, "The single most outstanding pheonomenon of our century is the flood of women into jobs. Its long-term implications are absolutely unchartable. . . ."[7] It is conceivable that Professor Ginzberg is correct in his assessment of the importance of the increased employability of women.

The thin crack in the wall through which some women are entering the field of management is paralleled by a crack in the belief system which holds that differences between men and women make the latter unfit for management.[8] The women's movement of the 1970s is revolutionary in that it questions the equality of employment opportunity and demands

[7] Sylvia Porter's syndicated column, *The Atlanta Journal*, Nov. 29, 1976.

[8] William E. Reif, John W. Newstrom, and Robert M. Monczka, "Exploding Some Myths About Women Managers," *California Management Review*, 17 (Summer 1975), pp. 74-78.

an equal share of social and economic responsibility and equal treatment in terms of talent and potential for both males and females. A flood of articles and books based on scientific research and clinical observation suggests that the sexes are more similiar than different in the ability to achieve in professions and managerial positions. But this attitude still is not generally held by either men or women.

When attitudes of the American public are obtained through research, we find that both men and women see males as being valued more highly than females.[9] Products and services are rated more highly when experimental groups are led to believe they were produced by men rather than by women. In one study, when men and women believed that large numbers of women soon would be entering a profession, the ratings of prestige and desirability of the occupation decreased.[10]

When men and women perform equally well, both males and females tend to ascribe it to skill for the male and luck for the female.[11] When females compete with males, the females have lower performance expectancies, lower self-confidence, and set lower goals.

More distinct achievement-striving in male-oriented activities is found in females who perceive themselves to be more like their fathers than their mothers. There is a tendency for women to fear success in achievement-oriented tasks that are, by nature, competitive and involve "aggressive" behavior because they see this as being unfeminine. Studies have shown there is a tendency for the competent woman who expresses masculine sex-role preferences (success-oriented) to be judged less attractive socially and less attractive as a work partner than an equally competent female worker who expresses "feminine" preferences related to non-success oriented activities.

These scientific surveys and experimental studies further reveal how masculinity and femininity are defined in our culture. Because all such studies involve relatively small groups of men and women, we must be careful not to read into them universal and absolute truths. But their results may help us understand the confusion and mixed feelings both men and women have as women, in increasing numbers, enter traditionally male-oriented occupations. Attitudes and opinions are not the same as performance. But if large groups of men and women think women should not be in management, then barriers will continue to stand. Once

[9] Virginia E. O'Leary, "Some Attitudinal Barriers to Occupational Aspirations in Women," *Psychological Bulletin*, 81 (1974).

[10] John D. Touhey, "Effects of Additional Women Professionals on Ratings of Occupational Prestige and Desirability," *Journal of Personality and Social Psychology*, 29 (1974).

[11] Kay Deaux and Tim Emswiller, "Explanations of Successful Performance on Sex-linked Tasks: What is Skill for the Male is Luck for the Female," *Journal of Personality and Social Psychology*, 29 (1974).

again society is duped by confusion about masculine and feminine identity.

When we look at actual measures of aptitude for business and business management, the similarities between men and women are predominant. The differences suggest that in some ways women may be able to function more effectively. Women show a tendency to grasp more quickly how the formal and informal aspects of an organization interact. Women may be more aware of important interpersonal aspects of the work environment. In testing for differences in ability and knowledge in 22 dimensions related to business, men and women tested the same in 14 categories, women excelled in 6 areas, and men in two areas.[12] On-the-job experience shows that men and women take about the same amount of sick leave a year, show about the same turnover rate at professional levels, and work for the same basic reasons.[13] The best comparisons between men and women as managers will come from long-term studies. Comparisons are difficult now, partly because men outnumber women in all management positions by 5 to 1 and, in top management, by 600 to 1.

The traditional view is that men are more responsible, rational, more able to handle crises, and are stronger in character. Objective evidence would suggest that women seem capable of as much objectivity, as much ability to think abstractly, and as much decision-making skill as men. As stated before, one difference seems to be women's greater ability in interpersonal relationships. Men and women appear equal in emotionality, although men are less likely to disclose their feelings about themselves and others.[14] Myths die hard. In the meantime, men and women seem to be creating self-made barriers, retarding the fullest functioning of each. (By the beginning of the 1980s, the Equal Rights Amendment still had not been ratified by a sufficient number of states to become law.)

STATUS, ROLE, AND SEXUAL-IDENTITY CONFLICTS

Since each of us is a member of many groups, each of us will have that many different status positions. There will be differences, also, in the role behavior we are expected to display. Our image of adequacy as either a masculine or feminine individual likewise will differ from place to place and time to time.

---

[12] Reif, Newstrom, Monczka, "Exploding Some Myths About Women Managers," *California Management Review,* 17 (Summer 1975).
[13] U.S. Civil Service Commission, *The Federal Women's Program: A Point of View* (Washington, D.C.: U.S. Government Printing Office, August 1972).
[14] Sidney Jourard, *Disclosing Man to Himself* (New York: D. Van Nostrand, 1968).

The life-insurance industry has a professional group for its top agents known as The Million Dollar Round Table. Only a small percentage of the nation's more than 300,000 agents qualify for membership in this organization, which is dedicated to industry excellence and the continued professional growth of the agent. With offices in Chicago and a top-rated staff, this organization—thanks to hundreds of the most qualified of its elite membership—ranks high in prestige among knowledgeable people in the life-insurance, banking, legal, and accounting professions. The president of this organization is selected carefully for maturity, leadership excellence, ability to be an effective spokesperson for the industry, and for his overall prestige within an already prestigious group. At the annual meeting, he will be acclaimed with a standing ovation and treated with the highest respect. He will be a sought-after speaker nationally. His articles will influence thousands of members and nonmembers. He enjoys very high status, indeed! When he returns to his hometown to resume the sale of life insurance, he may well have the following brief telephone conversation with a business owner who does not know him but with whom he would like to make an appointment for a sales presentation:

> Hello, Mr. Byers? This is Mori Sales of the Mutual Life Insurance Company. I'd like to . . .
> Oh, no! Not another salesman. You guys are comin' out of the woodwork. You're the third one today. I just don't have time to talk now. And I have all the life insurance I need. I'm sorry. Just take my name off your list.

That weekend Mori and his wife attend a cocktail party hosted by a good friend, but everyone else is a stranger:

> Hey, I'd like you to meet my friend Mori and his wife Muriel. Mori is this year's president of the Million Dollar Round Table!
> Million Dollar what? What's that?
> Well, it's a professional organization of life underwriters . . .
> You mean life insurance salesmen? You sell life insurance?
> Yes, I do . . .
> Oh, well, you know I have a lot of life insurance already. I don't think I'd better talk to you. Ha-ha! You might try to sell me something. . . .

Mori remembers his standing ovation of last week. What a difference!

The physician with a general practice will probably be ranked extremely high among her neighbors. However, at a medical conference, she may rank quite low as she chats informally with a group of surgeons.

A woman who has become the first female vice-president of a corporation may be seen by her colleagues as "really superior to have even been considered." Yet, with her nonemployed female friends, her announcement of the promotion may be greeted with, "Oh, do you have to work?"

An elder of a large, well-attended church is still working as a clerk; at work he is almost twice as old as the other clerks. He experiences status inconsistency in several different ways: he experiences the low status of a clerk, which is inconsistent with the tendency to give higher status to an older man, and which is inconsistent with his status in the church as a high-level official.

There is nothing unusual about the female department head who is expected to get the coffee and take notes at the department-head meetings "because she is a woman."

Most of us experience a different status depending upon which of our different groups we are with at any given time. We can adjust to these differences if we are with only one group at a time. It is when we are caught in cross pressures between different statuses of different groups at the same time that we feel the emotional strain. The mother taking her children to the family reunion, where she herself is considered "the baby of the family," may have to make some choices about which role to play. Enjoying high status with her family of procreation and low status with her family of orientation, she cannot possibly play a single role to satisfy the two different status requirements. The conflict is resolved usually by moving emotionally toward that group offering the highest status. The mother role will be maintained, even though that is inconsistent with "baby sister."

A person plays many roles during the day. Wife during those minutes before the children are up. Mother during breakfast. Chauffeur in the car pool. Employee during the day. Parent in a brief exchange with the children's teacher. Chairperson of the district charity drive. Answering service and message-center coordinator for the entire family. Purchasing agent, delivery service, and inventory-control clerk for household supplies. Mother again after school. Wife for a moment again. Then, cook. And mentor for school-, business-, or socially related problems. For a period of time—simultaneously—wife-mother-cook-answering service-adviser-soundingboard-nurse. And all of this while reviewing the frustrating and satisfying events of the working day. It's those times of simultaneous role-playing, where the various roles are incompatible, that strain the role-player to the utmost.

Some roles are easier to play than others. We experience greater satisfaction in some. Greater pain in others. What works well in one role is disastrous in another. It helps if we are aware of the incompatibilities and inconsistencies in the status-role-playing nature of our life. If a person is consistent in personality and behavior throughout the day, this very consistency will produce both appropriate and inappropriate role-playing, depending upon the situation. The former football coach and current sales manager has learned through both roles how to intimidate the opposition, how to manipulate situations and people so that there is more winning than losing, and how and when to blast someone apart if necessary, or to push, humiliate, shame, praise, kick, or hug for the proper effect. But sometimes the same techniques are brought home, where the opposition becomes wife and children. At least at the office, a salesperson can be fired or can quit. At home there may be hell to pay, now and later. The person who "bulls ahead," doing things the way he or she wants, may not realize the havoc involved until it's too late.

Some roles are new, unfamiliar, and poorly "written." Not everyone has a copy of the script. Conflict results. The woman entering the world of business management may not know how to handle her femininity. Does it conflict with being managerial? How does she become "one of the boys?" Or should she? Can she call her boss by his first name as readily as the rest of the managers? What do you do during an after-hours drink? And how do you handle taking a client out to lunch if *he* feels uncomfortable having a woman buy *his* lunch? What about trips out of town? Will her husband react the same as wives do when their husbands are out of town? Are there differences? Should there be? These are the types of questions which create and surround the role-status conflicts we experience.

Managing Status-Role-Identity Conflicts

Conflict between status positions, role expectancies, and identities seems inevitable in our complex society. We are pulled in different directions by social forces largely invisible and only partly understood. Let's look at a few ways of managing these conflicts to avoid being tyrannized, trapped, or duped by them.

Conflicts may be managed by

1. identifying and defining the conflict
2. discussing the issues with the conflict partner
3. ignoring and avoiding the conflict situations
4. compromising and establishing priorities
5. integrating conflicting elements
6. conforming and compartmentalizing
7. scheduling temporal and spacial intermissions
8. relying on rigid rules
9. changing the situation
10. changing the person
11. modifying and balancing situational and personal variables

Identifying and Defining the Conflict. A major aim of this book has been to identify and define personal and social influences which make up the collection of selves we are. Becoming more sensitive to status-role-identity conflicts may help us recognize the next one we face. Organizations are full of such conflicts. Detailed job descriptions, procedural manuals, written marketing and production plans, and written performance appraisals are attempts to identify who does what, how it should be done, and what has been accomplished in the past. One highly successful financial consultant keeps careful notes on each meeting with a client and dictates a detailed narrative record of issues discussed, actions to be taken, and agreed-upon responsibilities of both consultant and client. A copy of the notes is sent to the client for approval. The client reads the account and may find unnoticed differences in viewpoint, which occurred during the meeting. The client also may see financial problems and opportunities in a new light by reading the notes. The possibility exists for detailed feedback to the consultant both on areas in which there were misunderstandings and on areas of agreement. Both consultant and client are helping shape their relationship and respective roles.

The same approach may be applied to the family arena, where status-role-identity conflicts can arise so easily. After a family discussion, members can write down their understanding of the agreements reached. They can compare notes and discover any differences in what each has heard. Some psychotherapists recommend that parents and children write out "contracts" concerning the expectations of the parents and the disagreements and commitments of the children. Of course, contracts are subject to negotiation. A contract in existence for some time may need to be renegotiated. But writing down expectations, agreements, desires, values, and perceptions is one way of discovering conflicts and defining the conflict areas in terms that all can understand.

When couples are asked to write their perceptions of self and spouse, interesting comparisons can be made. The husband may discover that his wife is not nearly as interested in his earning a huge income as he thought, especially if it takes him away from her and the growing children. The wife may discover that her husband feels deeply about some matters he previously has not been able to verbalize. Both may recognize more clearly slight value differences they have but never have discussed. Value differences in a relationship can cause status and role conflicts; until the basic values are understood, the apparent conflicts may seem to have no solution. Research by one of the authors of this book, which involved thousands of couples, attempted to explore this area by asking each husband and wife to answer questions about what they wanted to do to change or grow as an individual and how they thought their spouse wanted them to grow or change. The degree of similarity of responses was often very low. Such couples conclude that although they talk about many things in their daily life, they tend not to talk about values and personal-growth aspirations. Thus, conflicts in their role expectancies of each other are bound to result.

   Discussing the Issues with the Conflict Partner.   It's difficult to have a status-role conflict with another person unless that other person agrees to cooperate in the conflict. In both marriage and management, however, we usually find someone willing to cooperate. In counseling with married couples or consulting with management teams, interpersonal difficulties often are reported. The difficulties may involve one or more individuals who feel that either they, or a significant other person, are not performing or behaving in the approved or hoped-for manner. "I wish my husband didn't always have to feel that he was right about every single thing. It really irritates me!" This might be said to a counselor to whom the wife went for marital guidance. The counselor's first question is likely to be, "Have you told him about your feelings?"; and, more likely than not, the answer is, "No, not really. He would probably say that he is usually right in what he says." This brief exchange does not begin to tell us what the real problems may be in that marriage, but it illustrates a common unwillingness to discuss the issues.

   In a business consulting session, a manager worried about a floundering subordinate doing only mediocre work may wistfully hope that he or she will finally catch on so that the unpleasantness of a firing can be avoided. "Have you talked in detail about those specific aspects of the work performance which are substandard?" the management consultant may ask. Again, the most common answer is, "No, I haven't had the heart to do it." The manager continues, saying, "It's tough to tell someone they're failing. But I don't see why I should even have to . . . . It should be obvious that the work is not getting done." Perhaps the biggest mistake we can make in interpersonal relationships is to assume that the other person sees the situation as we do. Discussion may be painful, but it may also be highly rewarding, since it can clear up uncertainities about how we expect others to act. It is a means of providing feedback to the other person, who may or may not use it to their advantage. But, certainly, feedback cannot be used if it is not given.

   Going back to our example of Sam eating lunch with the group of corporate officers in the boardroom, the sooner someone talks to Sam to help him understand that there is a conflict between the way he is acting and the way he "should" be acting, the more likely it is that the conflict will be resolved. Of course, Sam may respond by objecting, "If my promotion depends on those kinds of nit-picking things rather than on how well I do my job, I think I'd better go elsewhere." And he may be right. It is better that the conflict be acknowledged and confronted than to let it do its damage without the person knowing that his or her progress is being damaged or even stopped for good.

The mother trying to play simultaneous but conflicting roles in her family can either silently anguish or openly share her conflict with children and husband. There may be times when both the husband and son want the attention of the wife/mother. To attend to one exclusively means ignoring the other entirely. Or to attend to both partially may satisfy neither. In families where discussions are planned involving all members, such a mother's dilemma would certainly be an appropriate item on the agenda. Discussion can help, but not all parties may be ready or able to handle the conflict by this means. There are still other ways that managing conflict can be attempted.

Ignoring and Avoiding the Conflict.   This is a more passive reaction to role-status-identity conflicts. It is less likely to be effective, but it is one of the most popular solutions people try. Sam's boss can ignore the slight deviations from the organization's norms for young executives, and can avoid embarrassment, by dropping Sam from the list of bright young men eligible for promotion. Unfortunately, this is often done with few people being the wiser—in more than one sense. Ignoring the problem seldom makes it go away.

The situation creating the status-role conflict may be very attractive even though the inner conflict is painful. A person soliciting funds or selling products and services wants to obtain the money but doesn't want to suffer rejection or rebuffs from the potential contributor or customer. There is a desire both to *approach* the conflict area and to *avoid* it. As the person gets closer to the conflict situation, the avoidance need will increase as the approach need decreases. Can you remember a time when you were going to make a call on someone, and just as you got close to the door you turned around and walked away—only to turn once more and approach the door? Or can you remember reaching for the telephone and then withdrawing your hand? If you are selling for a living and desperately need the money from a sale, the approach need may become strong enough to overcome the avoidance need, and the door will be reached. Unfortunately, the strong need to make the sale may decrease your sensitivity to the customer's needs, thus reducing the chances of making the sale. On the other hand, you may be able to reduce the avoidance need in the sales situation by remembering that the product is worthwhile and probably needed by the customer; you also may recognize that the customer may turn down the product but know that this doesn't mean you are being rejected as a person. Further insight into yourself may help you see that being turned down by just one of many customers is not so important, and the avoidance need is lessened.

Compromising and Establishing Priorities.   Attempts at resolving differences in expected behavior often reach a stalemate because the parties to the conflict continue to maintain their extreme positions. To help adjust contradictory demands, a third person may be brought in to act as an arbitrator. This has some chance of working if all agree to abide by the judgments of arbitration. Obviously, the arbitrator must not have vested interest or show favoritism. Asking a third party to make the decision seems to provide some face saving for both adversaries.

Establishing priorities can also help reduce conflict. For example, imagine a secretary who is trying to do the work of eight college professors, all of whom believe their individual work is of utmost importance. If, by chance, each gives work to the secretary one at a time, and if the project can be done before the next request arrives, all goes well. But, more realistically, seven or eight may have "urgent" requests late in the same afternoon. Each expects the secretary to play her expected role and do the urgent work immediately. To say, "I'm sorry, I can't do it now; I'm busy with Professor Pate's work," can create several problems. Suppose Professor Pate is the junior professor in the department and his work was given to the secretary earlier than another professor with seniority? Who comes first? Whose status is challenged? And who has an aspirin for the bewildered secretary?

Everyone's urgent work cannot be done at once. A compromise is in order. Perhaps the definition of the word "urgent" needs to be discussed during a department meeting, with the secretary present. Perhaps priorities can be established: announcements of quickly called committee meetings come first; letters from school administrators requesting information come second; examinations, third; manuscripts, fourth; and so on. If a senior and junior professor arrive at the same moment with an examination to be typed, the senior professor's request comes first. But even with such understood priorities, trouble will arise if there is no flexibility for unusual circumstances. Judgments are still necessary, and conflicts may occur without adequate solutions. Perhaps some other means of conflict management may be tried.

Integrating Conflicting Elements. When there are conflicting sides to an issue, usually there is merit on both sides. Let us illustrate this problem with an example. The new supervisor of a data-processing department was proud to be chosen from among her former co-workers, but there were some problems. She wanted to retain the friendships and camaraderie she had enjoyed before, but she also was expected to oversee their work and take disciplinary action if necessary. Her friends were delighted with her promotion because the former supervisor was a strict, fussbudgety young man, who was always "on the go" trying to create a good impression by running a "tight ship." His ship may have been tight, but the crew felt oppressed. All that, they imagined, would change now that their colleague was in charge; she would be more lenient and would let them bend the rules. On her first day as supervisor, she saw the prolonged coffee breaks, increased private telephone calls during work time, and heard the shrill laughter as groups gathered to celebrate their new freedom. But when she noticed work stopping thirty minutes before quitting time and some workers leaving early, she knew she had to do something. She wanted to play the role both of friend and manager; she wanted to feel on an equal footing with her friends, but she recognized the changed status as their boss; she wanted to eliminate the former sense of oppression but also wanted to do well as the first woman supervisor of the data-processing group. She made a plan.

The next morning she called a meeting of the group. She identified the status-role-identity conflicts as she saw them in herself and the potential conflicts she saw between herself and the group. She asked for their feedback to see if they understood what she was trying to say. She led a discussion of the department's various policies and procedures and sought consensus on the priorities or relative importance of each. She noted that the former supervisor had been overly strict, but she added that if she were overly lax that could be just as bad. "Let's avoid extremes," she said. She also pointed out that it would be to the advantage of every woman in the group, as well as herself, that the performance level of the group stay as high as it had been. "Or could we do even better, do you think?"

This sensitive young supervisor had avoided a "me versus them" situation. She had avoided using power over her group and had tried to find ways to get the group to use power together, as a team. Because of the conflicts she faced, she had resorted to a confrontation rather than ignoring the situation. Out of this confrontation came ways of managing the conflict; but an even more remarkable result was obtained. Much of the previous sense of oppression came because the former supervisor had overreacted to occasional private telephone calls; to him, any laughter had meant that the group was not serious in their work; he had made it a rule that no one could come in late or leave early for any reason unless they were docked a half-day's vacation time or a half-day's pay. The new supervisor, in discussing the performance of the group, emphasized their professional contributions to the company and asked for their help in maintaining and even improving the performance level. Attention was diverted from less important issues and focused on the more important matter of quick and accurate work. It would be nice if this approach worked every time in all organizations, but, of course, it doesn't.

Conforming and Compartmentalizing. Trying to be "all things to all people" can become a way of life. If our boss expects compliance, if our spouse expects dominance, if our minister or rabbi expects morality, and if our close friend expects company in extramarital activites, we may experience role conflict. Depending upon our needs, we may try to conform to each situation. Having to be different people in different situations, we will also experience internal value conflicts. We cannot value both marital fidelity and "swinging" experiences without experiencing cognitive and moral dissonance. Something usually has to give. Either we change our behavior in one situation so there is less conflict, or we change our moral structure so there is less conflict. But there is another approach to this kind of conflict which may be tried. It is a less healthy way of managing conflicts, but it is common. We can conform in each situation, but doing so by resorting to a mental defense mechanism known as *compartmentalization.*

Through compartmentalization we maintain mental separation between each status-role situation and fool outselves into believing there is no conflict. People seem to have a capacity (not infinite, but extensive) to avoid seeing contradictions in their role decisions. For example, we play the role of the honest person but still cheat on our income tax ("everyone does it"). We can be scrupulously careful to return the exact change to a neighbor when we grocery shop for her but still remove a pocket calculator from the offices of our employer ("It's a big company; they can afford it"). We may carry a heavy package for a colleague ("It's important to be helpful") but let our spouses struggle with the groceries from the car to the kitchen ("Our marriage is fifty-fifty"). We know that if someone tells us something in confidence, that confidence should be respected; so, when we pass it on to others, we caution them "not to tell anyone." We may believe in equality of opportunity, but also believe that "it's not what you know but who you know."

Providing Distance in Time and Space. Separating people and events may help avoid or even resolve conflicts. For example, a common problem is how to treat the divorced couple when both remain our friends. We may not be comfortable being friendly with both when they're together, because that upsets them both. A solution may be to continue seeing them, but separately. Giving a party, we might invite one but not the other; at the next opportunity, we reverse the invitation. For another example, imagine the couple whose parents live in the same distant town. There may be status-role conflicts during a visit. If the wife usually plays the dominant role in planning social events, she may assume this right in deciding how much time to spend with each set of parents. If the husband's father believes his son should "wear the pants in the family" and not be bossed by his wife, the stage is set for a conflict-filled visit. The visiting son, who plays the passive role with his wife but who also wants to live up to his father's expectations, may be uncomfortable in either letting his wife make the allocation of time or insisting that he make that decision. Such a role-status conflict may be ameliorated by agreeing ahead of time that exactly one-half of the visiting time will be spent with each set of parents. Or, the couple may agree, "You stay with your parents and I'll stay with mine." But these solutions introduce rigidity into the situations. Even though this rigidity may minimize status and role conflicts, the rigidity itself may introduce other problems.

Relying on Rigid Rules.   Our status in a group carries with it certain rights as well as obligations. What those rights are to each group member is a matter of individual perception. Our status itself may fluctuate from time to time or situation to situation. It is not a fact of certainty but a matter of judgment, which can be as subjective and whimsical as people themselves. Our roles (those behaviors we think others expect of us) are often uncertain, temporary, and highly dependent upon our situation.

Such uncertainty can be unsettling and provide a source of conflict and stress. Establishing rigid rules of conduct may appear to be a means of reducing that friction, but just as often they create new difficulties.

In a sales office, both clerical and sales personnel may agree that the salespersons have higher status than the secretaries and clerks. The salespersons may earn more money, have more freedom of movement, and appear to be doing more important work. This does not mean that the lower-status clerical people are happy with this status difference, but they may be resigned to it. But a point of contention may be the time for reporting to work. Imagine that the clerical people are required to be at work promptly at 8:30 A.M., and tardiness causes criticism and even a loss of pay. The salespersons are employees too, but they arrive in the office later, at times they seem to choose for themselves. The office manager gives the "rational" explanation that sales requires odd hours, depending upon customers' needs, and that after a late-night appointment the salesperson should not be expected to report in until 10:00 A.M. or even later. This does not necessarily make a clerical worker feel any better, especially if he or she has just been rebuked publicly for being ten minutes late—while one of the salespersons has sauntered in an hour later. If there is enough of an uproar from the office staff, the regional manager may decide that for the sake of morale (or in an attempt to reduce an element of status conflict) *all* personnel will report at 8:30 A.M. promptly. This rigid rule may please the office staff but may alienate salespersons.

People are different. Individuals are unique. Situations vary. Circumstances change. Status-role conflict is an almost inevitable result of such difference and variability. Imposing rigid rules may be an answer, but it is rarely a good one. Instead of one inflexible rule, a better solution to the problem of our hypothetical sales office might be "Flexitime," an organizational concept which means that, in certain circumstances, an employee can begin the workday at either 7:00 A.M., 8:00 A.M., or 9:00 A.M. and end it eight hours later. This can be helpful for the working wife who wants to coordinate her day to fit her husband's, or vice versa. It can allow a working mother to make plans for child care, which might be otherwise impossible. Flexitime still requires a person to work eight hours, but the precise hours can be adjusted to fit the individual circumstances. Rigidity is replaced by flexibility. Employee conflict often is reduced and morale improved as a result.

Changing the Situation. Being "called on the carpet" is an unpleasant experience. It means that a subordinate has been ordered to come to the office of a superior for criticism. An office carpet, itself, is associated with superiority. To move from a tiled office floor to a carpeted one usually involves an increase in status; just as a walnut desk suggests more status than a metal one. For a manager to ask a subordinate to come to the manager's office implies that the manager, with superior status, has the right to put pressure on the "inferior" subordinate. The subordinate will feel at a disadvantage and may react defensively.

The manager who wants to minimize possible status conflicts might consider visiting the office of the subordinate for a consultation. Changing the situation does not change the relative positions of the participants, but the manager's willingness to meet in the subordinate's office may help open up lines of communication.

Political diplomats often decide to hold talks at a neutral meeting place—that is, neither's home country—to avoid a suggestion of status inferiority or superiority. Adversaries in a legal battle may find it easier to negotiate in an attorney's office than in either of their respective business offices. A round table may ease strains in complicated negotiations because, unlike a rectangular one, no one sits at "the head of the table." Status depends largely on the situation. Changing the situation may help solve status-conflict problems.

Changing the Person. If we cannot change the situation, we might try changing ourselves. Status is our rank position in a group. But our reaction to our status depends upon how we perceive that status in a given situation. Our perception is largely under our own control. *Perception* means giving meaning to a stimulus of some sort. If we perceive that being asked to meet in our manager's office puts us in an inferior position, then we will probably react by feeling inferior, and we will behave accordingly. If we perceive it as merely a convenient place for conversation, then we will not be trapped or tyrannized by a status-role expectancy.

Our status functions in a group only if others agree with the same rules of ranking. If you and I meet, and you believe you are superior to me, this will affect me only if I also believe you are superior. If you believe you are superior and I see us as being equal, your reaction will be tinged with feelings of superiority and mine by feelings of equality. Both of us probably will be surprised at our interactions. You will be surprised because I seem not to show proper deference. I will be surprised because you apparently expect a deference I am not ready to give. Conflict!

If I make less money than you, I will feel inferior in status only if I perceive that money makes a difference in the essential worth and dignity of people. If I do feel inferior because you make more money, I can try to make as much as you do, or I can change my way of thinking to see that money itself does not equal moral worth or value.

The way we think about ourselves and our status can make a bad situation worse, as we see in the following example. But help in changing is available.

> Richard was the victim of a merger. He was a controller with 32 years of service with the company. He was 52 and not eligible for early retirement. He was asked to leave. He was fired! He felt shame, remorse, guilt, and inadequacy. He hardly knew how to tell June, his wife. For a week, he left home at the usual time, as if he were going to work. But he only wandered the streets. He climbed to the top of the town's observation tower and stood at the railing. He looked down and wondered if he had the courage to step over. Uncharacteristically, he went into a bar at noon and ordered a double drink. And another. He felt worse!
>
> When he came home Friday night, he told his wife the whole story. He couldn't help crying. He didn't really believe her when she said that she still felt the same about him, that they'd just have to start again, that they would make out all right. That weekend, a neighbor asked Richard how things were going at work. He answered, "Oh, just fine, thank you. Well, excuse me. I have to get to work on some reports . . . ." And with that, he fled.
>
> Richard was suicidal. He didn't know it, but he was a likely candidate. He felt pessimistic about finding a job that would pay anywhere near what he had been making. He was convinced that he would lose everything he had worked for and that, as the news got out, everyone would view him with contempt. At June's urging, Richard went to his banker to discuss how to handle the mortgage and other installment notes they had. Unexpectedly, the banker was understanding, sympathetic, and personally concerned.
>
> "Richard," the banker said, "you're really coming apart over this. I've never seen you this upset. I think we can work things out. But maybe you should see somebody and get yourself straightened out. Maybe you can get some help in finding a new job and also get out of this depression you seem to be in. Let me give you a couple of names of therapists I've heard of . . . ."

Richard had a narrow view of himself. He saw his total worth as a person in being employed and earning a certain income. With the loss of employment and income, his perceived status dropped to zero, and he was unprepared to play that role. There was nothing he could do about the merger situation. There *was* something he could do about his employment situation, and there was even *more* he could do to alter his view of his own worth. In counseling, he realized that he enjoyed the love and support of his family, valued his friendships, and prized his inner certainty that he lived a life of high morality. He was helped to realize how often he had been supportive of others and how many times he had been able to demonstrate outstanding performance in his professional field. Richard was able to change his perception of himself so that his status and sense of security did not depend solely on a job position and a certain salary. To conclude the story, Richard did find other employment, but he also freed himself from a status-category trap.

Balancing Situational- and Personal-Status Variables. For most of us, status and role expectancies are a way of life. Whether we recognize it or not, we frequently are trapped, tyrannized, and duped. We are made less effective because we allow ourselves to be confined and inhibited by societal pressures. Socialization is essential to group life, but slavish conformity to status and role expectancies can be self-defeating. We can free ourselves to be more productive and happier in our work if both situational and personal variables are modified to reduce the restrictions of status.

The worker on the assembly line frequently is bored and dissatisfied with the work. The status of the occupation is low, as perceived by both outsiders and the jobholders themselves. The perceived status is low because the worker can make few decisions regarding the work itself or the workplace. Assembly-line work has been labeled as "dehumanizing" because so little of a worker's full talents and resources are used or even recognized. The worker feels little control over the situation or the outcome of personal efforts. Someone else makes decisions regarding work methods, the speed of work, when the work will start and stop, and when changes will be made. The worker is likely to feel controlled by the assembly line. Sometimes, out of frustration and rage, workers will deliberately sabotage the line and force a work stoppage. It is not unusual to hear cheers when the line is finally stopped—or at least to see many grinning faces. At that moment, morale may be at an all-time high because the workers were able to engage in planning, decision making, and group action to cause a meaningful event. Beating the system can be satisfying not only to assembly-line workers but to most of us occasionally.

Perhaps more of us work on an assembly-line type of job than we realize. The laboratory technician engaged in typing blood, the clerk checking application forms for completeness, the telephone solicitor trying to make appointments for salespersons, the toll-booth operator endlessly collecting money from drivers, are clearly assembly-line workers. The young attorney checking library references for the senior partners, the auditor verifying all the figures in a company's accounts, and the army physician performing in repetition one part of an initial medical screening of recruits may also be considered assembly-line workers. Ordinarily, we do not think of a lawyer, accountant, or physician in such a way, and, indeed, even if they are engaged in routine work, their extensive and broad professional knowledge is constantly necessary in making routine decisions. But professionals who are, even if temporarily, performing routine work may well begin to feel the same loss of status and dehumanizing effect because more of their talents and resources are not being utilized.

During the decade of the 1970's, there was a growing awareness that America's work force is more sophisticated, better educated, and has higher expectations than ever before. During this same time, efforts have been made to enrich various jobs by changing the work situation to allow and encourage the fullest utilization of worker talents, decision-making ability, and responsibility. Assembly-line operations have been changed so that teams of workers function as a unit, making work-related decisions and sharing the responsibility for both the quality and quantity of the work. Experiments have been conducted such as allowing individual workers to assemble an entire radio, check it for quality, package it, and even receive and handle complaints. Some auto factory teams assemble an entire automobile transmission. Teams working in coal mines cooperatively plan and execute safety measures and are trusted to make other decisions regarding production methods. The change has been philosophical as well as practical. Increasing a worker's authority to act and to make decisions concerning his or her own work responsibilities, and broadening the kinds of work a worker can do—so that the worker finds more meaning and satisfaction in the tasks—often produces significant results. Production may go up, while accidents go down. The workers' sense of being trusted will increase. More work may be accomplished with less fatigue. Such results have not always been uniform, but the beneficial effects of the experimental work done so far have encouraged thousands of firms to change the structure of their workplace, to make it a more satisfying, meaningful, and productive organization of people.

We have learned that status is a rank position in a group. We each have many such ranks, depending upon our various group memberships. We are affected by the status position assigned to us by others, but even more by the status position we assign to ourselves. Our status is affected by both our situation and our perception of that situation. There is much we can do to free ourselves from a status trap and move to higher status or higher satisfaction.

STATUS MOBILITY

It is assumed that most of the readers of this book are interested in either keeping their present status position or increasing it. *Status anxiety* is that feeling of dread or apprehension associated with the anticipation of change. Change, itself, is always with us. Even 2,500 years ago the Greek philosopher Heraclitus was convinced, "There is nothing permanent except change." It is easy to assume that "People naturally resist change." But it is too much of a generalization. How many of you would resist a change in salary in an upward direction? Do we not delight in our changing circumstances when we win a prize, receive a gift, obtain a degree or certificate, or are welcomed as a new member of a club? We accept moments of change more readily because they include an increase in status. On the other hand, some persons with low self-esteem may resist such "good" changes precisely because they do not confirm the existing low self-evaluation. It is as if the low-esteem person would rather confirm this self-image than risk the unknown in a changing situation. But ordinarily change is feared and anxiety is aroused when change has the possibility of lowering our status. *Status anxiety* is associated with uncertainity about our future status and especially with the fear that our status may be lowered.

If America is known as the "land of opportunity," it is because upward status mobility is possible. But only a small percentage of people actually achieve an upward shift in their social status during their lifetime. Sociologists maintain that ". . . the amount of vertical mobility in the United States today is only a very small percentage of what it would be if people born at all levels had a truly equal chance to attain any given status."[15]

Upward status mobility is associated with awareness, opportunity, and effort; lack of upward mobility is associated with ignorance, denied opportunity, and indifference. Some of this is under a person's control and some is not. You can increase your awareness, and you can increase your effort; but whether you can influence opportunity is a matter of circumstances, legal efforts, and public opinion.

Occupation is one of the most important elements in determining our social rank in a community, as well as in determining our degree of self-actualization. One of the most prized freedoms is that of occupational choice, although many factors may keep us from making our own best choice. Occupational-guidance specialists may free a child of high native ability but lower-class expectations by helping the child become aware of a wider range of available occupations. This alone may not be sufficient to counteract the subtle and pervasive social conditioning of the child's early background, but it could be a start. Occupational guidance is indicated not only for the young before and during high school, but for the 40- or 50-year-old individual who may not have found the most fulfilling work.

Such guidance is available in most communities, from high school and college counselors or from private psychologists. The decision about what

[15] David Popenoe, *Sociology* (Englewood Cliffs, N.J.: Prentice-Hall, 1971).

to do is directly limited by the awareness of the occupational possibilities. Of course, lack of money for training and education is also a limiting factor. But if we don't know what is available, we certainly cannot choose it. Here is a do-it-yourself plan for either escaping your present occupational-status-category trap or verifying that what you are presently doing is exactly what you should continue to do.

1. Seek counseling from a qualified specialist in occupational guidance. A licensed psychologist in your community is a good place to start. The psychologist you contact initially may not specialize or be interested in vocational guidance but can probably refer you to someone who can help.

Vocational-interest tests such as the Kuder Preference Record or the Strong-Campbell Interest Inventory are standard measures which compare your pattern of interests with those of people presently active in a variety of occupations. If your interests are similar to those now engaged in a particular specialty, the possibility is that you would enjoy and do well in that field.

No test or vocational-guidance specialist can tell you for sure what occupation is best for you. They can provide hints, but not definite answers. The best answers for you are the ones you provide for yourself.

2. After vocational-interest and aptitude testing, which should give you only broad directions in your search, increase your knowledge of the enormous number of occupations which exist. Go to your local library and request *The Dictionary of Occupational Titles.** In it are listed more than 20,000 occupational titles with brief descriptive paragraphs. Browse through this volume and read the descriptions of those vocational titles which catch your interest. Read about the occupations whether you presently possess the necessary education or skills or not. Make notes of those which seem to be the most interesting. Then proceed to the next step.

3. For each interesting occupation you found in the dictionary search further in the library for additional information. Ask the librarian for help. Read about the entrance requirements of each occupation. Find out what training or education is required. Look up the starting salaries. Read the trend reports showing whether there is an increasing or decreasing demand for those occupations. Keep looking. Libraries have the information. Don't give up!

4. By this time, you have narrowed the possibilities. For those occupations you have discovered—and which seem feasible for you to pursue—start looking for people now doing those things! Go talk to someone doing what you think you might enjoy as a life work. Call them up for an appointment. You will be pleasantly surprised at how willing most will be to talk to you and to try to help. Of course, some will not want to bother. But most people are eager to talk about what they're doing. Go talk and learn. And make a choice!

* *Dictionary of Occupational Titles*, Fourth Edition, 1977, U.S. Department of Labor, U.S. Employment Service.

There's absolutely no reason why you should be stuck in a dead-end job which gives you little satisfaction. You can explore new occupations, new opportunities, and new status categories. You can remain in your present status trap if you wish, but you do have a chance to move out and up.

We found earlier that each person initially acquires the status of the family they were born into. This *acquired status* may well be the one you own for the rest of your life, especially if you happen to be black, lower class, poor, or female. Race, class, and sex are social categories that often affect status, role, and identity characteristics, ones which can lead to denial of opportunity and self-induced feelings of doubt, despair, and apathy. But an *achieved status*, which depends upon your own efforts and aspirations, may give you the additional freedom that allows you to go beyond your early socialization, becoming the person you are truly capable of being.

Becoming the person you are capable of being is a lifetime job. It is a journey rather than a destination. It is an act of self-actualizing which depends greatly upon your understanding of human *communication* and *motivation*. The next four chapters will study these two important human processes in detail.

SUMMARY

In this "land of the free," it is not nice to think that we may be trapped in a status category, tyrannized by role expectations, and duped by overreliance on our masculine or feminine identity. But the one thing worse than realizing how our freedom is limited is to not recognize its limitations at all. Because we are members of many groups, we are expected to display different kinds of role behavior; inevitably there will be conflict. We will experience conflict within ourselves about what we think is expected of us. There will be conflict between the role we want to play and that which is expected or demanded by others. Conflict may be inevitable, but there are ways of managing or coping with conflict so that we gain more freedom as individuals.

Coping with conflict may not be easy, but there are a series of strategies we may try. Identifying and defining the conflict may be the most important first step to take. Discussing the issues involved, compromising, attempting to integrate conflicting elements, and trying to change either the situation or the persons involved are some of the major means of managing conflict.

QUESTIONS FOR REVIEW
AND DISCUSSION:

1.   In our society we are free to do whatever we want. True or False? Discuss, using the theory of socialization.

2.   How are we tyrannized by our expected roles as a male or female in our society?

3.   What are social controls and how do they affect us?

4.   Conflict between role-expectations may be managed or resolved in a number of ways. Which of the methods of conflict management seems most likely to work for you? Explain.

5

SELF-MOTIVATION

The life which is unexamined is not worth living.

SOCRATES*

To be what we are, and to become what we are capable of becoming, is the only end of life.

ROBERT LOUIS STEVENSON**

What is life all about? What does it mean? Why do people do what they do? The human being is a curious, creative, achieving, socially-conditioned, and meaning-searching-animal who uses a written and spoken language to communicate what is learned from his or her experiences. Human beings are especially concerned about *why* they do *what* they do.

Why we do what we do, at a given moment, depends upon our *self-image* and the level of *needs* and *wants* presently experienced. It depends,

*Apology, 38.
**Familiar Studies of Men and Books, 1882.

too, on the *alternatives* we can see or create, on the *perceived probability* that certain actions will result in the achievement of goals and satisfactions, and on our perception of the *situation* we are in. The italicized words suggest only some of the factors and complexities involved in self-motivation. In Chapter 1 we saw how the reliability and validity of our observations influenced our ability to predict how individuals will behave in certain situations. In Chapter 2, the tyranny of the image we have of ourselves was seen as a lifelong process that we partially manage and control depending upon our awareness of how this image is formed. The personal identity we think of as our "self" and the conflicts between our personal needs and society's demands were examined in Chapters 3 and 4. Now, we need to see how all these conditions and pressures come together to create the environment which we respond to and which determines how we and others shape our lives for better or worse.

How do we make those decisions which minimize failures and bring us the greatest satisfactions? How can we motivate others to do what we want them to do? The next three chapters are especially concerned with understanding and influencing the behavior of individuals as they live and work within the limits and opportunities of both small groups and larger organizations.

All motivation is essentially self-motivation. What we do at a given moment in a given situation depends primarily on our *perception* of the desirability of the various courses of action available. We move toward those sources of satisfaction which appear to meet our needs. Others may think they know what is best for us, but we tend to do things for *our* reasons, not theirs. We do not live in isolation, however. We are members of small groups, such as families and clubs, and larger organizations, such as companies, government agencies, churches, schools, and professional and union associations. Organizations pervade our lives and provide those circumstances and opportunities which form the menu from which we pick and choose our physical and emotional nourishment. Organizations seem to have personalities of their own. Some are protective and benevolent; others are demanding and severe. Some organizations seem to enhance the development of the individual; others are dehumanizing. (The dynamics of organizations and their influence on individual growth and decision making constitute an area of study that is largely beyond the scope of this book.)[1]

---

[1] For those interested in understanding the influence of organizations on individual behavior, the following references are suggested: Abraham K. Korman, *Organizational Behavior* (Englewood Cliffs, N.J.: Prentice-Hall, 1977). H. Randolph Bobbit, Jr., and Robert H. Breinholt, *Organizational Behavior: Understanding and Prediction* (Englewood Cliffs, N.J.: Prentice-Hall, 1978). Stephen J. Carrol, and Henry L. Tosi, *Organizational Behavior* (Chicago, Ill.: St. Clair Press, 1977). J. Clifton Williams, *Human Behavior in Organizations* (Cincinnati, Ohio: South-Western Publishing Co., 1978).

MOTIVATION AS A STATE OF BEING

Motivation is a state of being. Because we are alive, we are motivated. It is common to hear someone say, "I'm just not motivated right now," but what is usually meant is that the person is not overtly doing something at the moment. One can be intensely motivated while being absolutely still. In fact, inactivity may be the result when so many motivational forces are operating from so many different directions that no one direction of movement seems feasible. We can be "frozen with fear" because of extreme motivational pressures. We may experience feelings of apathy or lethargy and think our level of motivation is low. But as will be discussed later, these may be defensive reactions in the face of unresolved conflicts between strong but opposing motives. *Motivation is a continuous process of interaction between needs within the individual and between the individual and the environment.* It never stops. This is just one of the reasons why motivation is so complex and difficult to understand. Figure 5-1 illustrates some of the complexities of being a continuously motivated person.

figure 5-1   The Motivated Person

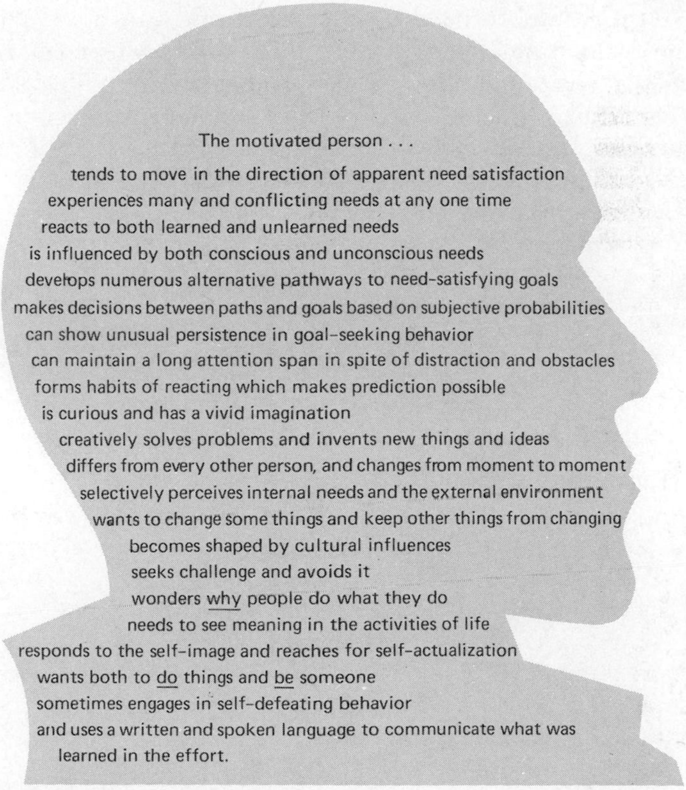

The motivated person . . .

tends to move in the direction of apparent need satisfaction
experiences many and conflicting needs at any one time
reacts to both learned and unlearned needs
is influenced by both conscious and unconscious needs
develops numerous alternative pathways to need-satisfying goals
makes decisions between paths and goals based on subjective probabilities
can show unusual persistence in goal-seeking behavior
can maintain a long attention span in spite of distraction and obstacles
forms habits of reacting which makes prediction possible
is curious and has a vivid imagination
creatively solves problems and invents new things and ideas
differs from every other person, and changes from moment to moment
selectively perceives internal needs and the external environment
wants to change some things and keep other things from changing
becomes shaped by cultural influences
seeks challenge and avoids it
wonders why people do what they do
needs to see meaning in the activities of life
responds to the self-image and reaches for self-actualization
wants both to do things and be someone
sometimes engages in self-defeating behavior
and uses a written and spoken language to communicate what was
learned in the effort.

If this verbal portrait of the motivated person sounds like a table of contents, it is so strictly by design. Each part of the portrait must be examined in detail to bring out the character of the entire individual. In this case, let that character be *you*—you who are holding this book right now. Why not take a look at yourself as we examine self-motivation and understand this process from a most personal view? Some of the examples may not fit your particular situation. So, think of examples from your own life, your own unique background of experiences, your own personal point of view. Why not try to use this reading time to better understand what makes you tick? And in so doing, achieve a better vantage point in the everyday effort to understand why others do what they do. As we pointed out in Chapter 1, understanding leads to better prediction, which in turn leads to more control. Perhaps the best place to start is with self-understanding, self-prediction, and self-control.

MOTIVATION IS GOAL-DIRECTED

Right now you have one thing in mind. In a moment it will be something different. What would you like to have right now? Something to eat? Or drink? Something that smells good and tastes good? Would you like a more comfortable chair? A cooler room? Or a warmer one? If you are alone, maybe you would like to be with somebody. Who? Let your mind wander and think about who you would like to have next to you, right now! Or if you are with someone, perhaps you would like to be alone. Or at least be left alone. And far away. Let yourself become aware of how your "goals" change from moment to moment.

Figure 5-2 illustrates three important principles of motivation:

1. Motivation is goal-directed toward need satisfaction.
2. Multiple needs and goals may exist at the same time.
3. Conflicting needs may create tendencies to move in opposite directions.

By this time in your life you have motivated yourself to reach for a great many goals. (Figure 5-2 suggests only a small fraction of the many and conflicting needs a unique person may experience at any one time.) These goals have been *material* things, such as food, shelter, and the thousands of possessions most of us desire. Some goals may have been *activities* such as athletics, the arts, professional achievements, leisure, daydreaming, etc. Goals also can be states of *being*, such as experiencing love, peace of mind, spiritual awareness, creative thinking, trust and integrity, and so on. Some of the goals you have reached you are proud of, and some, perhaps, make you ashamed. Some of your behavior you take

figure 5-2   Motivation of the Unique Individual

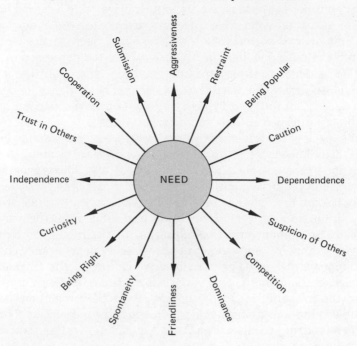

credit for, and some you blame on someone else. You understand perfectly why you have done certain things but are puzzled by others. You may have thought to yourself, or said out loud, "Now why did I do that?. . . I don't know what's gotten into me . . . I don't know what I want to do . . . or be. I don't even know how I feel about that . . . or him . . . or her."

Our daily behavior may be goal-directed, but we are not necessarily always aware of what those goals are. We are not always satisfied with the goals we have reached. Some goals remain important to us even though we are repeatedly frustrated in our attempts to reach them. Most of us have had the experience of giving up a desired goal because it was in conflict with still another goal which seemed more desirable.

Moving in the Direction of Need Satisfaction

We *tend* to move in the direction of apparent need satisfaction. *Tendency* suggests a readiness to act or move but not a certainty that action will take place. The awareness of hunger pangs may create a readiness to eat, but other factors in the motivational process may prevent movement toward the goal of food and the action of eating. Much depends upon our perception of the situation. For example, we may be hungry but not eat because we are more motivated to lose weight and appear more attractive to others, because we have arrived at our hotel room late and believe no restaurant will be open, because the food that is available is not appealing, or because we are too depressed to eat.

The tendency to satisfy the hunger need is there, but the motivated behavior to satisfy that need does not occur. The tendency, or predisposition, is or is not followed by need-satisfying behavior depending upon a combination of perceptions and circumstances.

We speak of the tendency to move toward need satisfaction in another sense. Our knowledge of human behavior consists of many *generalizations* about how people act in certain situations. These generalizations are useful in predicting how groups of individuals *may* react, but we can rarely be *sure* just how one individual *will* react. Individuals are unique. They differ from all other individuals and differ from themselves from moment to moment and from situation to situation. Sometimes they behave rationally and sometimes not. Uniqueness and change are continuous states of being. The best we can do at the current state of knowledge about motivation is to look at generalizations, try to understand the probabilities involved, and make the predictions as well as possible. Thus, our first generalization about the motivational process involves a tendency to move toward need satisfaction rather than the actual attaining of that goal.

We tend to move in the direction of *apparent* need satisfaction. The word apparent indicates that it is our perception of the value of a need-satisfying goal which is involved. You may have been motivated to buy something for your home only to discover it was the wrong color, didn't fit, or didn't please other members of the household. The initial perception was enough to engage in goal-directed behavior at the time (you bought it), but the purchase did not satisfy the related goals of looking right and pleasing others. If, through some mental trial and error while in the store, it became apparent to you that the article was not suitable, then satisfaction of the need to add furnishings to the home would have been postponed. From a personal point of view, reality is whatever we perceive it to be now. We may learn later that our perception of reality at the time was not "real" because a later perception has given us a different view of reality.

Referring again to Figure 5-2, any individual can be seen as a collection of needs. These vary in strength and in the way in which they are combined. Longer arrows suggest stronger drives toward need satisfaction. Some of these needs are relatively dormant, and others are currently felt with some urgency. Some of these needs are conscious, and others, unconscious. Some needs are learned, and others, unlearned. Some needs we are willing to acknowledge, and others we pretend we do not have. From this collection of needs, pressures for their satisfaction are created.

A particular goal may satisfy several needs at the same time. Being promoted to manager may contribute to the satisfaction of needs for prestige, control over others, higher income, self-satisfaction, and so forth. The hunger need combined with the prestige need may motivate someone to eat lunch in a fine restaurant, even though that action leads to paying a large bill, which conflicts with another need to conserve money.

Needs Are Often in Conflict

A third principle of motivation suggested in Figure 5-2 is that we often deal not only with multiple needs but with needs which are in conflict. For example, a salesperson may need to make a call on a prospective customer and also need to avoid another rejection. The felt need to make the call may be very strong while the salesperson is in the office getting ready to start the day. The need to avoid rejection may be there, but it may not be particularly strong. As the salesperson approaches the office of the prospect, the imagined rejection may loom so large that the earlier need to make the call is overwhelmed. The desire to *approach* the prospect is overwhelmed by the desire to *avoid* the possible rejection. We can easily imagine this salesperson getting near the office of the feared prospect, hesitating, retreating, hesitating again, walking back to the prospect's office, hesitating . . . Ambivalence! Can you understand why this person might step into a nearby coffee shop to summon up more courage to make the call—or to reflect on the possibility of getting out of the sales field?

Our simplified model of motivation suggests an individual with tendencies to move in sixteen directions at once (Figure 5-2). Our best guess is that the individual will move in that direction which tends to maximize the satisfaction of needs. But moving in the direction of, say, a need for cooperation with a competitor may mean moving away from the potential satisfaction of competition. This is not to say that cooperation and competition are always in conflict. But sometimes cooperating with a competitor may lead to losing when we would much rather win. In Figure 5-2, if we let the length of each arrow suggest the relative strength of the drive toward need satisfaction, our hypothetical individual has a slightly stronger need for cooperation than for competition. There is also a slightly greater need to satisfy the need for curiosity than for caution. The need for dominance is stronger than the need for submission, and so on. And all of these needs are likely to change with time and depending upon the situation. If we picture our individual as being in the center of a web of multiple and conflicting needs, then, reducing or increasing the strength of a drive or the level of satisfaction may immediately change all the other drive strengths and the relationships between the various needs. Moving strongly toward showing that we are right on an issue may conflict with our need to be popular. We may increase our drive toward aggressiveness in demonstrating that we are right but find that this conflicts with our desire for friendliness from those around us. Our strong need for independence of action may conflict with an opposing need to be dependent upon certain important individuals in our social situation.

We need to look at further complications of this motivational process. The entire combination of needs, apparent satisfactions, and the interactions of needs with each other change when:

1. A particular satisfaction goal begins to seem more appealing than before

2. There is an increase in the perceived probability that one of the goals can be reached more easily (more about probability later)

3. An outside source of stimulation (such as advertising) catches the attention of the individual and highlights one of the satisfactions

4. Certain needs have been relatively satisfied and momentarily have lost some of their motivational appeal

Making choices between conflicting need satisfactions and choosing when to react to either an internal or external stimulus will be discussed in detail in Chapter 6.

Attention and Imagination

Attention and *imagination* are extrinsic and intrinsic factors in the motivational process. Attention-getting devices impinge upon us from outside and tend to get our attention. A blinking light is more attention arousing than a nonblinking light. Intermittent sounds attract us or distract us more than steady or regular sounds (although a steadily dripping faucet can be powerfully distracting). The lighthouse lamp rotates. The train's headlight swings back and forth. The ambulance siren or air-raid-warning siren wails up and down in pitch. The skillful speaker introduces variation in voice and subject matter to keep the audience awake. The worn out joke about training the mule involves the application of a two-by-four to the head to first get its attention. Kitchen sounds attract our attention when we are hungry but will go unnoticed after the meal (unless we are the one making the clean-up sounds). Hearing our name being paged rivets our attention to the message. The motivated person can be seen as a collection of needs waiting for an attention-getting source of need satisfaction to come along. But this suggests a passive role in the motivational process. Much human activity is active in seeking known sources of satisfaction and *imagining* new sources which can be created.

Imagination is a human talent which allows us to invent labor-saving devices and to engage in mental trial and error. We can visualize a conversation we are about to have and make corrections in our approach before we are actually in the situation. This same imagination produces needless worry and apprehension about troubles that never happen. The skillful TV advertiser appeals to our imagination in talking about a certain food or drink, and we move toward the refrigerator or store in search of the taste delights we all too vividly imagine. Imagination moved humankind to invent a language, a printing press, and mass distribution of newspapers and magazines. Just imagine the impact of human imagination! Imagination produces mental images of different sources of satisfaction for any one need. It suggests different pathways to reach any one goal. It leads to exploration and discovery: new frontiers, new sources of energy, new solutions to old political problems. Imagination leads us both to self-enhancing and self-defeating ways of living. It is a blessing or curse, depending upon how we use it.

Learned and Unlearned Needs

A need may be defined as some requirement for survival or adjustment to our environment. At a most basic level we need water, food, air, and protection from danger. These needs are not learned but are innate or natural. In response to these needs or requirements for life, we experience a tension or drive to satisfy those needs. The infant experiences these tensions at birth but is helpless to move actively toward a source of satisfaction. In some cases even breathing must be started with a slap.

In response to a biological need or requirement, the human being experiences a tension to satisfy this need. Obtaining the goal or object which satisfies a biological need tends to reduce the strength of the tension. When we are thirsty, we start looking for water and continue until we find it. As soon as we have a drink, we have less interest or desire to search for more water. The longer we go without water, however, the greater is this biological need and the stronger is the tension. If we are without water for an abnormally long time, we become frantic in our efforts to find it and may think of little else until we are successful in our search.

Biological needs continue to be a major source of motivation, but other needs are learned throughout our lifetime and become as important—or even more important—as motivators. In his famous theory of motivation, psychologist Abraham Maslow stresses that these physiological needs for sustaining life are fundamental and must be largely satisfied before other higher-level needs become prominent as motivators of human behavior. Maslow suggests that a hierarchy of needs exists. As physiological needs are   satisfied, the need for safety or protection from external threat becomes more prominent. As the safety need is satisfied, it fades as a motivator and the need to be included in affectionate relationships with a family and others moves into prominence. Then desires for self-esteem, esteem from others, and recognized competence become predominant motive forces. And finally, Maslow's highest level of need is that for self-actualization, self-fulfillment, or the realization of one's ultimate potential as a human being.[2]

There is a common-sense appeal to this explanation of motivation, but it is easy to think of some exceptions. And the exceptions occur because of some very powerful *learned* needs. Learned and unlearned needs are intermingled in sometimes subtle ways. Our unlearned need for food motivates us to learn efficient and effective ways of satisfying our hunger needs. We may learn how to hunt it, grow it, make money to buy it, or steal it. We learn to prefer it cooked or raw. We learn that social status is associated with eating certain foods. But on a more serious and life-threatening level, we learn that certain social and status issues are worth dying for. The rejected suitor may commit homicide and/or suicide. The executive passed over for promotion may drink heavily to try and blot out some of the despair and become involved in an automobile accident. Attempting to prove his masculine adequacy (a culturally learned idea), the mightily motivated male may jog too long, push himself beyond endurance in his work, or refuse needed medical or psychiatric help until it is too late. Literally, learned needs can become just as important for survival as the unlearned needs at the biological level.

Learning an Assortment of Responses

A major step in the motivational process is the establishment of an *assortment of learned responses* that can act to satisfy needs. The need itself impels the individual to activity, but it is through a learning process that the most efficient ways of satisfying needs or reducing their tensions are discovered. The motivational process entails the location of a goal object and the decision as to which of a number of possible activities might be used to reach the goal. The repetition of need-reducing activities results in these activities becoming learned as habits. The strength of any habit will ordinarily be greater as the strength of the need and the frequency with which it must be dealt are increased.

---

[2] A modification of Maslow's theory of motivation has been developed which emphasizes three basic needs: existence needs, relatedness needs, and growth needs. See: C.P. Alderfer, *Existence, Relatedness, and Growth: Human Needs in Organizational Settings* (New York: Free Press, 1972).

EMOTIONAL MOTIVATION

Emotions play an important part in our lives as powerful motivators of human behavior. Advertisers and salespersons hope to arouse emotions of delight, greed, fear, urgency, affection, disgust, excitement, and anger and show that a purchase will help the buyer achieve or avoid a continuation of the aroused emotion. Emotions motivate behavior in some of the same ways as biological needs. The presence of an emotion tends to produce a tension or drive toward or away from an object, situation, or person. Obtaining the goal objective satisfies the emotional need and helps restore a balance. Biological needs motivate the individual toward activities that assist in survival. In the same way, emotions such as fear help keep the individual away from threatening situations. Emotions such as affection attract us to individuals or groups, where we may experience security, protection, and freedom from loneliness.

Emotions produce changes in us at three levels. First, we have the conscious experience of feeling something. Something happens *to* us, and, in that sense, we are passive recipients of a change in our internal condition. We can be seized by fear, overwhelmed by depression, uplifted by joy, and torn apart by jealousy. Emotions have the capacity to devastate and disrupt our normal functioning, or they can produce some of our most sublime moments and lead to unparalleled achievements. Second, emotions are accompanied by behavioral expressions. Nonverbal facial expressions and posture often clearly indicate the emotion, such as hostility, guilt, or delight, being experienced. Verbal and vocal squeals, grunts, gasps, and stammers—with or without words of delight, indifference, astonishment, and embarrassment—tend to communicate the existence of emotion. We have virtually no *control* over the existence of the emotion and our experience of it, but we do learn ways of *concealing* any bodily expression of the emotion. One may experience strong emotion but give no outward sign of it. Conversely, one can display behavior suggesting strong emotions, even though the emotion is not being felt. The good actor portrays emotion through voice sounds and behavior but does not necessarily experience it. Third, emotion is a physiological process. During the presence of emotions, there are definite activities in the portion of the nervous system that controls those smooth muscles which make up the blood vessels, sweat glands, heart, and all the rest of the visceral and glandular systems. This *autonomic nervous system* functions in an automatic way to maintain body systems such as blood temperature and other homeostatic mechanisms. During the presence of strong emotion such as fear or joy, we will notice an increased heart rate, perhaps sweaty palms, rapid, shallow breathing, and a flushed face. These are signals that the body is rapidly making internal adjustments which might be appropriate either for *flight* from the situation or to *fight*, if that is necessary. We may not permit ourselves either to flee or fight, but the body's internal preparation is going on anyway. Our awareness of this physiological activity may be heightened excitement, slight confusion or distress, or even a "bursting" sensation as with happiness or joy.

Emotions Are Often Overlooked Or Denied

With the pulse pounding in the ears, the stomach tied in knots, the palms dripping with sweat, and the mouth dry, it is amazing that someone is able, apparently, to "play it cool" and appear nonchalant. In our culture, it is "normal" for strong emotions usually to be hidden, denied, or at least minimized in behavioral manifestations. Let's look at an example. A young manager has been on the job only six months when it becomes apparent that a subordinate is functioning so far below standard that dismissal is necessary. The manager has never fired anyone and is understandably upset at the prospect. "How will I handle this?" the manager wonders. "How can I tell him that he is fired when I know that he has a family, has just bought a more expensive house, and has no savings? I know the employment market is tight, and he will have trouble finding another job. Will he raise his voice and shout at me? Will he accuse me of throwing my weight around and using my newly granted authority? What will I do if he gets ugly and makes a scene? How will I handle all this?" The next morning, the new manager cooly summons the subordinate into her office and begins.

> John, I first want to tell you how much I appreciated your efforts to do good work, but . . .
>
> Well, thank you, Ms. Price, I certainly enjoy working here.
>
> But . . . what I am trying to say is that you have not been working up to standard and I . . . I . . . uh . . . well, I think . . . that is . . . don't you think you'd be better off doing something else . . . somewhere else, that is . . . don't you, uh . . .
>
> Ms. Price, your face is red, and I guess you're pretty uncomfortable.
>
> Indeed I am not! I am simply pointing out to you that your work has not been satisfactory, and we must do something about it.
>
> Well, I figured that the first female supervisor we've ever had here would need to have a show of strength sooner or later.
>
> Now see here! It's not like that at all! I'm just trying to do my job, Jim . . . I mean John. And it is my decision that it would be better for everyone if you were to relent . . . I mean relocate . . . and do your . . . use your talents in a different sitting . . . setting.

We can imagine Ms. Price still trying to appear in control of the situation and, after reaching for a cigarette, casually lighting the filter end.

And all the time reminding herself of the admonition from her boss: "Ms. Price, you're moving into a position of management responsibility. It is important to learn to make good, logical decisions and keep your personal feelings out of it. Business is business. Remember, keep feelings out of it!"

Emotions are a continuous influence in our work and private life whether we acknowledge them or not. Literally, we cannot keep feelings out of business or any other part of our lives. We can *pretend* that we do not feel, or *deny* that we feel, or, worse yet, *not even know* that we feel. But, regardless, we experience feelings of varying intensity throughout the day and night. Ignoring or denying feelings will not lessen their impact on us as prime motivators. In the case of Ms. Price, it appears that the strong emotions she is experiencing are mildly disrupting her ability to articulate what she wants to say. Trying to deny that she feels uncomfortable creates additional strain, which is added to her inital discomfort about firing John. In this case, John sees the redness of her face and infers some degree of discomfort, which Ms. Price denies. In a more open, responsive relationship, the feelings of both individuals could be acknowledged and, perhaps, used in a constructive manner.

Let's continue with our example. In the six-month period of her new management position, Ms. Price was often uncomfortable and tried not to show it. The need to mask her discomfort, uneasiness, and uncertainty about being a new manager—and the first female manager—motivated her to wear a facial expression of coolness, calmness, and detachment, which she saw as properly managerial. But she also masked much of her ongoing feeling, concern, and urgency about John's below-standard work. In the brief and infrequent talks she had with him, she mentioned the importance of double-checking work for errors, but without any show of feeling. John heard the suggestion, but he had no hint that it was important enough to lead to his firing. Pretending a calmness instead of the concern she really felt resulted not only in John not getting the entire message but also in a lost opportunity to create a motivational climate for him.

We have already seen in Chapter 4 that our culture teaches one set of emotional lessons to boys and another to girls. As adults, males are supposed to behave in reasonable, logical ways and avoid showing much feeling. It is generally not acceptable for a man to cry or show signs of distress when he feels frustration, grief, or despair. At the funeral of a loved and respected friend, most men will struggle to control their emotional expression. Tears still seem to be regarded as unmanly, although there are signs that this slowly is changing as a cultural trait. The behavior and attitudes of respected public figures provide examples of the humanness and acceptability of disclosing emotions. John Cappelletti, receiving the Heisman trophy in 1973, openly wept as he described the courage of his younger brother, who was dying of leukemia. The late Hubert Humphrey said, "A man without tears is a man without a heart." But at the same time, the usual expression used to describe such emotional reactions is that the person "broke down" and cried. We may refer to someone "crying like a baby." Both expressions connote a departure from the expected norm of a mature adult. As long as there are cultural sanctions against such emotional expression, individuals will continue to cover up and deny them. Even expressions from the manager of joy and ecstasy regarding achievements are often muted or denied, especially in a business setting, as being unseemly or undignified; this could mean some loss of motivation for those who helped reach those achievements.

Appropriate Emotional Expression

The person who cannot freely show genuine feeling may be losing a very potent source of motivation. Of course, we cannot allow a completely unrestrained venting of feeling, for this could often be disruptive and counterproductive. We need to find a balance between being too emotional and too suppressed. We need to find ways of expressing emotions appropriately. The word *appropriate* suggests an expression suitable to the situation.

This, of course, is a matter of judgment. When is it appropriate to laugh or cry? When is it appropriate to disclose uncertainty, fear, affection, trust, excitement, disappointment, anger, etc.? Because appropriateness is a matter of human judgment and depends upon the situation, precise rules of appropriateness cannot be formulated, but some general guidelines may be considered.

What properly is considered to be appropriate emotional expression differs as the individual matures from childhood to adulthood. In fact, our judgment of the emotional maturity of an adult may be a measure of the degree to which the individual behaves differently from the child along several dimensions of emotional reaction. The degree of *frustration tolerance* usually increases with maturity. The child, frustrated because two pieces of a toy do not fit together, may cry, scream, or break the pieces. The adult has learned to accept or adapt to sometimes extreme and repeated frustrations and failures, while continuing to work toward the solution of a problem. With maturity there is a *decrease* in the *frequency* and *intensity* of emotional expressions. There is less *impulsiveness* and less tendency to engage in self-pity or in behavior designed to obtain sympathy. With growing maturity there is *less overt manifestation* of the emotions. The child growing toward adulthood learns to be more controlled in the spontaneity and intensity of outward signs of inner emotional activity. But the growing individual may learn the culturally shaped lesson of controlled emotional expression all too well.

An increasing tolerance for frustration would seem to be an appropriate measure of the maturing individual. We do see examples, however, of the frustrated motorist yelling, screaming, and pounding the steering wheel, generally carrying on in a manner similar to a preschool child. But, too much tolerance for frustration may be just as bad. The existence of unfair employment practices, or corruption in government, or inadequate public schooling, or poor workmanship in manufacturing, can be frustrating. Unless there are some who will *not tolerate* these kinds of frustration, the unfortunate circumstances may continue. On a personal level, visits to the physician or confinement in a hospital may include the frustration of not knowing basic details about an illness or surgery. The busy physician or nurse may not take the time to explain to the patient what to expect during examinations in a room full of awesome and perhaps frightening equipment. The patient may complain, "The doctor didn't tell me what to expect"; but why didn't the patient ask? There is a tendency for patients to be so awed or intimidated by medical settings that they tolerate the frustration of not knowing; they needlessly experience anxiety associated with the unknown. A too high level of frustration tolerance may indicate not emotional maturity but, in fact, the opposite. Apathy, lethargy, and indifference can be defense mechanisms suggesting the presence of conflict that is being tolerated rather than handled. The need to deny the strong emotion of frustration, thus, can become a powerful emotional motivation itself, which results in self-defeating rather than self-enhancing behavior.

In a similar way, the absence of impulsive or spontaneous emotional expressions, or the excessively controlled manifestation of emotions, may not indicate maturity but instead a learned control with potentially harmful results. Suicide, mental illness, cardiovascular disease, ulcers, and death may be the extreme end results for the individual who too strictly suppresses emotional expression. Experiencing anger, disappointment, frustration, love, joy, etc. but pretending not to feel them produces continuing strain and stress, takes energy to suppress, and increases the likelihood of breakdown. The constant monitoring and careful planning necessary to successfully hide one's emotional self becomes an enormous distraction in attempting to think clearly and function effectively. In addition, the levels of trust that are established between individuals depend upon how open and disclosing they are. A closed individual who cannot be "read" by others is less likely to be trusted. Emotions are powerful motivators of behavior. Overlooking or denying their existence seriously reduces human potential.

Emotions May Become Generalized as Motivators

We experience many frustrations and punishments in the process of maturing. In response to these frustrations and punishments we may experience the emotions of anger and fear. As a child, we see a parent as a source of authority. Later, we meet other adults who are also authority figures. These might be a teacher, police officer, or employer. The anger or fear first experienced with the parental authority figures can become generalized to other authority figures. A salesperson may have the same emotional reactions to an older fatherly looking prospect as he or she originally experienced with the real father. This could explain some salespersons' fears of calling on anyone in a position of authority. Perhaps all of us feel a certain amount of discomfort when we are in the presence of a high-ranking official. It is probable that some of our discomfort is an earlier learned fear which has generalized from our parent-child relationship.

Our reactions to authority figures provide a good example of the way emotions can become generalized from one situation to another. In the literally hundreds of learning experiences we went through as children, we often received punishment or praise from our elders. Most of these experiences occurred while we were with our parents and were literally looking up to a person who appeared to be a giant in terms of our own size. We, thus, associated correction, punishment or fear with the presence of someone bigger than us or above us. Later in life, whenever we encounter an individual who is physically above us, we may tend to react to them as a child does to an authority figure and feel the earlier learned emotional reactions of fear, anger, or respect. It is not just coincidence that a speaker stands on an elevated platform. The judge in the courtroom sits high above the defendant. The physical relationship, especially the vertical distance between the two people, may have much to do with the creation of fear and respect. In an office, even something as apparently superficial as the height of the chairs may affect the outcome of a business conference. The person sitting in a lower chair may feel subordinate or inferior, although usually on an unconscious level. The boss who rises from the chair to lean over the desk of the vice-president while making a point may gain some "authority" in the eyes of the subordinate and may "motivate" more than if the boss had remained seated. Unfortunately, the vice-president also may feel intimidated by this and have a negative reaction to the boss. Most of the time these physical relationships, with their emotion-arousing effects, operate unconsciously on both persons involved.

The boy who experiences a negative and traumatic relationship with his mother may have difficulty forming a healthy interdependent relationship with women later in life. The girl who enjoys a warm and supportive relationship with her father is more likely to have a successful marriage. You, too, may think of many examples from your own childhood in which you experienced certain emotions in one specific situation only to find, now, that other similar situations generally evoke the same emotions. The child does not readily make fine discriminations between people, events, or things. Having a gentle dog for a pet makes all dogs seem approachable. A near drowning at the lake can make the bathtub, a public fountain, or a shallow swimming pool seem dangerous. One cruel babysitter can make all strange adults seem frightening. As an adult, with greater ability to see the difference between people, we can see that one crooked politician does not mean all politicians should be suspected. One management-trainee failure with a degree from the state university does not mean we should avoid all future applicants from there. This is logical. Yet the adult mind may still have some thinking and feeling patterns more characteristic of a child. The child in us may fail to discriminate at an adult level, and the emotional reactions appropriate to a childhood experience may generalize to produce inappropriate behavior as an adult. Emotions do generalize as motivators. Inappropriate reactions to present situations may be the result.

SOCIAL MOTIVATION

Biological motives tend to operate in a relatively mechanical way. A biological need arises, it creates a drive toward some source of need satisfaction, and then it subsides. Emotions are aroused in a relatively automatic way in reaction to internal or external threats and attractions. The arousal of emotion is not under our conscious control in most situations; but we learn a variety of ways of consciously expressing what we feel. Social motives are never completely separate from biological needs or emotional states, but they are overwhelmingly created and shaped by learning experiences. *Biological* needs are unlearned; *emotional* states are aroused automatically; but modes of *expression* are culturally shaped and *social* needs and desires are mostly learned. We do not learn the hunger need. Feelings of urgency or excitement impinge upon us as the hunger need grows. But we learn ways of obtaining food and manners of consuming it. Socialization is that process whereby we learn how to express our biological needs and emotions.

When we talk about social needs and motivation, we use the word *need* in a different sense. For survival, we do not need a large expensive house, a new car every two or three years, clothes of the latest fashion, or a color TV set. But, we do learn to "need" these things. We cannot be truly isolated from the influence of society. Much of what we do is related to cultural pressures and our desire to be an accepted part of society. To differentiate between unlearned needs and what we have learned to want, it may be helpful to use the term *desire*. We learn that it is important to get along with people and that many of our satisfactions can come only from others. We, therefore, desire to be included in groups in order to achieve close relationships, to achieve relationships of affection, and to achieve some measure of control over others and situations.

By the time we reach adulthood, we learn to want or desire a great variety of things. We want to have material things, to be a particular kind of person, and to do a variety of things. As with any learning, we tend to learn first or best the things which seem to lead to reward. This basic principle of learning, called the *law of effect,* states that behavior which seems to lead to reward will tend to be repeated. Behavior which seems to lead to no reward or to punishment will tend not to be repeated. We use the word "seems" because we usually act on the basis of what we believe to be true and not necessarily what is objectively true. Learning what to want or desire is essentially a part of the process of assimilating the culture in which we live.

The Desire for Inclusion

The social motive to be with people and to be included in a meaningful group is one of our first learned motives and continues to be one of the strongest motives influencing our behavior. The infant quickly learns that discomforts of hunger, cold, wetness, and skin irritation are relieved by something done by mother or a mother substitute. For many years to come, rewards and punishments will shape the child's desire to be favorably included in a relationship or a group as a means of benefiting from others. For the child, standing in the corner or being isolated from the family can be a punishment worse than spanking. Solitary confinement is not only feared by prisoners but can lead to a loss of sanity. For anyone, a symptom of increasing mental illness is the tendency to isolate oneself from others. The need for being favorably included in a group meaningful to us, or the fear of exclusion, creates almost irresistible motivational pressure.

College freshmen being "rushed" by a fraternity or sorority not only will be on their best behavior (as learned from the past) but will look carefully at how others act and will conform as much as possible. The waiting period until the new pledges are announced can be excruciating. Even the person who does not really want to join may still want to receive the invitation. Current vernacular expresses this need for inclusion when we talk about the "in" thing to do or wear. The cry "You're out!" can be upsetting in other places besides the ballfield. Our desire to be included in important groups motivates us to buy a home in an exclusive neighborhood, attend a college because it has a good name, join social, civic, and professional groups, and engage in much consumer behavior because desirable "others" are known to buy this or drink that. Of course, there are additional reasons for doing these things, but the desire to be included and to be a "member" is basic.

Closely related to this is the desire to be accepted, respected, and loved. If we can identify ourselves as being a member of the same group as a new acquaintance, our reception is likely to be much warmer. The desire to be liked can be much more important for some than money or promotion. We may even compromise some of our other important values because being liked is so important. The dilemma of choosing between doing what we think is right and doing what will make us popular can be difficult to resolve. Many employees will work harder and more conscientiously for the respect and affection of their manager than to earn more money.

Growing out of the desire for inclusion and for warm relationships is the desire to be helpful. We learn that it is rewarding to be affectionate toward others and to take care of or support them emotionally. Altruism, the unselfish giving to or regard for another, can be a strong social motive. We can receive an intrinsic good feeling from doing a good deed, as well as receiving recognition from others who admire our selflessness. The desire to help others probably cannot be entirely separate from the desire to help ourselves; our behavior is motivated by more than one desire or need at a time.

The Desire for Control

A strong desire for power and influence may be learned early in life when we discover that we are more likely to have our needs and desires satisfied when we are in control of a situation than when we are being controlled by it. We have already talked about the growing desire to control the expression of our own emotions and of the consequences of that control. Our attempts to control or influence the behavior of others also may have wanted and unwanted consequences. We perfect our ways of influencing others through giving advice, arguing, actively fighting, subtly misleading or tricking, and a whole array of coercive or persuasive maneuvers. Our efforts to influence the lives of others may not work and, in fact, may result in alienating the very people whose respect, cooperation, or love we were trying to get. The quest to find the proper balance of power and influence in our relationships is a major social motivation in work, family, and social activities.

Power is basically a combination of personal abilities and social position, which allows someone to influence others.[3] Authority is the *right* to command or compel others to do what we want them to do, while power is the *ability* to influence behavior. One can have authority without power and power without authority. The police officer has the authority to command an unruly crowd to disperse but may lack the power to make them move on. If they become threatening, the police officer must call for enough reinforcements so they will have sufficient power to carry out their authority. A robber with a gun has no authority to command the teller to fill the sack with money, but the threat of loss of life becomes the power that influences the action.

Legitimate authority is that assigned to a person who occupies a recognizable position in an organization. The manager of a department has legitimate authority, as delegated by superiors, over the activities of that department. This conferred authority is effective in influencing the members of the department depending upon their *acceptance* of that legitimate authority. Let's look at the manager of a clerical department, who has the legitimate authority to request clerical workers to perform activities as listed in their job description. Such a description may include duties such as ". . . typing, filing, and such other duties as may become necessary for the proper functioning of the department. . . ." One morning, the manager approaches a busy worker to say, "Would you mind cleaning out the coffee maker and starting another pot?" Imagine the manager's surprise when the reply is "No! This morning I don't feel like it, and I don't have to do it." If the frustrated manager insists, "Listen, this is part of the job here. You do it or else," then anything could happen, from simple hurt feelings to a formal grievance filed. The formal, legitimate authority possessed by anyone is effective in influencing behavior depending upon what has been called the *"zone of acceptance."*[4] If the acceptance of legitimate authority is extremely high, there is a danger that the followers will follow orders like automatons, with no degree of personal initiative or creativity in doing the work. If the degree of acceptance is very low, either threats of punishment may produce minimal cooperation, or actual sabotage may result. Either extreme carries with it some unwanted consequences. Other means of power and influence must be tried.

Competence in performing some task exceedingly well can be a source of power. Frequently, although not always, people admire excellence and

[3] For a discussion of the different bases of power, see: J.R.P. French, Jr., and B. Raven, "The Bases of Social Power," *Studies in Social Power*, D. Cartwright, ed. (Ann Arbor: Research Center for Group Dynamics, Institute for Social Research, University of Michigan, 1959). See also: David C. McClelland, *Power, The Inner Experience* (New York: Irvington Publishers, Inc., 1975).

[4] For an interesting discussion of the relationship between the degree of acceptance of authority and the effectiveness of various types of leadership, see: Manley Jones, *Executive Decision Making* (Homewood, Ill.: Richard D. Irwin, 1962).

tend to respect and be influenced by an outstanding expert. The desire to be competent is a strong social motive not only because of the inner joy of achievement but because a person who is "one of the best" often acquires unusual powers of influence. Outstanding athletes, and to a lesser extent outstanding scientists and artists, are sought for commercial advertising because of their appeal and influence upon the buying public.

Competing and winning, the demonstrations of competence, are such strong social motivators that injury and even death may be risked in the effort. Winning a sales contest may become a stronger motive than the extra money to be earned by the increased sales. To be number one can be a motive inspiring greater and greater effort for an entire lifetime. The Guiness Book of Records does not list the millions who strive for the records contained in it. Winning is not just seeing who is best at some skill. It often becomes the larger issue of establishing personal adequacy and esteem. Losing a hotly contested tennis match becomes a "blow to the ego." Two joggers overextend themselves, not just for exercise, but to see who is the first one to quit. Arguments over questions as insignificant as who is right in the definition of a word can lead to blows.

A seemingly paradoxical social motive is the desire to submit or yield to the control or will of an authority figure. Of course, cooperation is necessary for any society to exist, and we must be submissive in certain situations, as in obeying traffic regulations, tax laws, or ordinary rules of courtesy. But in some individuals, the desire to be submissive is a predominant social motive. Some wish to have authority figures make both major and minor decisions for them. Decision making can involve some agonizing choices and the bearing of heavy responsibility. All this can be eliminated by abdicating personal responsibility in deference to an authority figure, whether it be a teacher, manager, spouse, salesperson, etc. It is not unusual for such a person to become a fanatic, exhibiting intense and uncritical devotion toward a religious, political, or profit-making cause. Once persuaded of the "rightness" of the cause, the motive of submission may become coupled with an authoritarian zeal, including the use of force to bend others to the same level of submission.

At a less extreme level, submitting to others in the sense of seeing others as being responsible for our own feelings and behavior is rooted in a common social motive. It is easy to blame others for "getting me all upset" or "driving me to drink" or "making me feel inferior," or any number of other conditions we really get ourselves into. In turn, we develop an "If only . . ." philosophy. The salesperson thinks, "If only my customers would see the value of my products . . . ." The teacher feels, "If only I had brighter students, I would be so much more effective as a teacher." The manager believes, "If only we could recruit some really hard working, conscientious people like we used to . . . ." The common theme in these fantasies is that our success or lack of it depends upon someone else. It is a belief that someone else is in control of our lives and results in an essentially submissive approach to life. The alternative would be to wonder what we can do to gain more control over our own attitudes and skills and to see how we can be more responsible for ourselves.

The Desire for Self-actualization

We seem to have a drive to make full use of our capacities or abilities. We need to grow, to develop, to improve ourselves, and to make the best use of our particular and unique talents. Unlike biological needs and social motives, the need for self-actualization seems only to increase in strength as it is satisfied. While we stop searching for food when we satisfy our hunger and we relax somewhat in our search for affection when we become a loved and respected member of a group, with self-actualization, we seem to want even more growth as we succeed in growing.

Growth means more than normal physical and mental maturing. It means the expanding ability to make use of the qualities that make us unique among animals. Growth or self-actualization is the creative, building urge in us to deal with others on a more mutually satisfactory level. Human growth involves becoming a responsible, self-directing, self-knowing person who moves toward becoming everything he or she is humanly capable of.

Growth implies a direction. But what is that direction for each of us? If self-actualization means reaching the height of our capacity or achieving an ultimate purpose, what is that purpose? What are our goals in life? Do we not need to achieve a better understanding of who we are in terms of our chief talents in order to move toward realizing the full use of those talents?

A MATTER OF LIFE AND DEATH

If you have ever said or thought, "It's a matter of life and death!" it must have been in a situation of extreme motivation and urgency. No discussion of the life enhancing process of motivation would be complete without a consideration of the psychological impact the awareness of death has on us.

Motivation *is* a complex process, partly because of the drives or needs for self-enhancing and self-defeating actions. We are moved by stories of heroic efforts to save a life. We are equally moved, although for different reasons, by stories of suicide. Side by side in the intensive care unit of any hospital may be two patients, one with a continuing, urgent need to die after a suicide attempt, and the other with an urgent need to live after a traumatic injury, heart attack, or stroke. The one may feel bitterness at the efficient and professional efforts of the hospital staff to maintain life; the other feels gratitude for these same efforts.

Life is sometimes a comedy and sometimes a tragedy. But death is no laughing matter. Or is it? Jack Benny's longest laugh reportedly came in a contrived situation where a robber approached him with the demand, "Your money or your life!" Benny's reaction was to place a hand on his chin and, in a contemplative manner, consider the alternatives. His characteristic "stinginess" and the common-sense notion of the value of life were presented in sharp contrast. Watching, we are caught up in Benny's dilemma and react with an explosion of feeling. It's a life and death matter. But which is more important? "Laugh? I thought I'd die!" is a phrase that unconsciously expresses the ambivalence that is life itself. Laughter is often the reaction to a situation that arouses anxiety but promises relief. The good joke raises the tension level in the audience but offers a way out in the punch line. Here is an example:

> It is midnight on a dark and lonely night. An inebriated gentleman is walking home and decides to take a shortcut through the cemetery. He stumbles into a freshly dug grave. Panic! The next few minutes are spent in frantic efforts to climb out, but he can't make it. It's pitch black and he can't see anything. What is there to do but settle down in a corner of the grave and wait for morning and a rescue attempt. It's quiet and eerie. Suddenly, from the far corner of the dark grave he hears the voice of another person who fell in earlier, saying, "You can't get out of here," but in one gigantic leap he did!

Talk about motivation! There is something about dying, death, and situations associated with the dead that stirs emotions from hysterical laughter to profound grief and despair. Death and dying are not the most pleasant subjects, but they are vital ones in the most literal sense of the word.

Intellectually, we know that death is inevitable and that shock, grief, and mourning are part of life. Emotionally, we may not be prepared for it. Ours has been described as a death-denying society in that we prefer not to talk about death or acknowledge it. The dying person is often frightened and unable to talk about the fears and uncertainties associated with a terminal illness. The family may share these fears but feel unable to mention them. Both patient and family may endure the last days or hours of life in a state of excruciating loneliness. Both need each other, but learned responses to death create alienation. A century ago it was likely that members of the family died at home, and the event was experienced by children and adults alike. Today, death is likely to occur in a hospital, where the family is often shielded from the last moments and the efficient hospital and funeral parlor quickly remove the body from sight. Our last view of the "loved one" who has "passed on" is in a strange room in a mortuary, perhaps labeled the "slumber room," and all too often the eulogy is pronounced by an official unfamiliar with the "departed." The words used and the setting tend to create an atmosphere of unreality. Death is no stranger to us, but strangeness is what we feel in its presence.

We may be uncomfortable with death, but the death of an old person seems more acceptable than the death of a child. The concept that it is the quality of life lived that is important rather than the number of years lived may be of some comfort to the family of the dead youth, but there is a peculiar sense of loss associated with the death of a child. Perhaps even more disturbing is the loss of a relative or friend by suicide. Annually in the United States approximately 25,000 children and adults kill themselves. At least this is the number recorded on death certificates. It is commonly supposed that the true number is more than twice this. Many suicides are concealed because of family or political pressure, and many more are improperly recorded because of the difficulty in detecting when deaths are really self-imposed. It is estimated that for every successful suicide there are six to eight survivors directly affected by the event. And for every death due to accident, homicide, or natural cause there are additional family members, friends, and colleagues who are confronted with dying and death in one form or another. With over 5,000 deaths every day and close to 1 percent of the United States population dying every year, most of us in our lifetime will be faced with death. Will we confront these events only with dread, anxiety, and repressed feelings, or can we learn to cope with death in life-enhancing and rewarding ways?

Concern is growing that our education for life is incomplete if we are not helped to cope with our own inevitable death and those of our friends and family. It is likely that as we better understand, talk about, and accept death we will better accept all other aspects of life, allowing us to live it to the fullest. Denying the intellectual, emotional, and spiritual aspects of death is likely to lead to denying these same inspiring aspects of life. A major contribution to a healthier awareness of death was the book *The Meaning of Death* edited by psychologist Herman Feifel.[5] He stressed that, contrary to popular belief, the dying person often needed to talk about his or her feelings, rather than being "protected" by the medical staff or family. The psychiatrist, Elizabeth Kubler-Ross, in her book *On Death and Dying,* provided another breakthrough by defining various psychological stages in the dying process and offering means of coping with each.[6] Her concern was at least twofold: that help should be provided to medical personnel, who are not always emotionally prepared to deal helpfully with the dying patient and family; and that the dying patient be more aware of his or her impending death, because she believed that knowing what is happening can be a source of comfort to the dying patient. She described the stages of dying as including: denial of the seriousness of the situation; anger that it could be happening; bargaining, in the sense of thinking, "Let me live a little longer and I will do those things I should or want to do"; depression, which comes with the realization of death's inevitability; and finally, acceptance of what must be. Not every specialist in death and dying agrees that these stages are experienced by all, nor is there agreement as to the meaning of the terms used to describe them. But these books have stimulated educational efforts in death and dying through courses offered in high school and college and through adult continuing-education lectures and seminars.

Many educators believe that death education, like sex education, should begin in the home. Since it often does not, the responsibility for this education increasingly is accepted by school systems. Educators Audrey Gordon and Dennis Klass have written a book to fill this need: *They Need to Know: How to Teach Children About Death.*[7] Aimed at parents, teachers, and "everyone who is involved with children and adolescents," it is a source of information about how children grow into an awareness of death and what can be done to help them cope with death as part of life. Information is provided to help dispel the anxiety often associated with children's questions about hospitals, doctors, patient rights, funeral services, and other matters involved with the dying and death.

We began this chapter with the question, "What is life all about?" In the following chapter we examine how we make choices in life depending upon the meaning we give to our existence. A full awareness of death and its implications may help life mean more to each of us. In life, we are motivated by our needs for inclusion, affection, and control. The dying person continues to have these same needs, but the satisfaction of them is often denied by well-meaning but unaware professionals, family, and friends. We can learn from the statements of dying individuals that it is the quality of life that is important, and not so much the length of life. Understanding dying can help us realize that important matters should not be postponed "until we get around to it," because the time available to us is always uncertain. Living without awareness of the inevitability of death makes it easy to postpone the things we know we should do. The mentally healthy, motivated individual perceives and responds appropriately to the world as it really is. Death is part of this real world. As Kubler-Ross has said, "This is perhaps the greatest lesson we learned from our dying patients: *live*, so you do not have to look back and say, 'God, how I have wasted my life.' "[8]

[7]A. K. Gordon, and D. Klass, *They Need to Know: How to Teach Children About Death* (Englewood Cliffs, N.J.: Prentice-Hall, 1979).

[8]E. Kubler-Ross, *Death, the Final Stage of Growth* (Englewood Cliffs, N.J.: Prentice-Hall, 1975).

"What do I want from life?" may seem a senseless question to some, and to others a terribly difficult but necessary one. But do we not need to answer this question to achieve a sense of direction in realizing our potential? These questions are worth reflection and thought. The answers you find may change your life.

SUMMARY

All motivation is essentially self-motivation because our actions depend upon our perceptions of a situation, and perception is an *internal process* unique to each individual. We must deal with a constantly shifting combination of needs that tend to move us in many and often conflicting directions. Some of these needs are learned and some are unlearned. Biological needs create tensions that rise until satisfied and that then drop to a lower level before rising again. Emotional and social needs are more complicated and less predictable but nevertheless are powerful in their motivational impact. How well we satisfy our strong desires for inclusion, control, affection, and self-actualization shapes the direction of our growth as a unique individual.

QUESTIONS FOR REVIEW
AND DISCUSSION

1.   We cannot motivate others because motivation is inner-directed. Motivation depends upon our individual and unique perception of the world around us. Do you agree? Discuss.

2.   Biological needs may be unlearned, but the means of satisfying them are culturally determined. Explain by giving an example.

3.   The inability to express appropriately a strong emotion may be self-defeating. Discuss, using an example from your own life experiences.

4.   The desire for self-actualization and the acceptance of our own death are bound together. Discuss.

6

THE FREEDOM AND COMPLEXITY OF CHOICE

*. . . I have set before you life and death, blessing and cursing:
therefore choose life, that both thou and thy seed may live: . . .*

DEUTERONOMY 19

*Afoot and light-hearted I take to the open road,
Healthy, free, the world before me,
The long brown path before me leading where I choose.*

WALT WHITMAN*

The difficulty in life is the choice.

GEORGE MOORE**

How many choices do you make every day? Would you guess dozens? Or thousands? Or even hundreds of thousands? Some are inconsequential and others crucial. Choices are conscious and unconscious, impulsive and deliberate, difficult and easy, and have short and long-range consequences. The mind is in constant activity as a receiver of information, a processor, a judge and jury, a planner, and an initiator of often fateful

*Song of the Open Road, I
***The Bending of the Bough,* Act IV

courses of action. Think of the choices you make as you go through the day. Will you get up with the alarm or not? What soap, lotion, tonic, paste, cream, perfume, or coloring will you use? What color, texture, style, and fit of dress will you wear? Why? Will you talk to your mate during these choices, and if so, what subject, words, and voice inflections will you use? Will you run for the bus or wait for the next one? Buy a paper? Which one? Even before getting to work (with its thousands of choices) your day has begun in a most human way: as the originator of simple, sometimes elaborate, often baffling choices.

The study of motivation also explores the question of *how* people create new and worthwhile solutions to problems or new pathways toward goals, and *why* they make the choices of the paths they do take.

CREATING ALTERNATIVES

Motivation is a process that involves making choices between alternate pathways, which lead toward a variety of goals that appear to satisfy inherent needs and learned needs. Generally, the more good alternatives we can think of, the more likely our final choice will be a good one.

Let's imagine that you are unemployed and looking for work. Or perhaps you don't like your present position and would like to obtain a better one. Your goal is employment in pleasant surroundings, associated with compatible peers, doing work which makes full use of your best talents at an income level which is equitable.[1] That goal would satisfy your needs for inclusion, control, and affection. Let's trace the motivational process involved in getting you from where you are now to where you want to be.

How do you expect to obtain that desirable position? Your mind begins to generate various alternatives or pathways that have a reasonable chance of leading to the goal. You could go the route of employment agencies, public and private. Perhaps the want ads in the local and national papers or in professional publications in your field are possibilities. Maybe you have some friends you could ask. One of your former classmates is the Personnel Director of a company that would be ideal, but you have never liked her and would hate for her to know that you're looking for work, so that's out. Or is it? Maybe you could swallow your pride and . . . . Well, what else could you try? Try to think of

---

[1] The Equity Theory of Motivation attempts to explain aspects of human behavior in terms of our perceptions of the fairness of what we receive as compensation for what we have contributed, especially as we compare our compensation with others doing comparable work. For a research-based discussion of this theory, see J.S. Adams, "Toward an Understanding of Inequity," *Journal of Abnormal and Social Psychology*, 67 (1963), 422-36.

something. Something *creative* perhaps. How about writing letters to the presidents of several companies requesting an appointment? Would that be too audacious? Or just call them directly. Perhaps, their secretaries would give you the runaround and not let you get through. Why not rent a billboard and design your own "employment wanted" sign? No, that's really getting ridiculous! But what *else* could you do? These mental ramblings illustrate an important step in the motivational process: the creation of feasible alternatives to solving problems.

Creativity: The Process and the Person

Conformity and creativity are important processes in making choices most likely to lead to satisfaction. There is a regularity in the way human problems repeat themselves, so turning to traditional solutions may be the best choice.

When changes do occur, such as moving into a new home, moving to another city, changing jobs, marrying or divorcing, adding a child to the family, or losing a family member through death, the stresses and strains produce feelings of uncertainty, confusion, or anxiety. At times like these, it may be more comfortable to conform to existing patterns or rituals of behavior, even if they are not as effective as a newer, more creative approach might be. Conforming to existing cultural patterns of job seeking, family rearing, education, or recreation help avoid the unsettled feelings often associated with new learning and adaptation. Conforming to "tried and true" alternatives avoids confusion, embarrassment, and loss of time and energy. But conformity to traditional alternatives to goal seeking may encourage mediocrity in performance. The cost of conformity may be in the loss of new and potentially effective ideas and solutions. Creating just one more alternative may make the difference between reaching a valued goal or not.

The Stages of the Creative Process. Creativity, as with most human talents, is a combination of inherited tendencies and learning experiences. While most people have some degree of creativity, there is a wide range of creative ability in the general population, from very low to extremely high. Each individual, however, is able to make more use of the creativity that is potentially there. Training programs which succeed in helping individuals to change their attitudes toward themselves and to learn techniques of generating additional ideas have helped many to make much more use of their creativity. With some, the fear of change or fear of deviating from the old ways of their important groups may keep them from using their creative talents.

Creativity is the capacity to innovate, invent, or place elements together in new ways. It seems to emerge most in situations of informality and in an atmosphere of acceptance and freedom rather than one of criticism and rejection. Creativity takes courage. To think of a truly new idea, or an idea new to those around you, tends to make you different or somewhat isolated from others. You may be labeled an "odd ball"—until your idea works magnificently and then you're a "hero"! To venture forth and try new alternatives to old personal and social problems is an act of human freedom at its finest: to face the ridicule and ostracism can be real agony. Creativity is risky.

The process of creativity consists of a series of stages. First there is a *sensitivity to a problem* or a possibility for improvement. In our example of seeking new employment, the problem is obvious. What may not be so obvious is that there might be a better way of doing it. The highly creative individual is not only especially sensitive to the subtle nuances of a problem but has the capacity to be puzzled by things that others take for granted. "Why should I do it the way it's always been done?" is a question frequently asked by the creative person. Questions such as "Maybe there's a better way . . . . Why not look for it?" or "I wonder what would happen if . .?" are characteristic of creative thinking. If, at this initial stage of the creative process, an influential person replies, "What makes you think you're so special? Why rock the boat or make waves? What's the matter, isn't the regular way of doing things good enough for you?", then the more timid person will stop right there. Who knows what valuable ideas are lost every day because of this kind of social pressure to conform?

The second stage involves *preparation*. It is a time for assembling in the mind information from past experiences—and yet going beyond that. The creative person seems to have a roving curiosity about a wide variety of subjects. Our job seeker might read widely not only about the employment market but also about techniques of selling and the processes involved in communication and decision making, advertising, interviewing, recruiting practices, etc. If interest were high in seeking employment with a specific organization, much library and field research could be conducted to learn about its financial health, its growth trends, consumer problems, public-relations strategies, the reputation of the organization, and many more bits of information. The highly creative person is much more likely to come up with feasible pathways to the employment goal just because of the intense preparation. One personal characteristic of highly creative people is their tendency to evaluate themselves and their ideas primarily from *within* themselves, rather than on the basis of others' opinions. Perhaps they can readily believe in their own opinions and work because they are simply better prepared with more information than their critics. The creative person is open to ideas and suggestions from others but does not let their doubts lead to discouragement.

The third stage of *incubation* is largely an unconscious part of the creative process. If we think of the brain as a storage warehouse of millions of bits of information and can picture these bits being continuously sorted out and combined with each other, we can imagine that once in a while several bits are combined in a new and unusual way, and a creative idea is born. The term incubation refers to the act of brooding over something to give it form and substance. We may consciously mull over the problem, turning it this way and that, trying to see it in a new light, and then, perhaps, we seemingly give up and "forget it." But the puzzlement remains alive in the unconsicous, where it is massaged and shaped, turned inside out and upside down, combined and reformed, with a solution ready to be "hatched." Most of us have had the experience of puzzling over some problem without success and then deciding to "sleep on it." It's not unusual that upon waking a solution is obvious. For some, creative ideas come during periods of reverie, daydreaming, or, apparently, when not even thinking about anything at all. It is as if a lessening of conscious effort at times allows the unconscious to do its work.

The saying "Comes the dawn, I see the light" illustrates the fourth stage, *illumination*. Cartoonists depict a character having an idea by drawing a light bulb over the head. Indeed, it is as if a switch were turned on and a creative idea comes as a flash with a suddenness that can be as surprising as it is delightful. The creative solution often appears in our conscious mind fully formed, with many intricate details worked out. The conscious and unconscious parts of the mind are not in opposition but work as a team. Consciously, we must be able to recognize the usefulness of the creative product from the unconscious and see how it fits in with our awareness of the problem. The term "serendipity" refers to that ability to recognize the creative and useful nature of a thought process when it occurs.

Verification is that stage where the new idea is tested or tried to see if it works. The highly creative person seems to be able to suspend judgment, temporarily, during the incubation stage, where the use of too much judgment, logic, or reliance on tradition might prevent the free and spontaneous and playful mixing of vague thoughts and memories. But precise and rigorous experimentation is what separates the bizarre thought from the creative and worthwhile idea. Depending upon the attitude we have toward ourselves, we may or may not proceed through the verification stage. Verifying the worth of an idea usually involves the combined efforts of others. Presenting our ideas to a committee or to a friend exposes it to possible censure as well as praise. There is always the risk that, in verifying the creative alternative we generated, we'll find that it doesn't work, or it will expose us to ridicule. If we don't try our new ideas, we will avoid failure, but we may also avoid unusual success. Our final decision in choosing between alternatives in the motivational process can be only as good as the best alternative. Research indicates that the more alternatives or ideas we can create, the greater the chance of high-quality ideas. The more the better!

Characteristics of the Creatively Motivated Person.   Motivation involves: (1) generating alternative paths to a goal; (2) accurately assessing the probabilities of success in reaching the goal, including each of the paths; and (3) estimating or foreseeing the relative values of the several goals which could satisfy our needs. In each step of the motivational process, the more mature, flexible, creative, and sensitive we can be, the more likely it is our motivated efforts will produce the desired satisfaction. Looking at the characteristics of highly creative people may give us hints as to how we may make the best use of our creativity.

Creative individuals tend to be "open" and receptive to a wide range of information. They are "open" in the sense of delaying judgment and not jumping to conclusions based on inadequate information. But they are also open to all learning opportunities, even from people they do not particularly like. All too often, if we do not like someone, we turn them off and assume we have nothing to gain by associating with them. Creative individuals are more likely to be receptive to ideas without letting prejudices get in the way. They are open in the further sense of being highly observant, noticing detail which may escape most of us. For example, we may see a red brick at a building site and think of its obvious use in building a wall or a walkway. The more creative person would be aware of its rectangular size, its weight, color, texture, density, sharp edges, and brittleness. Sometime later, our creative person might use such a brick as a doorstop, bedwarmer, marker, weapon, fulcrum, wheel chock, art object, ballast, water displacer, toy, hammer, anchor, knife sharpener, bookend, plumb bob, footstool, and so on. This habit of thinking is an asset in imagining solutions to unusual problems.

Creative individuals tend to be more self-reliant, independent, flexible, spontaneous, and playful. They are not playful in the sense of playing practical jokes but in a manner similar to that of a child playing with a toy. The child will carefully examine every part of a new toy, exploring it with eyes, fingers, and mouth and becoming thoroughly familiar with all its aspects. The child will use the toy not just as it was "intended" but will combine it with another toy or pretend that it is something else. The natural fantasies and vivid imagination of the child are talents all too often lost as we "grow up."

Creative people are exceptionally able to see patterns in information, to see how knowledge from one field is related to other fields. They sense more complexities in the world and are more complex themselves. They are more tolerant of ambiguity and lack of structure in their surroundings, but at the same time, they possess a need and ability to bring order out of chaos. They have unusual intellectual persistence and concentration. Biographies of creative people tell of their intense work,

figure 6-1

employment agency, public
employment agency, private
want ad, local paper
want ad, national paper
want ad, professional publication
friends
former classmate
writing letters
direct telephone call
rent a billboard
what else?

Need for Work

Desirable Employment

lasting for decades without let-up, to finish a particular machine or process or work of art. The ability to concentrate amidst distractions suggests not only a dedication but a relative freedom of concern about the impression they may be making on others. For the less creative person, the need to look well in the eyes of others creates such self-consciousness and readiness to conform to their expectations that creative thought is often buried. The highly creative person tolerates both psychological and physical isolation. Having an opinion different from others, or being physically alone, seems not to threaten the creative person. A need for a variety, willingness to act on a hunch, and acceptance of the wild and seemingly irrational thoughts which flit through the mind, are further characteristics of creative people. Being different does not mean that the person is creative, but creative people *are* different!

Evaluating the Alternatives

We started with the problem of locating employment. Figure 6-1 illustrates the alternative pathways to a goal that are generated as a result of remembering traditional approaches, as well as some additional alternatives generated through the creative process. Having more alternatives gives us more freedom of choice and adds complexity to the choice process. We do have to make a decision, but the decision process may include feelings of uncertainty, doubt, and apprehension. Some of the pathways will seem like good chances for success, while others will seem remote possibilities. As we look over the alternative pathways, we mentally calculate the probabilities of success for each. Our estimates of probable success depend upon our past experience, what we have read or been told, and on our creative imagination. Our estimates are *subjective*

141

probabilities because they are usually based on limited experience and on our individual perception of alternative actions and the situations in which they may occur.

Remembering our discussion in Chapter 1 of the use of probabilities in predicting human behavior, the greater the number of observations or experiences we have had, the greater our confidence in predicting outcomes of human events. Also, the more creative person engages in exceptional preparation in the process of creating good solutions to problems. We increase our ability to understand and influence human behavior as we know more about the role of subjective probabilities in the motivational process.

PROBABILITIES AND CHOICES

How often have you said, "But I had no choice! I just had to do it!" You may also have thought, at other times, "I don't *have* to do anything." But there is no such thing as having no choice, and there is no such thing as not having to do anything. We always have choices, and we always have to do something. Taking no action is a choice and is something we do. Recognizing that we have choices and that subjectively perceived probabilities are involved in choosing among alternatives are further steps in understanding the motivational process.

Subjective Probabilities

Let's continue with our hypothetical job search and determine some ways of meeting our goal. The subjective probabilities of success you assign to each of the pathways toward the goal of employment depend upon your assessment of your knowledge, skills, attitudes, the situation you will be in, and the imagined reactions of the other people involved. You may think that going to your former classmate, the Personnel Director, is one feasible way of obtaining employment, but, since you doubt that you have the skill to make the approach without your negative feelings showing, you will try almost anything else first. Combining your assessment of the knowledge, skills, and attitudes necessary for that pathway—and imagining the reaction of your former classmate in the situation of the Personnel Office—you give yourself about 1 chance out of a 100 to make it work.[2] In the language of probability, you assign that path a value of .01.

---

[2] For more about determining the probable success of different pathways to a goal—and about determining the *value* of each goal for yourself—see: John P. Campbell and Robert D. Pritchard, "Motivation Theory in Industrial and Organizational Psychology," in the *Handbook of Industrial and Organizational Psychology,* Marvin D. Dunnette, ed. (Skokie, Ill: Rand McNally, 1976), chap. 3.

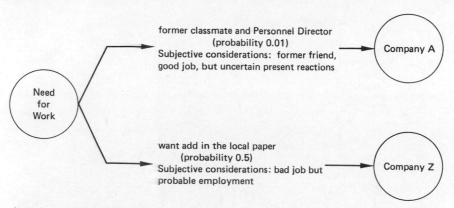

figure 6-2 Employment Possibilities from A to Z

Another goal pathway is responding to a local want ad. You know that a position is being advertised, you have the skill to write a good résumé and a covering letter, and you feel comfortable doing it. Subjectively, you give yourself a fifty-fifty chance of getting a job that way. The probability is 0.5. The choice between these two pathways is easy. You choose answering the ad.

The Perceived Value of the Goal

The choice making becomes more complicated when we begin to consider the differences in the desirability of employment with different companies. Referring again to the same two pathways to employment but considering the relative value you place on working for two different companies, we illustrate the situation in Figure 6-2. Company A, where your former classmate is Personnel Director, has just created a position which suits your talents exactly, and the pay is excellent. Company Z offers a job in the want ads, but it's demeaning work, and the person you would work for has the reputation of abusing employees with sarcastic and cutting remarks. Now what? Should you try the low-probability pathway toward the ideal company or the higher-probability pathway leading to a job where you're sure you would be miserable? Your subjective estimate of the probability for the path toward the ideal Company A may begin to change as you think about it. Maybe your former classmate has changed over the years. Certainly you have. So give it a try. With a slight change in your own attitude, your estimated probability for path A may go up enough for you to be motivated to go for an employment interview. To your surprise and relief, she seems immediately to be glad to see you and is delighted that your talents are exactly what the company is looking for. This story has an idyllic ending, but the point is that the subjective probabilities which motivate our behavior may have little to do with the

figure 6-3   The Motivational Process

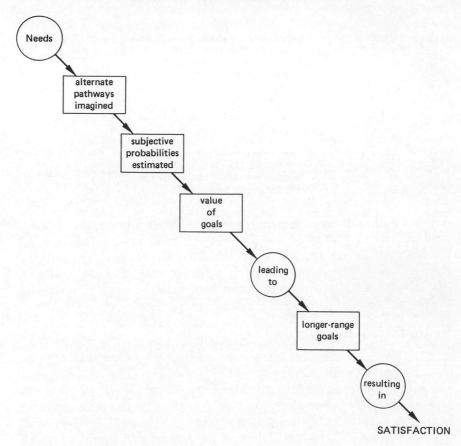

reality of the situation. We move in the direction of *apparent* need satisfaction. What we do at a given moment is determined by our perceived probabilities that certain actions will result in desired outcomes, multiplied by the estimate we make as to the desirability of the expected outcome.

The motivational process illustrated in Figure 6-3 involves subjectively perceived elements which are likely to be changing as we estimate the risks and values in each situation. We are continuously changing in the knowledge we have, the skills we acquire, and the attitudinal frame of reference which influences our perception and behavior.

The culture in which we are immersed is also changing continuously, as well as changing as we move from place to place. This presents us with an unending stream of new problems, challenges, and opportunities with which we must cope in new or creative ways. As choice makers, our success depends upon how well we make use of our distinctly human talent of creativity, our subjective probabilities of successful actions, the situation we are in, and the overall meaning of what we are doing, or plan to do. Let us examine how our choices may be limited or expanded depending upon the characteristics of the situation or the organization within which we work.

ORGANIZATIONAL INFLUENCE ON INDIVIDUAL CHOICES

When we discussed the socialization of the individual, we showed in an illustration (Chapter 3, Figure 3-1) the various social and cultural characteristics that influence the development of the unique individual. The illustration included the impact on us of our chosen occupation. A high percentage of our waking time is spent within the organization that employs us. Depending upon the *structure* of this organization and the *processes* which make up the interpersonal dynamics there, we will perceive a degree of personal freedom which ranges between a great deal and very little. Most of us will prefer having a wide range of choices available and will resent having almost no say as to how we do our work. Our experience at work can vary between feeling like a prisoner in an institution to feeling the joy of self-fulfillment and the satisfaction of making choices which improve the effectiveness of our organization.[3]

Organizational Structure and Process

The structure of any organization is that arrangement of people, groups, functions, and systems which determines *where* and *when* decisions will be made. It is the relatively stable and predictable framework of communication systems, of levels of authority, of various interdependent functioning groups, of systems of reward and status, and of all other aspects of the formal organization which help it reach established goals. Questions of who should have decision-making responsibilities, who reports to whom, who is invited to participate in discussions leading to decisions are matters of organizational structure, and they influence an individual's range of choices regarding his or her work. The processes of any organization have more do with *how* things are done. The manager may have the formal authority to make an announcement (structure),

[3] For a comprehensive review of current theories of motivation in an organizational setting, see: John P. Campbell and Robert D. Pritchard, "Motivation Theory in Industrial and Organizational Psychology," in the *Handbook of Industrial And Organizational Psychology*, Marvin D. Dunnette, ed. (Skokie, Ill.: Rand McNally, 1976). chap. 3.

but the way in which it is announced (process) may have as much or more impact than the content of the message itself. Organizational processes include communication, methods of influence, how change is brought about, the style of management, the levels of coordination and competition, and many other matters related to how people actually behave with each other. Organizations are complex, and the varieties of structure and process, as well as the possible interactions between them, contribute to this complexity. The employee's perception of a particular manager's authority within the organization and the manager's method of exercising that authority will widen or narrow the range of choices involved in that employee's self-motivation.

Organizations are not alike either in structure or process, even within the same industry. Each possesses a unique "culture" which provides rewards and satisfactions for certain behavior. Some organizations are concerned for the quality of life of their employees; others stress only the importance of getting the work done, almost regardless of how people feel about the work or themselves. But individual employees are unique, too. Despite working for an authoritarian, demeaning manager, an employee may concentrate on the meaning and satisfaction of the work itself and still achieve a high level of self-fulfillment. Another employee doing the same work may be so distressed at the perceived inhumaneness of the manager and the organization that illness or mental distress may result. In the behavioral sciences, the debate persists as to the relative importance of the environment versus the self-determination of the individual in shaping patterns of human behavior.

"Organizational design" is the activity of diagnosing and modifying the structure, processes, and other situational and environmental variables in an organization so as to increase its effectiveness.[4] To some degree, organizations may be modified by the persistent demands of individuals in their self-motivated attempts to increase their need satisfactions. Certainly, the collective-bargaining power of individuals who have formed themselves into a union has changed significantly the structure, processes, profitability, and longevity of many organizations. This does not mean that such changes are always good for either individuals or the organization.

Organizations influence individuals, and individuals influence organizations. If the individual perceives that no change is possible, and no attempts are made, the prophecy is likely to be self-fulfilling. But if an individual believes that change is not only possible and desirable but also

---

[4] Organization theory and organizational design are separate fields of study which depend heavily upon behavioral sciences such as psychology, sociology, anthropology, economics, and political science. The interested reader is referred to: Pradip N. Khandwalla, *The Design of Organizations* (New York: Harcourt Brace Jovanovich, Inc., 1977).

that individual effort can be influential, then sometimes "mountains can be moved." A study of the science and theory of organizations may give an individual a much greater measure of control over present and future achievements.

Managerial Style

The impact of an organization is felt by the employee through the actions of the manager who is his or her immediate supervisor. While there may be a certain work climate which characterizes the overall organization, the individual manager will use a style of leadership which may or may not be consistent with that climate. If we are an employee, one of the most influential persons in our life is our immediate supervisor. It may be obvious that the style of leadership exercised by our supervisor has much to do with our own self-esteem, our willingness to give our full effort to the job, or our choice to maintain a low profile and get by with a minimum of effort. What is not so obvious is the relationship between different styles of leadership and the overall productivity of the group or individual being managed.[5] Douglas McGregor, in his classic, *The Human Side of Enterprise,* stressed the importance of the manager understanding his or her own values, attitudes, and assumptions about people and how they affect the response of employees to actual managerial behavior on a day-to-day basis.[6] McGregor pointed out that ". . . people react not to an objective world, but to a world fashioned out of their own perceptions, assumptions, and theories of what the world is like. Managers, like all the rest of us, can be trapped by these assumptions into inappropriate and ineffective decisions."[7] It was his contention that being aware of how we create our own work worlds increases our freedom to make self-enhancing rather than self defeating choices.

As a result of scientific research into understanding the relationships between organization structure, process, leadership styles, and individual performance, the trend over the past fifty years has been toward greater consideration for the personal needs of employees, as well as for the profitability and growth of the organization. We are a highly mobile society, with much freedom to live and work where we choose. Changing jobs for greater opportunities is a right and a privilege. But changing jobs because of broken promises, misunderstandings, mismatching of talents

---

[5] For a review of research on the effectiveness of various leadership styles in different situations, see: Victor H. Vroom, "Leadership," in *Handbook of Industrial and Organizational Psychology,* Marvin D. Dunnette, ed. (Skokie, Ill.: Rand McNally, 1976). chap. 34.

[6] Douglas McGregor, *The Human Side of Enterprise* (New York: McGraw-Hill, 1960).

[7] Douglas McGregor, *The Professional Manager,* Caroline McGregor and Warren G. Bennis, eds., page xii of the Introduction by Edgar H. Schein (New York: McGraw-Hill, 1967).

and job requirements, inept management, and employee exploitation becomes extremely costly for organizations and employees. What organizational climate will attract and keep competent people? What climate and management style will encourage creativity? What are those combinations of values, attitudes, and behavior on the part of the management "climate makers" that lead to the optimum of individual satisfaction and organizational effectiveness? What contributes to work groups being effective and achieving high levels of performance?

Effective Organizations

One example of an extensive and long-range research effort to determine differences between effective and ineffective organizations is the work of social scientist Rensis Likert, of the Institute for Social Research at The University of Michigan.[8] The results indicate that certain conditions are likely to lead to the fullest possible utilization of individual and group resources, especially in making responsible choices. It is, of course, in the subjective perception of the employee that these conditions exist, which leads to individual choices in the motivational process, which in turn leads to more effective work performance. The following brief description of these conditions is not meant to be a complete one. The conditions that are likely to promote organizational effectiveness include: (1) high levels of trust and confidence between leaders and subordinates, so that ideas and suggestions can be freely discussed; (2) encouragement and satisfaction of economic, social, and individual growth motives through cooperative participation of employees at all levels of the organization; (3) free communication throughout the organization, with employees feeling responsibility for its accuracy; (4) interactions are extensive and friendly, and teamwork is effective; (5) decisions are made throughout the organization, not just at the top; and (6) much participation is encouraged in setting goals, and a sense of accountability in measuring and improving performance is widespread throughout the organization.

Ideal as this may sound, the theory *is* being applied in a number of organizations, while careful research measures the results. Increasingly, research supports the assumption that individuals are motivated and capable of making responsible creative choices to the extent that they work and live in an environment which supports and encourages individual responsibility. We ended our discussion in Chapter 4 with the observation that we each could explore and move toward an occupation and organization which would allow us to become that person we are

---

[8] Rensis Likert, *The Human Organization: Its Management and Value* (New York: McGraw-Hill, 1967).

capable of being. Our choices will depend upon the alternatives we are aware of or can creatively generate; choices depend upon the subjective probabilities we assign to various alternatives; choices depend upon the degree of perceived support for the worth of our individuality; and choices depend upon the perceived meaning of our lives, of what we are doing and of what we might be doing. Discovering or remembering this meaning becomes an exceedingly strong motive toward achieving the freedom of individual choice.

MEANING AND MOTIVATION

The "essence" of something is its basic underlying entity, substance, or form. The essence of motivation is finding meaning in what we do. Throughout our discussion of biological, emotional, and social motivation, we stressed the essential idea that how we behave depends upon the various meanings we attach to things, events, and life itself. We need to know *why*.

In Search of Meaning

Dr. Viktor Frankl, a Viennese psychiatrist who during World War II was imprisoned in concentration camps at Auschwitz and Dachau, has had a significant impact on our understanding of the importance of finding meaning in life.[9] From his first-hand experience in Nazi concentration camps, he saw that as long as people had a sense of purpose they survived extreme conditions of torture and deprivation. When they lost their sense of purpose, they weakened and died. He helped many retain the will to survive by stressing the meaning of continued existence. For example, with a fellow prisoner who was an author, he kept reminding the man that he had an unfinished manuscript to complete. For another, he emphasized the importance of the man's family and how much they needed to see him again. These were extreme conditions of living, and it is easy to see how those prisoners could doubt the importance of survival.

> It is reserved for man alone to find his very existence questionable, to experience the whole dubiousness of being. More than such faculties as power of speech, conceptual thinking, or walking erect, this factor of doubting the significance of his own existence is what sets man apart from animal.[10]

[9] Viktor Frankl, *Man's Search for Meaning: An Introduction to Logotherapy* (Boston: Beacon Press, 1962).
[10] Viktor Frankl, *Doctor and the Soul* (New York: Bantam, 1965), p. 21.

Even though most of us have never experienced the debilitating and demoralizing existence of a prisoner of war, questioning the significance and meaning of what we do has a daily impact on how we are motivated.

The first questioning of the meaning of life is most likely to occur during our adolescent years. A not-so-incidental statistic is that suicide (the ultimate renunciation of life and its meaning) is one of the four leading causes of death among teenagers. The adolescent with newly acquired knowledge and skills, finds courage to rebel against the very family (and other social institutions) upon which he or she so tenaciously depended such a short time ago. Growing awareness of inconsistencies, superficialities, and hypocrisies in our society may be followed by disillusionment and cynicism. This can be agonizing as the adolescent tries to make choices between two equally undesirable courses of action. Relief from the agony of shattered trust, broken promises, and fallen idols may be sought in a variety of ways. For some, a renewed religious faith may bring back a sense of one's personal significance and meaning. For others, relief from the pain of life's difficult choices may come from "dropping out" or "turning on" to a variety of drugs.

One of our strongest needs is the need to believe! Even the cynic who maintains that there's nothing to believe in, believes that. Do you remember how it felt to discover there was no literal Santa Claus who came down the chimney bearing gifts, or that the Easter Bunny was also a fantasy? As adults, believing in the importance of the work we do becomes a powerful source of motivation. Losing that belief, or not having it to begin with, makes work a drudgery. In every type of organization, one of the most common complaints of managers and other employees is that they are often told *what* to do but seldom told *why*. They suffer from insufficient information about the meaning and significance of their work. It is hard to believe in the importance of what we do if we can't really see what difference it makes.

When we wonder about the meaning of what we do, it is a way of speculating about the immediate and long-range consequences of our actions. The significance of even a small act can be enormous if we are able to see how one thing can lead to another to produce a result of greater importance. Benjamin Franklin has said:

> A little neglect may breed mischief; for want of a nail the shoe was lost; for want of a shoe the horse was lost; and for want of a horse the rider was lost.

Let's consider an example that could easily occur to any of us: A mechanic rotating the tires of your automobile may be distracted while tightening the lug nuts of a wheel. Because of the pressure of time and the distraction of another customer at the gas pump, the mechanic loses track

figure 6-4

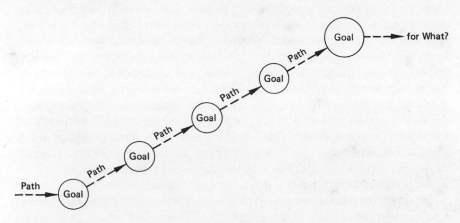

of the job, and the hub cap simply is slammed in place; you drive home pleased that you didn't have to wait very long. Three months later when the loose nuts and the wobbling wheel contribute to a sliding, skidding lurch into a ditch, you may well reflect on the meaningfulness of living. "It was sheer luck that I wasn't killed," you may exclaim. Somewhere in that confused, thankful mood following the accident, you may find yourself making vows for the future, or perhaps reexamining your values. It is unlikely that the mechanic is having a similar experience!

The Value of Larger Perspectives

Motivation is the process of selecting pathways which have the best chance of leading to need-satisfying goals. Goals reached become the means of reaching other goals. A book may be read not only for its knowledge or pleasure but because it is necessary to pass a test. Passing the test contributes to passing the course, which leads to a degree required for employment, which is the beginning of a career leading to . . . what? We can imagine this process as a series of steps, such as in Figure 6-4.

Frustration is as much a part of daily life as motivation. We are often blocked somewhere along the path toward a goal. We may react to frustration by redoubling our efforts to overcome the obstacle, by searching out another path to the goal, or by giving up the desire to reach it. One of the fascinating aspects of frustration is that it seems to make the unattained goal even more desirable. While we are engaged in an even more intense effort to reach the blocked goal, other goals may seem to be temporarily less important. We lose perspective. Two motorists arrive at the single remaining space in a parking lot at the same time. Both want the space so they can enter the store and do their shopping. Before this event, parking the car for one of the persons was a routine event (goal) leading to grocery shopping (goal) so that some extra delicacies could be part of the dinner (goal), which needed to be special (goal) because it was to be the happy (goal) celebration of an anniversary. But now! Imagine the two drivers inching their cars toward the space until the bumpers touch. Windows open and claims of being first are made by both. The goal of occupying the space has become so important that blows are exchanged. Imagine what mood the anniversary celebrant will be in at dinner time. Temporarily forgotten is the fact that another space may become available soon, that there are other stores, or that the purpose of the whole trip was to make the celebration just a little more joyous. A *larger perspective* has been lost.

Maintaining a larger perspective is one way of coping with the anxiety so often aroused in goal-seeking activity. "To err is human, to forgive, divine." This idea is easy to accept while reading it, but it's harder to remember when we've made a mistake. Mistakes will occur whenever and wherever people are involved. It is how we interpret the meaning or significance of the error which blocks or facilitates our motivational effort. If we let one mistake make us think, "I can't do *anything* right," then we've lost the larger perspective. One rejection can make us feel unattractive and unlovable. We can choose to become depressed. But we can also choose to remember others who love and respect us. One mistake does not make us a failure. But one success should be seen in a larger perspective, also. "Resting on your laurels" can be tempting but also can be an inhibitor of motivation. The person deserving the term "laureate" because of an honor such as the Nobel prize seems always to be continuing efforts toward larger accomplishments. The creative person, as we saw, bases a sense of self-worth not on the opinion of one or even many persons but on the larger perspective of superior preparation.

RESPONSIBLE CHOOSING

Motivation depends upon *our* individual perception of what will satisfy our needs. Perception is the meaning *we* give to those events and people impinging on us. The meaning we give to events and people depends upon the countless successes and failures we've experienced as we *motivate ourselves* along the pathways we choose. And choosing is an act of personal responsibility: ours, and no one else's. We can choose to abdicate our responsibilities and blame our motivational failures on others, but that choice does not make others responsible for us. We can choose to take the responsibility for our own feelings, thoughts, and perceptions and recognize that both wanted and unwanted consequences are their result. More than any other animal, we human beings have the freedom to make self-enhancing as well as self-defeating choices. The important thing is to know what is important to us. Keeping this in mind gives us the freedom to make short-range choices leading to meaningful and self-fulfilling lives.

SUMMARY

The study of motivation explores the question of how and why we make the choices we do. Creating good alternatives and evaluating the probable success of each is a process both conscious and unconscious. Those organizations within which we live and work both limit and expand the choices we make. The structure, the processes, and the managerial style can be designed so as to increase the levels of motivation and personal satisfaction. The essence of motivation is finding meaning in what we do. The individual perspective we maintain, and the level of responsibility we assume, leads to that freedom of choice we identify with maximum human self-fulfillment.

QUESTIONS FOR REVIEW AND DISCUSSION:

1. Motivation begins with the process of generating several good alternatives to a problem. Discuss how this may be done.
2. The creative person tends to be "open" to the ideas of others. Could this lead to rigid conformity or passive acceptance of the status quo? Discuss in the light of the theory of creative behavior.
3. What is the role of probability in making personal decisions? Give an example and show how subjective probabilities may determine the action taken.
4. Frustration may block motivation. How may we cope with frustration so that we achieve the maximum in self-motivated self-realization?

7

THE PROCESS OF INFLUENCE

Knowledge is power.

FRANCIS BACON*

What you are stands over you the while, and thunders so that I cannot hear what you say to the contrary.

RALPH WALDO EMERSON**

The country is the richest which nourishes the greatest number of noble and happy human beings; that man is richest who, having perfected the functions of his own life to the utmost, has also the widest helpful influence, both personal, and by means of his possessions, over the lives of others.

JOHN RUSKIN***

All of us need people for what they can *do* for us and what they can *mean* to us. That need may be personal and direct or impersonal and remote. But we have no choice. We cannot live in a society without needing others. We have previously defined a society as an enduring and cooperative social group whose members have developed organized patterns of relationships through interaction with one another. Those interactions range from the ridiculous to the sublime and from murder to

Meditationes Sacrae, "De Haeresibus."
**Letters and Social Aims.*
***Unto This Last,* Sect. 77.

nurturing. We need each other, and we need to influence the attitudes and behavior of each other. How we do that and the consequences of what we do are the subjects of this chapter.

Manipulation, brainwashing, and seduction are methods of influence, as are coaching, teaching, and counseling. Power is that combination of personal abilities and social position which allows one to influence behavior. Power may be used for good and evil purposes. The process of influence is, therefore, an ethical issue.

ETHICAL INFLUENCE

Ethics is the study of what is good or bad, right or wrong, and is concerned with moral duty and obligation. The ability to influence the behavior of one or of millions is awesome. Influencing a generation of people to receive vaccinations against smallpox has virtually eliminated that dread disease. The influence of one person who subverts the law and fraudulently misuses government agencies can lower the trust of a nation of people. How can we judge when the power of influence is used for good rather than bad? When is it right and when wrong? By what standards do we judge? And who should judge?

Criteria of Ethical Influence

Caveat emptor, or "let the buyer beware," is defined in *Webster's Third New International Dictionary* as "a warning principle in trading: the purchaser should be alert to see that he gets the quality and the quantity he is paying for." And what's wrong with that? If someone will buy it, sell it! After all, business is business. Of course, what's wrong with that principle of influence is that the consumer often lacks the knowledge, skill, and judgment to *know* either the quality or quantity of the purchase. To protect the consumer, laws and regulatory agencies have been established to make it easier to recognize the worth of a product or service. Truth in advertising, fair credit reporting, disclosure of interest rates, food and drug safety standards, pollution controls, regulations governing medical, psychological, legal, accounting, and other professional services, and a multitude of legal and moral sanctions place more of the responsibility on the supplier of goods and services rather than solely on the consumer. The emphasis is moving away from what will "sell" to what is fair and right. But there is still much gray area left to worry about. What regulates the influence of the manager who has the power to coerce, exploit, and mislead the employee to work at a speed and intensity injurious to physical and mental health? What agency can *prevent* the battered child, or wife, or husband? Who can interfere in the cooperative venture of the con artist and victim? It is difficult to *prevent* an unethical crime of influence, but some guidelines may be suggested for the enlightened self-interest of those who want to use influence ethically.

Some form of the Golden Rule is a common denominator of all major religions: do unto others what you would have them do unto you. It also means: if you don't want it done to you, don't do it to others. Codes of ethics for professional, social, and civic groups usually include this basic idea of *reciprocity*.

The law is a guide, but ethical behavior means more than mere conformity to it. "The law is a floor. Ethical business conduct should normally exist at a level well above the minimum required by law."[1] What is legal is essentially what the majority of a population believes to be moral behavior. The majority, as represented by Congress and the courts, may not always be right according to those individuals who see religious, professional, scientific, or business imperatives as being more important. But public opinion of the actions of individuals becomes a powerful influence.

> Possibly the best test for a person with a family might be to think whether you would be happy to tell your spouse and children the details of the action you are contemplating or whether you will be willing to appear on television and explain your actions in detail.[2]

Unfortunately, one can think of individuals who eagerly appear on television to espouse racial discrimination or to defend sales or promotional schemes of which the majority disapproves. Thus, what one believes to be right cannot always be a reliable guide for ethical influence.

It may be easier to reach agreement about practices that are not ethical. The Ten Commandments is essentially such a list. It is easy to agree that lying, stealing, or killing is intrinsically bad. But some would pose many exceptions to these religious injunctions: Shouldn't untrue statements sometimes be made to dying patients to maintain their hope? And isn't killing in self- defense judged to be morally right as well as legally sound? What is ethical, then, does depend somewhat upon the situation. Consider these statements of unethical conduct:

1. It is unethical to falsify or fabricate.
2. It is unethical to distort so that a piece of evidence does not convey its true intent.
3. It is unethical to make conscious use of specious reasoning.

---

[1] Quote from *Worldwide Business Conduct* (Caterpillar Tractor Company), as cited in *The Ethics of Corporate Conduct*, Clarence Walton, ed. (Englewood Cliffs, N.J.: Prentice-Hall, 1977).

[2] Clarence Walton, ed., *The Ethics of Corporate Conduct* (Englewood Cliffs, N.J.: Prentice-Hall, 1977), p. 5.

4. It is unethical to deceive the audience about the speaker's intent.[3]

To fabricate means to make up something for the purposes of deceit. As an example of its usage, Webster's Dictionary includes the phrase, "the unconscious fabrication of an honest man trying to put his best foot forward." This suggests that without realizing it, we may engage in deceitful attempts to influence by doing what comes "naturally"; in other words, presenting only the "good" sides of our personality and hiding the rest. A television commercial shows a woman examining two piles of washed laundry, one washed by her regular brand and the other by the brand being touted. These supposedly "scientific" comparisons have one thing in common: the advertised brand *always* cleans better. Amazing? Another example: the manager eager to hire a desirable recruit may talk only about the benefits of the job and not the strains or unpleasantries.

Specious reasoning is that which presents a superficially beautiful, attractive, right, or proper view of an issue that is not so in reality. It makes good sales sense to "sell the sizzle, not the steak," to talk about what the product will do for the buyer rather than discuss the product itself. Selling the benefits is ethically proper if the benefits are real as they are presented. Children may demand the advertised toy because the illustration in the magazine or on TV makes it appear as if it will be bigger than it really is or to do more than it really does. Adults often buy larger or more expensive toys such as automobiles, furs, and diamonds because of the promised sexual attractiveness or popularity the ad associates with the purchase. How ethical is it to suggest that a decathlon winner achieved his Olympic success by eating a certain cereal? The literal wording of the cereal advertisement does not claim a cause-and-effect relationship, but that implication would seem to be the intent.

By working definition, ethics is the study of the *criteria* of good and bad actions. Criteria are standards by which decisions or judgments may be based. Decisions must be judged by their short and long-term consequences. Increased knowledge of long-term consequences bears directly on our study of the process of influence.

Knowledge and Accountability

Knowledge leads to greater freedom, and sometimes agony, of choice. The freedom of choice gained through knowledge gives us power to influence, and power is inseparable from responsibility. The brilliant Disraeli, former prime minister of Great Britain, said, ". . . all power is a trust—

[3] Wayne C. Minnick, *The Art of Persuasion* (Boston: Houghton Mifflin Co., 1957), p. 284.

that we are accountable for its exercise—that, from the people, and for the people, all springs, and all must exist." The more we know about the long-range consequences of our power to influence, the more precisely we may define our individual accountability for our actions.

Science and ethics are partners in shaping our destiny. The science of ecology has made clear the intricate systems of interdependence which make up our world. Standard industrial practices of waste disposal a generation ago are now known to result in damage or destruction to the environment, as well as to humans. Ethical concerns of citizens sometimes have resulted in halting or delaying scientific experimentation on genetics, nuclear products, mind control, and other areas of controversy. Moral decisions by citizens may help determine the allocation of funds for research on diseases and other medical research. Scientific research has helped us understand why brainwashing is so effective in altering values and behavior and how individuals can be prepared to resist such efforts. Understanding and influencing human behavior, likewise, is a partnership of scientific information and ethical concern.

The behavioral sciences of psychology, sociology, and anthropology have generated much information about the human being on an individual, group, and cultural level. This information helps us predict and control behavior by relying on probabilities. And science is based on assumptions and statements of probability rather than certainty. The probabilities of one event following another may be very high, and we may think of it as a certainty; but that does not make it so. People are not alike, do not think or react alike, do not value the same things, and even change while we are in the process of examining them to see why they are different. There is regularity in the way people behave, and this creates predictions of how they will behave in the future; but our best predictions are merely statements of probability. The findings of the behavioral sciences have a significant impact on what is considered ethical by helping us to see the probable consequences of our actions in influencing the behavior of others. The more we know about the consequences of our actions, the more realistically and stringently we can be accountable for the influential power we use. The rapid growth in knowledge of human behavior not only helps us improve our predictions but also increases our power of influence and thereby our responsibility for our own actions.

Responsibility means to be accountable *to* someone *for* something which we are able to cause. What can we cause to happen? How likely, or how probable, is it that certain actions we take will be followed by the actions of others? The problem of causation is not easy to deal with, because of the uncertainties of what really does cause what. This is especially true with human behavior. We have discussed motivation as a process which depends upon how we perceive various sources of satisfaction. Perception is a personal mental process. No one else can perceive *for* us! How we perceive our environment influences our behavior. Literally, we *cannot* motivate another person to do anything. What we can do is to so thoroughly understand the needs and motives of another that we are able to alter their environment partially so that their perception of it increases the probability that they will act as we desire them to. We can create a climate which increases the probability that a person's perceived need satisfactions will be followed by movements toward specific goals. If they are goals we hoped they would pursue, we might feel we have "motivated" them. If they are goals we didn't want them to move toward, we probably will think that we failed to motivate them. The only way we can definitely cause someone else to behave in a certain way is to "manipulate" or physically handle them.

The process of influence which would seem to be the most effective in helping a person motivate themselves toward goals of need satisfaction and in their own best direction, would be that of professional counseling. Two people working together in a collaborative instead of an adversary relationship are more likely to achieve mutual satisfaction.

A COUNSELING APPROACH

Solitaire is a game designed for one person to play alone. Other activities can serve a similar function. Gardening can be a game of solitaire. Puttering and pruning, watering and fertilizing, can help us to relax, to mentally sort things out, and to prepare again for the inevitable, unavoidable, and often exciting interactions with people that fill our lives. Working a crossword puzzle, doing needlepoint or knitting, painting, making pottery, reading, writing letters, prose, or poetry, listening to music, or just musing are games of challenge, intrigue, and contemplation. They engross us as individuals. We can feel a sense of fulfillment and pleasure. Or maybe just the passage of time. And perhaps, a tinge of loneliness. Games of solitaire are not without vexation, but they are personal times. Alone times. Fun times. Thoughtful times. Times when we often feel free, secure, with our guard down and spirits up.

But people! Introduce one other person into our bubble of private space and alarms go off! Interactions are necessary. Certain facial expressions are required. Rules of good manners must be observed or the consequences must be faced. The game, now, is to listen, inform, teach, show, threaten, defend, love, hate, help, hurt, compete, cooperate, coerce, comply, win, lose, sell, buy, survive, or die. And much more. Reacting to people is stressful in both good and bad ways. It's risky. We can gain or lose in playing the people game. But we do have some choice in the matter.

How we choose to relate to people depends primarily on the assumptions we make about them. And the assumptions we make about people bear a close resemblance to the assumptions we make about our own nature and needs. The cynic will have self-doubts. The person with high self-trust will tend to trust others. The suspicious person will assume others are, too. Since people are different, no one set of assumptions will be right all the time. But we are going to make some (hopefully useful) assumptions about the process of influence and the readiness of people to respond to influence, so that the goals of ethical behavior and self-fulfillment may be realized for as many as possible.

The Concept of Professional Counseling

Our first assumption is that successful and ethical selling, managing, parenting, and person-to-person relating can best be accomplished by following common *guidelines* of professional counseling. Many types of counseling are being used in the helping professions. We will describe one approach; although it may be considered professional in nature, it does not require that the influencing person be a member of a profession. Specifically, we will discuss applying the role of counselor to management, sales, production, teaching, marriage, child rearing, or friendship. We should acknowledge that the *content* of what we counsel with others about depends on our competence. Without training, we should feel hesitant to play the role of counselor in trying to help someone with medical, psychological, or legal problems. A person trained in those professions should be consulted instead. It is the *process* of professional counseling which may be used as we try to improve our competence in interpersonal relationships.

Any profession is characterized by at least three elements:

> 1.   A body of knowledge and a range of skills in applying that knowledge. It is assumed that one has the best and most current knowledge available.
> 2.   A relationship of responsibility to the client. This relationship is guided by a code of ethics and assumes that the client is of paramount importance in the relationship.
> 3.   A governing body which exerts control over who shall enter the profession and under what circumstances one should be removed.

A professional person enjoys the highest respect partly because we feel *trust* and can depend upon and obtain strength and courage from that person. When we follow professional advice, it is because we *feel* that our best interests are being considered and protected. We assume that the professional is following ethical practices and are assured by that; the layman usually cannot judge the professional competence of the practitioner. We realize that some in a profession will not behave ethically, but our hope is that most will. Everything that has been said about professional behavior can potentially be true about anyone. Professional status in action comes not from claiming it, or from being licensed, but by behaving in a professional way. The professional person tends to minimize self concern and has maximum concern for the welfare of the client.

Professional counseling, as we use the concept, aims at helping others to expand and strengthen their abilities, uncover and maximize talents, stimulate their creativity, and assist them toward self-actualization. The professional salesperson can use professional counseling skills to assist the customer in making decisions in the customer's best interest. The professional manager can contribute to the development of the human resources of a firm. The professional parent can find ways to help the child make growth-inducing choices and to feel responsible for those choices. Friendships can flourish on the basis of mutual concern, respect, and responsibility. Is this idealistically impossible? No. Difficult to achieve? Yes. But it *is* possible.

Assumptions of Collaborative Influence

The basic orientation of this approach to the process of influence is away from *deciding* for others and toward *helping* them decide for themselves. It is away from an adversary and toward a cooperative relationship. It aims for a win-win rather than a win-lose game. It deemphasizes the use of power and intimidation *over* others and reaches for ways to create power *with* others. Two or more individuals pooling their talents and resources can create a great deal of power to make things happen. This orientation assumes that people can be oppressed and misled, but only for a time and at great cost. People do respond to threats and deceitful tactics, but at the cost of destructive resentment, loss of trust, and lowered self-satisfaction.

The consequences of human actions are far reaching and long lasting. The manager can apply pressure through threats and sarcasm to speed up production for the moment, but later consequences may include a higher error rate, deliberate slow-downs, and perhaps greater absenteeism and personnel turnover—not to mention difficulty in recruiting because of unfavorable information passed around about the department. The salesperson may coax the customer to overstock an item but lose the account when the customer finds that styles or trends have changed and the item is not selling. Parents may be nonaccepting of a child's feelings and needs and then wonder years later why there's so little communication from the child.

Whether humankind's basic nature is aggressive and warlike or cooperative and sharing is a philosophical argument we will not attempt to debate here. But there are known positive consequences of sharing rather than combating. Much human energy is used in establishing and maintaining superior-subordinate status relationships, but the consequences are not mutually beneficial. Establishing psychological partnerships also takes energy and careful planning. We believe the consequences of this effort are overwhelmingly, mutually beneficial. When two or more people become involved in a growing psychological partnership, these consequences have a higher probability of occurring:

1.   Extensive emotional and social exchange; shared control of events in situations of work and play

2.   Higher growth rates of people; increase in responsible and accountable behavior

3.   Higher levels of trust

4.   Recognition of conflict and resolution by mutual efforts

5.   Optimally uninhibited two-way communication

6.   Mutual participation: the rule rather than the exception in decision making and problem solving

7.   Marked increases in individual and group creativity, innovation, and adaptability

8.   Appropriate risk-taking in groups and organizations

9.   Emphasis on self-appraisal and appropriate requests for help

In 1973, a group of 120 noted religious leaders, philosophers, scientists, writers, and social scientists from around the world signed a 4,000 word document called Humanist Manifesto II. This document stressed our responsibilities to solve the problems which threaten human existence on earth. Economic systems, according to the Manifesto, should be judged by ". . . whether or not they increase economic well-being for all individuals and groups, minimize poverty and hardship, increase the sum of human satisfaction and enhance the quality of life." It was declared that the "ultimate goal should be the fulfillment of the potential for growth in each human personality."[4]

This ultimate goal cannot be accomplished by signing a document, or by government fiat, but it can succeed by individual actions. It is a path which can be freely and responsibly chosen by us if we understand the consequences involved in the process of influence.

[4] *New York Times,* August 26, 1973, p. 51, col. 1.

ACHIEVING GREATER SENSITIVITY TO INDIVIDUALS

We want certain individuals to do things for us and to feel and think things about us. We want to influence their attitudes and behavior. A major problem is that what we want them to do may not be what they want to do. The greater the difference between what we and they want, the more resistance to change will be aroused. But people change, and often willingly, because they learn to see the change as being better for them than the status quo. We would be mistaken to assume that people automatically resist change. Variety, freshness, newness, and surprise can be attractive *if* our needs seem to be better satisfied with the change. We can be effective in the process of influence to the extent that we know what the unique individual's needs are at this moment and to the extent that we can predict how that individual will perceive those changed conditions which we can control in the environment. The teacher can create a learning environment with a high probability of stimulating learning if the student's needs, interests, and level of readiness are known. The manager can effectively plan and organize how money, materials, and people should be combined if the diverse motives of the different people are understood. The physician can help patients plan for healthy lives to the extent the professional interest, caring, and listening skills influence patients to trust and talk openly. The salesperson knows that understanding the customer's short- and long-range goals and demonstrating how certain products and services can help satisfy those goals can lead to an economic and social exchange beneficial to both.

What hampers our awareness of others? What increases our sensitivity to their needs? How can we improve our predictions? Sensitivity is not used here in the sense of being thin-skinned. It refers to a heightened awareness, a more acute perception, and an ability to understand complex motives with a minimum of cues. Photographic film varies in sensitivity. Highly sensitive film allows us to take clear pictures with less available light. Human sensitivity is a skill which can be practiced and improved with effort. Let's look at some common obstacles to sensitivity in individuals.

Obstacles to Sensitivity

We are hindered in understanding what unique individuals need by some factors beyond our control, but most obstacles to our ability to "read" people are created by ourselves. To understand what people need and want, a logical first step would be to ask them. This is complicated by three things: (1) they may not know what they want; (2) they may know but be reluctant to tell; or (3) they may know but be unable to express themselves. These obstacles are largely beyond our control.

We manage to get in our own way in achieving greater sensitivity through a variety of attitudes and habits formed over the years. A partial list of these would include:

1. Self-centeredness and egotism
2. Distractions
3. Assuming others want what we want
4. Errors in perception
5. Preconceptions and false inferences
6. Dominance, control, and hidden feelings
7. Overenthusiasm for *our* own product, service, or treatment

Self-centeredness and Egotism. What arrogance, to think that we can motivate someone other than ourselves! But arrogance, self-centeredness, and egotism are very human characteristics. It is as egotistical to assume that we can motivate another as it is to assume that we can make a flower grow. We can supply water, fertilizer, proper soil conditions, and the right amount of sunlight. But we must depend upon innate tendencies of the flower for growth. Similarly, we can supply stimuli in the form of knowledge, opportunity, and feedback, but the human must interpret, respond, and learn for motivation to take place. What we *can* do is attempt to understand the innate and learned tendencies of others and see if we can help nurture them in their own best directions.

Distractions. Distractions plague us. They are the bane of our existence. Outside noises and irritating interruptions cut into our concentration. Inner noises in the form of worries, suspicions, fears, and desires are equally effective in diluting our ability to attend to what is in front of us. Meeting people for the first time and remembering their names is a chore for most of us. Our memories are good; it's the attention that's at fault. If we weren't so preoccupied with making a good impression and attempting to control our facial expressions and vocal tones, we just might have enough attentiveness to *hear* those names in the first place. We can't hear the evening news if the kids are making a ruckus. In the same way, we can't hear the needs and desires of others if we are creating our own mental ruckus. We distract ourselves with prejudices and illusions, unresolved conflicts and frustrated desires. What we want screams so loudly inside that we can't hear what the other person needs.

Assuming Others Want What We Want.   People do things for *their* reasons, not *ours*. A serious obstacle to our sensitivity to the needs of others is to assume that what is good enough for us is good enough for them. A sales manager initiates a contest. The winner gets a prize. Because the manager likes fishing, the first prize is a deep-sea fishing trip in the Gulf. Some salespersons seem to increase their efforts, but others don't. Do we wonder why? If money is important to us, we are likely to assume others will be motivated to make more money, or to save more. Sometimes we're right, and sometimes, wrong. And that is because people are different.

Errors in Perception. These can decrease our sensitivity to others. Perception is determined partly by the needs, expectancies, and attitudes that we have at any one time. Research on how we observe indicates that we frequently see what we want to see, what we expect to see, and what we have learned to see. We "see" what fits our previous beliefs about a person rather than what may actually be true. We observe characteristics of a person until we have him or her "pigeonholed," and then we tend to overlook other characteristics which conflict with our neat perception. We frequently "see" in people not what they feel and need but what we feel and need. We tend to see in people what they can do for us or what we can get from them. Less often do we see what they feel, need, or want. Our frame of reference, or mental set, distorts our perception of events and people. If money is no problem for us, we may fail to be sensitive to another's concern over too small cost-of-living increases or delayed raises in salary.

Preconceptions and False Inferences. Preconceptions color our perceptions. The manager who feels that the average worker needs to be coerced to get work done will relentlessly pressure employees to avoid social conversations and "get back to work." Another manager who thinks people in general want to do a good job and want to be given more responsibility and significant work will permit and even encourage discussions between employees as a means of getting them to stimulate each other to produce new ideas and effective work methods. Our attitudes determine how we see people and the kind of influence approach we use.

Dominance, Control, and Hidden Feelings. Dominance and control are personality traits many assume are associated with success in selling, managing, and parenting. Being "cool" and detached in analyzing problem situations and being unmoved by emotional displays sounds like a logical approach to effective influence. In fact, these characteristics may interfere with the ability to know and understand how others are reacting internally. The strong, aggressive salesperson and the forceful, dominant manager do frequently enjoy success. We have seen that some individuals have a need to submit and be controlled. If the dominant salesperson or manager happens to be dealing with clients or employees who need to submit or be controlled, then sales or work productivity are likely. It could be argued that some people will buy anything from a forceful salesperson, and that some employees will put up with almost any kind of working situation or unfeeling treatment from their supervisor. On the other hand, it might be deflating for some salespersons to realize that occasionally a person will buy from them in spite of their pressures or attempts at dominance.

Overenthusiasm for Our Own Product, Service, or Treatment. Another obstacle to achieving sensitivity to the values, feelings, and needs of others is our own enthusiasm for the product we are selling, the service we are rendering, the goals of our organization, or the form of treatment or help we are offering. Enthusiasm would seem to be a vital ingredient to the successful exercise of influence. But enthusiasm for what we can do can keep us from seeing that another person is not enthusiastic about having it done. The small child given a new hammer finds that almost everything needs to be hammered. The manager fresh from a training course in participative management assumes that everyone wants to and should participate in all decisions. The surgeon thinks of surgery; the chiropractor thinks of joint manipulation; the attorney thinks of legal solutions; the psychologist thinks of behavioral changes; the minister or rabbi seeks spiritual solutions. Our own expertise narrows our perception and limits our sensitivity to the whole person we are trying to influence.

We have come full circle. Our self-centeredness and egocentric need to rush in to fix things with our special knowledge and skill makes it difficult to be sensitive to what our patient, client, customer, or employee needs and wants. If we could only get out of our own way!

Enhancing our Sensitivity

Sensitivity is our ability to understand and predict the behavior of others based on the observations and attitudes we have of them. It is a skill that can be improved with training and practice. It takes practice, as does any skill, and techniques of observation may be helpful. People vary in their levels of sensitivity, depending upon past experiences, their occupations, and their sex. When comparing groups of males and females, more females than males achieve higher scores on measures of sensitivity and ability to predict behavior. The differences between the groups is not great, but even a slight difference can be significant. More females than males show a greater interest in people and social situations. More females than males disclose more about themselves to others. The greater interest in people and more openness in disclosing self apparently allows one to be more open in receiving information and observing more accurately. Sensitivity is an ability we all have, but to different degrees. Sensitivity is likely to be quite specific to the person, the situation, or work we are observing. An executive may be able to predict which engineers are more likely to develop patentable products but unable to predict which sales managers will be best in marketing the product. The sales manager may be sensitive in selecting recruits who will be successful salespersons but inept in selecting a secretary.

Observation skills and attitudes can be altered in a number of ways to enhance our sensitivity:

1. Look past the general impression and be alert to the specifics which make a person unique
2. Use mechanical and analytical methods of feedback to test the reliability of observations
3. Talk less and listen more
4. Use the scientific method in improving the accuracy of your perception
5. Reduce your own defensiveness and practice more emotional disclosure of your self

People are so complex that it can seem, at times, as if it is impossible to know them well enough to predict their behavior with any real accuracy. It is not surprising that we tend to make quick, first impressions and stick to them. These first impressions may be wrong, but if we do not attempt to look past them to see the specifics—the inconsistencies and contradictions which make up every unique person—we will remain low in our sensitivity. There are at least six levels of information about people that we use to achieve understanding of them:

1. Appearance
2. Memberships
3. Activities
4. Beliefs
5. Values
6. Feelings

A person's appearance can "tell" us a lot; but appearance can be misleading, also. With our first glance at a person, we notice the obvious characteristics such as race, sex, age, size, posture, facial expressions, mode of dress, neatness and cleanliness, and what they are doing. Every one of these factors of appearance can trigger in the observer many past experiences, associations, prejudices, misconceptions so that our immediate conclusion can be quite erroneous. We are not sensing the person so much as reviewing broad generalities. We may assume an old person is rigid and unwilling to change, missing entirely the presence of a still active mind eager to learn. Or we may assume a young person we see is irresponsible, unstable, and so on. Our insensitivity here may keep us from even giving that person a chance to demonstrate the level of maturity that does exist.

We make judgments of an individual based on memberships. The place of work, the political party, the religious affiliation, the family, and social and civic memberships evoke general impressions of the kind of person who would belong to those various groups. We know that not all accountants or Republicans or Jews or Shriners are alike, but our assumptions about these groups may overwhelm our sensitivity to the individual.

In our search for clues as to what someone is like, we pay attention to the things that a person does. A man who hunts and fishes creates one impression. The man who likes to knit or do needlepoint will undoubtedly bring different images to mind. The woman who jogs and the woman who practices belly dancing both may thoroughly enjoy the movement and exercise. Are your images of what these two women are like different because of what they do? Just as with appearance and memberships, the activities we observe people doing may produce generalizations which obscure sensitivity.

We increase our sensitivity as we deliberately move deeper past appearance, membership, and activity to try to understand what a person thinks, values, and feels. There are social barriers which seem to keep us from doing much sharing of ourselves at these more intimate levels, but this is precisely where our sensitivity to others can be sharply improved. Even in intimate relationships such as marriage, the family, business associations, and friendships, conversation may center overwhelmingly on matters of appearance, membership, and activity. Talk concerning items of clothing, hair styles, problems with committees, the week-end tennis or golf game is more common than discussions of values and feelings. It is not uncommon to discover after years of marriage or business associations that one person will say of another, "I don't think I really know that person at all!" We all wear masks to some extent. The sensitive person attempts to understand the thoughts, values, and feelings behind that mask. In the next chapter on communication, techniques for listening to that person behind the mask will be discussed.

We can practice increasing our sensitivity by using mechanical devices such as tape and video recorders to improve our powers of observation. All too often we see only what we want to see or what we think is happening rather than what is actually taking place. It would be helpful to use a tape recorder during a conversation with a friend or during an employment interview (with full knowledge and permission, of course). At the same time, take notes as carefully as you can; try to write down all the facts, ideas, phrases, or points of view being expressed. Then listen to the recording while scanning your notes to see what you failed to write down or forgot. Notice the differences between what you "heard" and the tape recording. Analyze the kinds of information you seem to overlook. Ask a friend to listen with you so that you get another perspective on your tendency to be less sensitive to certain kinds of information. Go to a meeting with someone else, and have both you and your partner take notes. Try to write a complete narrative of the meeting, separately, then compare versions with your companion. Notice what you agree you both saw and heard and what only one of you observed. It is a way of beginning to see how you might unconsciously be distorting facts or perhaps, projecting your own feelings into the situation. As we mentioned in Chapter 1, three eyewitnesses to a single accident invariably report three slightly different versions, yet each is likely to think their version is correct. We become more sensitive to others when we become a little doubtful about the accuracy of our observations and make strenuous efforts to improve.

Our sensitivity can be enhanced when we talk less and listen more. The old sage who said, "You ain't learnin' when you're talkin' " may have a point. The individual who is strongly expressive in social situations tends to be less aware of others than one who is more reserved. As we will see later, good listening is more than remaining silent. To the extent that we need to dominate the conversation, or keep others entertained with our remarks, we will know less about what others are thinking and feeling. The experienced and highly talented comedian can entertain and still be sensitive to audience reaction, but it takes enormous energy and concentration. Trying to avoid interrupting the other person may give us more time to think over what is being said, as well as allowing the other person to be more disclosing.

The scientific method, as discussed in Chapter 1, ". . . can help us move away from superstition and toward reality; from costly trial and error toward efforts which are more often right the first time." The major point we reemphasize here is that, in an attempt to be ultra sensitive to the facts as they are, the scientist observes carefully and systematically, obtains all relevant facts (not just the ones that are convenient), and repeats the entire process to be even more sure of the results. The scientist makes detailed observations while delaying judgment and then comes to a conclusion. The nonscientist all too often forms a conclusion then observes selectively to support the conclusion.

The defensive person who is charged with being "defensive" is likely to respond in just that way. When our point of view is questioned, or we are accused of not doing our share, our first inclination is to defend ourselves. We may continue a debate even after we've changed our view to that of our opponent's because we don't want to seem to have "lost" the argument. This seems only human, and it is. But defensiveness makes us less sensitive to the other's point of view. We can make a choice not to be defensive and to ask the other person more about their views, their reasoning, and their feelings. If we avoid arguing and continue to encourage the other person to go into more detail, we will not only understand more and be more sensitive, but, with our acceptance, the other person may begin to modify or soften his or her stance.

CHANGING ATTITUDES AND BEHAVIOR

Social or economic exchange can bring mutual benefits to two people, or it can be a gain for one at the expense of the other. Sometimes we are aware we are choosing the first approach, but at other times it is not clear. Professional counselors are aware that using their influential capacity to assist clients in their growth also becomes a growth experience for the counselors.

In our discussion of techniques of influence, we will refer to the possessor of influence as the *counselor* and will refer to the recipient as the *client*. The counselor may be a schoolteacher, preacher, rabbi, parent, manager, stockbroker, engineering consultant, sales clerk, or, in fact, anyone who works with others where change is expected or possible. The client may be our child, a student, an employee, a spouse, a customer, or anyone who may be influenced by us.

If it is the intent of the counselor to influence clients ethically, the guidelines on page 156 are a beginning. Because counselors have an impact on the total person, we suggest some additional aims for the counselor-client relationship where influence is the intent:

1. Do the persons involved become more realistic in seeing themselves and their situation?
2. Is there a gain in their ability to make responsible decisions for themselves regarding matters which directly affect their lives?
3. Do they become more flexible, adaptable, and creative in their perceptions and actions?
4. Are there gains in self-esteem and satisfaction with their work and in their private lives?
5. Do the individuals accept more realistic goals for themselves?

Each of these aims deals with personal growth. Both counselor and client can share in the benefits.

Establishing Credentials and Competence

A public speaker's influence (like a counselor's) depends on how expert or competent the listener feels the speaker is. The introduction of a speaker becomes critical in getting the attention of the audience, arousing their interest and readiness to be influenced. Introductions often are boring listings of honors and memberships, but a good one indicates why the speaker should be believed. In the same way, the counselor is more influential when office documents and certificates and the testimonials from other clients suggest competence. The third-party influence of a satisfied client can do much to build an initial feeling of trust.

Trust in a counselor-client relationship is important, but it must be warranted. It is possible that in the introduction of a speaker, or in a testimonial regarding a counselor, specious reasoning is used. We may be impressed by an Olympic gold-medal winner, but is he or she competent to speak to us about principles of motivation? The president of a highly successful company, of which we are an employee, is not necessarily an expert on national or international economics any more than an economist is an expert on business management. Our talents as counselors are likely to be beneficial but limited. We should help the client understand that. In the long run, we are most likely to build images of competence and confidence in the eyes of the client if we are careful to point out the limits of our competence.

Building Rapport

A close, comfortable relationship of confidence has its beginnings in the initial assumption of adequate credentials and confidence, but it must be sustained and built further if maximum influence is to be used. Rapport is a *feeling*. It is the comfort we feel in the bedside manner of our physician. It is the feeling of liking and respecting another. Good rapport means that counselor and client are "in tune" and ready to confide in each other and work together. Feeling good about the teacher, manager, or therapist does not mean that good teaching, managing, or treatment will result. But it helps. We know that many transactions take place in business organizations without rapport being necessary. Orders are given and followed, items purchased and services rendered, not because of rapport between individuals but because legitimate authority is perceived or the product and service speak for themselves. Rapport, however, is crucial when change and growth in individuals is desired. Rapport can be built to the extent that the counselor:

1. Is genuine or authentic
2. Shows acceptance and unconditional regard for the client
3. Demonstrates empathic understanding
4. Maintains attention primarily on the client
5. Avoids embarrassing or belittling the client
6. Attempts to speak the language of the client

Genuineness cannot be pretended. Of course, that is a redundant sentence, but its obvious truth is often ignored. The sales trainee may be advised to "lean forward in your chair, smile slightly, lift your eyebrows, and nod your head frequently to show the customer you're interested." Try doing that in a mirror and see how interested you look! Not only is pretended interest a form of deceit, but it takes energy and concentration to remember how you should look to appear interested; it also heightens attention on yourself, which reduces sensitivity to the needs of the customer. Genuineness is not a way of *looking* but a state of *being*. It means to be congruent in what you are experiencing and what you are communicating with your words and behavior. It is to be transparent so that the client will know where you stand and how you are reacting. But can we be completely genuine in this real world? Sometimes we can, and sometimes not. There are consequences either way. If we sense lack of genuineness in others, we will be wary and less inclined to respond to their influence. It works both ways in the counselor-client relationship. The need to be genuine is often determined by our goal. The physician is often less than candid in predicting the progress of a serious illness *if* it maintains hope and contributes to the patient's willingness to fight for recovery. But for the attorney not to express doubts about the success of a suit may take some responsible decision making out of the hands of the client and may lessen the preparedness to testify. To be less than genuine when it serves our interests but detracts from that of the client would be less than ethical.

We feel a rapport when someone seems to accept us as we are. They may not agree with our ideas or what we are doing, but if they see value in us and accept us as the wondering, groping, conflicted, uncertain person we are, we sense an atmosphere of freedom conducive to change and growth. Being accepted is being free of being judged. Judgments have a ring of finality to them. They seem absolute, and we wear them like a scarlet letter. And judgments tyrannize! Let someone call us "irresponsible!" and we may feel and even begin to behave irresponsibly. Judgments sting and make us feel inferior to the judge. We withdraw and plan ways of protecting ourselves from further judgments. But acceptance! Acceptance means acknowledging reality—what we really feel, want, and care about. To feel that someone respects, regards, or loves us because of who we are, and not for what we can do for them, is a powerful influence in learning to have that same feeling about ourselves. If it is raining outside, we don't fight the reality of the rain; that would seem stupid and self-defeating. It's raining, so accept it and cope with it. Take an umbrella or wear a raincoat. Or stay inside. Acceptance means letting reality be our guide rather than being guided by illusion or wishful thinking. Acceptance helps build rapport, but it is also the beginning of readiness to change and learn. The counselor can accept the client but point out the positive and negative consequences of the client's actions. Knowing that accepting or rejecting the advice will not jeopardize the relationship, the client will probably feel increased rapport, sensing that the counselor's interest in the client's welfare is paramount.

It is not enough that the counselor understand and accept the client. This must be clearly demonstrated. If the counselor can accurately articulate the client's feelings, needs, and objections to a sale or a change in behavior, the client receives direct and immediate feedback that demonstrates the counselor's understanding. Empathy is that ability to see the world from the client's point of view. Empathy means putting aside our own preconceptions and seeing those of the client. We have biases and so does the client. We have needs, and they may or may not coincide with our client's. Rapport is diminished and our influence weakened if our own needs blind us to the needs of our client. Needing a sale may prevent the salesperson from correctly reading the buyer's needs. Needing to *push* employees toward faster production may blind the manager to the existing needs for meaningful work and recognition. Pushing is likely to create resistance rather than faster work. We cannot always empathize. There are times when we simply do not understand the needs or motives of the client. Research and clinical evidence suggests that if the client perceives that we genuinely *want* to understand, that is almost as satisfying as if we *do* understand. Empathy is not only demonstrated understanding but is an attitude of wanting to know as well.

A key element in all professional activities is a relationship of responsibility to the client. The client is of paramount importance. Professional psychotherapy is patient-centered; professional teaching is student-centered; selling can be customer-centered; and managing can be employee-centered. We would hope that parenting is child-centered—not in the sense of the child dominating the household; this is not helpful to the child or family. But if parenting helps the child feel lovable, respectable, worthwhile, and dignified, that child will more likely grow into a highly influential counselor too. To feel lovable makes it more likely that we will love. Self-respect is an attitude which fosters respect of others. Being cared for helps the individual learn how to care for others. The language of a caring rapport involves more "you's" than "me's." It is always tempting to talk about ourselves and our problems. But if this is a need, then take yourself as a client to a counselor trained to help.

There are all kinds of "tricks of the trade" in the business of persuasion. Most of us have been subject to, or have subjected others to, embarrassment or belittlement as a means of changing attitudes or behavior. "Shame on you!" can cause cringing and, perhaps, immediate obedience, but at a probable cost in self-esteem and respect. Teenagers, and us "old" folks too, can be goaded into deviant and regretted behavior through the embarrassment or humiliation of an individual or group. Guilt can be a bludgeon which leaves us bleeding *and* bowed. Guilt is a form of tyranny that is sometimes praised as a means of getting someone "in line." A groan and a "Oh, what you do to me!" is a form of hocus pocus which attempts to shift the responsibility of feelings from the groaner to the victim. But guilt sells. It motivates. It devastates. And it weakens rapport. It is a not uncommon scene that a husband will allow himself to be embarrassed into a purchase by a successful guilt-inducer only to have it returned immediately by his more dispassionate wife. We should hastily add that it works the other way around, too. Guilt may result in a sale or a change of behavior. Guilt can also lead to resentment, which terminates accounts or ends relationships. Guilt can be a feeling of morbid self-reproach, which is bad enough when it comes from one's own failure or mistake; if it is something we have directly caused, we can attempt a remedy. But if we feel guilty because of someone else's feelings or behavior, we have just lost control of the ballgame. We are like the manager with assigned responsibility but no authority. Part of our aim as a professional counselor is to help the client feel responsible for his or her own behavior. We should not burden clients with ours.

Traveling in a foreign country is exciting, but there is confusion and anxiety if no one speaks our language and we do not speak theirs. What a relief to run into someone from our own country! Or, better yet, from our own state or hometown. In foreign territory we may feel more rapport than if we were to run into that same stranger on the streets at home. Here at home we have the same problem, but it's less obvious. English may be the native language for most of us, but we speak in different tongues. The engineer has a vocabulary strange to the social worker, who has difficulty following the television repairman trying to explain the needed repairs. We expect these differences due to technical or professional specialties. What is less obvious is the variety of meanings different people give to even ordinary words. (Our last chapter on communication will expand on this concept.) We build rapport with another when we understand their meanings and their usages of words. It is tempting to impress clients with our technical terms, and we may succeed. But our efforts to impress may interfere with our desire to express. Trying to speak the language of the client does not mean that we "talk down" but instead that we strive to talk *with*. Entering someone's life is like entering a foreign territory. There are customs and expectancies with which we may be unfamiliar. We could choose to be arrogant and expect them to speak our language, or we could take the initiative in building rapport by learning theirs. Only the second choice is under our control.

Modifying Perspectives

With good credentials and a solid rapport, the competent counselor may choose means of helping to modify the client's perspective so that attitude and behavior changes may occur. The basic steps toward helping to modify change include:

1. Getting and sustaining attention
2. Examining both sides of an issue
3. Repeating the message enough times
4. Showing connections between actions and goals
5. Reviewing all possible objections to change
6. Asking for the change to occur

Early in our discussion of self-motivation in Chapter 5, we saw that attention and imagination are extrinsic and intrinsic factors in the motivational process. We notice blinking lights or changing sounds more than constant ones. Internal worries or anticipations can be so vivid that we are momentarily blind and deaf to what's happening around us. Generally, we notice only one thing or idea or feeling at a time. Our mind works so rapidly, though, that we appear to focus on many things at once. The motion picture is a series of still photographs, but our mind interprets them as motion. The flickering of the incandescent bulb 60 times a second looks steady to our eye. The mind flits from this to that and back again so rapidly that we can seemingly listen to the symphony and read the program notes at the same time. The clash of cymbals may jerk us upright, stealing our attention from thoughts of the composer's biography. But in a moment, worries about the new baby-sitter may drown out the loudest of crescendoes. We attend to a running stream of images and sensations. Anyone seeking our attention has some real competition.

If clients come to us, their attention is focused on the appointment—and probably has been for some time. If we go to the clients, who may or may not be expecting us or wanting to see us, our first problem is to get their attention. If we have been referred by a mutual friend, that name is an attention-getter. If the company we represent, or the product or service we offer does not immediately interest the client, something else must be tried as an attention-getter. Something unusual. One salesperson carried his product right into the office of the buyer; it was a 90 pound road barricade with a blinking yellow warning light. We should add that this salesperson was big and strong enough that carrying it was little effort. He was an attention-getter himself.

The creative person is effective because of unusual preparation. The effective and creative counselor will research, gather information, talk to people, and understand as much as possible about the client's situation prior to making the approach. Knowing the technical language, understanding the problems specific to the client's industry, and being familiar with some of the history of the client's firm can supply clues as to what the client is likely to notice. Bringing solutions, or even partial solutions, to the client's problems can help arouse and sustain attention.

There are usually two sides to every issue. More intelligent persons seem to respond more favorably to being given both sides so that they can form their own conclusions. For less intelligent or less educated persons, attitudes are more likely to be changed by presenting only the side we wish them to believe. While research lends support to these observations, our goal of encouraging clients to make responsible decisions for themselves would suggest using the two-sided approach. Products will not do everything. They all have limitations. The salesperson showing both the advantages and limitations of the product may lose occasional sales but is more likely to build credibility and long-term customers. New employees who have been told the pleasures *and* irksome details of their work are less likely to become disillusioned and quit early in their tenure.

Repetition can be influential. And boring! Standard advice to speakers is to tell the audience what they will say, say it, and then tell what has been said. Repeating a thought can be attention-getting and influential—not boring—if the thought is varied or different examples are used. It takes some of us a long time to understand something. We may hear a notion discussed or may read about it many times before it finally "sinks in" and becomes usable. But practice makes perfect unless we practice the wrong thing; then we become perfectly wrong. Radio and television commercials that seem to depend upon unending repetition to gain product recognition may "convince" many buyers. If the repeated slogan or ditty upsets us, the repetitions make us vow to *never* buy that product.

Learning takes place when we make mental connections between certain actions and goals. The good teacher, tennis pro, consultant, or manager helps the client recognize effective actions and differentiate them from ineffective ones. "Oh! I see!" is an excited response we make to an influential coach who has helped us recognize what we are doing right, or wrong. We have seen that the Law of Effect suggests that actions that are rewarded will tend to be repeated. Praise is a reward for many. Praising someone for what they have done is a method of influence, rewarding the one who has performed well. Both praise and punishment are externally applied sanctions to the client, and they are commonly used to shape the behavior of children, employees, spouses, customers, and friends. They are judgments made about the client's behavior and often about the client's character. Judgments, even positive ones, tend to make the client dependent upon the judge—and somewhat defensive. We are defensive even with positive judgments about us (although the defensiveness is probably unconscious) because what someone gives us they can also take away. Depending upon others' praise for our own motivation is still dependency rather than self-determination. On the other hand, helping clients realize the consequences of their own behavior is a solid form of influence, a fundamental principle of learning, and an action which increases self-determination and responsibility. The joy of learning, the pleasure of accomplishing, the satisfaction of helping are all *intrinsic* rewards. These rewards depend upon our own efforts rather than on the opinion of others. The caring, influential counselor will help clients discover the links between their actions and the self-enhancing or self-defeating consequences of those actions.

Of course, people object to some changes. They object a lot. They may have many objections, only some of which they mention in the opening stages of a controversial conversation. The counselor may try influencing the client to change by answering the objections one by one. Adamant and clever clients may think of new objections to a sale or behavior change while the counselor still is trying to overcome the last one. Like the mythical Hydra, each objection cut off makes two new ones sprout. It's a stalemate. Try something else. Ask the client to think of all the possible objections there could be to the suggested course of action. Ask if there are any more. Prod. Probe. Try to find every last resistance to change. Two things may happen. First, a client, after having unlimited opportunity to talk against the proposed change, may realize the case is somewhat overstated and begin to soften his or her stance. Second, the counselor has a larger perspective of how the situation appears to the client and is now more sensitive to the whole person. If the counselor asks, "If we can find satisfactory answers to each of these objections, will you be ready to take action?" the client who says yes has a commitment to the process of influence.

Experienced salespersons look for the right signs and try for the "close." They then ask for the sale, the decision, or the action. Even a gentle "Try it" may encourage the undecided to take the plunge. "What've you got to lose?" may give the client a larger perspective and the supportive nudge needed to take the first step. One disservice we do to our clients, whether children, employees, spouses, or customers, is to expect too little from them. It is showing some lack of regard for their potential and can discourage them. Asking for more than one expects to get is a ploy used by every manager who submits a budget. "They're asking for more than they need" is the inevitable thought of the executive reviewing those budgets. The results cancel out, but both parties are involved in a form of deceit. We can ask too much and make a mistake. We are mistaken, also, when we expect too little. We should ask our clients to reach their maximum potential. As influential counselors with the capacity to affect the lives of all those we reach, we should expect no less of ourselves.

SUMMARY

With knowledge of how to influence others comes the power to do so, and with power comes the responsibility to use it ethically. Professional counseling is only one of many forms of influence; this concept can be a useful guide in other fields such as selling and managing. Using a professional-counseling approach assumes a relationship of responsibility to the client, prospect, or employee. This relationship is based on mutual trust and cooperation.

The more we are sensitive to and aware of the circumstances and needs of others, the more we can design our influence to be helpful. The ability to understand others is a learned skill that can be improved systematically.

QUESTIONS FOR REVIEW
AND DISCUSSION:

1. Why is public disclosure one criteria of ethical influence? What are the individual and social pressures involved? Is willingness for public disclosure always an indication that the intended influence is ethical? Discuss.

2. Why does a professional person often encourage trust and confidence in the client who may not be able to judge the competence of the professional person?

3. We often create our own obstacles to being sensitive to the needs of our client. What are the psychological and emotional explanations of this?

4. How does following the scientific method help us be more accurate in assessing the needs of others with whom we may be counseling?

5. How does the effective counselor encourage new learning on the part of the client, customer or employee?

8

COMMUNICATION: A PROCESS OF HUMAN EXCHANGE

This desire for interpersonal fusion is the most powerful striving in man. It is the most fundamental passion, it is the force which keeps the human race together, the clan, the family, society.

ERICH FROMM*

No man is an island, entire of itself; every man is a piece of the continent, a part of the main; . . . any man's death diminishes me because I am involved in mankind; and therefore never send to know for whom the bell tolls; it tolls for thee.

JOHN DONNE**

With the shout "Play ball!" the great American pastime baseball enters our lives. We all play games, as players or spectators, and generally agree that what counts is not how you play the game but whether you win or lose. Or is it the other way around? It may depend upon how much you want to be "a winner" and avoid being "a loser." When we "make a pitch," we hope for a specific result. Most of us know that it takes much effort, and some luck, just to "get to first base." If we can't do that, someone is sure to think of us as a "foul ball." If your aim is not to be "home free," maybe it's because you're "out in left field." Let's look for

The Art of Loving, copyright © 1956 by Erich Fromm. Reprinted by permission of Harper & Row, Publishers, Inc.
**Devotions,* XVII.

the "signals" that help us decide whether to throw "a fast one" or "a curve ball." Play ball!

On radio and television the words and pictures push everything else out of our mind.

> Well, folks, this has been one exciting series, climaxing one of the most exciting seasons in recent memory. It's the seventh game. It's the last of the ninth. The score is tied. Two out. The count is three and two. The tension is unbelievable! You can't even hear yourself think! Everyone's on their feet. This could be it! He leads the league in home runs, and he hit the home run that won the sixth game and kept them in this series. Will he do it again? Or will we go into extra innings? The pitcher shook off the sign. He nods. The stretch. The wind up. The pitch and . . . it's a hit . . it's a high one . . . it's going . . . it's going . . . it's . . .

Can you imagine static on the radio or the TV picture replaced with the message: "We are experiencing technical difficulties . . . please do not adjust your set." Frustration? Certainly. The same frustration we experience when we make our "pitch" in the form of a statement or question and receive an unclear reply or no reply at all. Communication is a process of human exchange frequently involving tension, sometimes involving frustration, and always including signs, signals, symbols, and significance. Communication is a game played on a field with certain rules, with players, with usually an audience, and with an outcome: win, lose, or rained out. Communication is the great human pastime, entering and altering our lives in all seasons.

Communication is a game different from baseball. It knows no seasons. Everyone plays. Batting averages are impossible to calculate and are not published. And you're not always sure which team you're on. Or whether you've won or lost. The rules seem to change with the situation. Coaches are everywhere giving advice, but *they* don't make the runs or suffer the penalties. In baseball, you can choose to buy a ticket or turn on the set or join the team and get involved; in communication, you have no choice. You are in the game whether you like it or not. You cannot *not* communicate.

We communicate with ourselves as well as others. We communicate consciously and unconsciously, verbally and nonverbally. We float in a sea of communication, and it is frequently a case of sink or swim. We begin the process of communication even before birth, and we continue after death in our writings or the memories of the living. Communication gives us the cloak of *culture,* which we never remove. It shapes our *identity* and gives us an "I." It *motivates* us with things real and ideal. It is the process of *exchange,* which gives us the *choice* of self-enhancing or self-defeating reactions. Communication is the exchange of information and understanding. It is an exchange of value, as in a sales transaction. We give and receive thoughts and feelings worth something to us. Sometimes the bargain is fair. And sometimes not.

STAGES IN THE COMMUNICATION PROCESS

"One way to understand communication is to view it as a people process rather than as a language process."[1] It is a series of actions and reactions, events and developmental stages. It is the yarn which weaves us into cohesive groups capable of doing far more together than any individual can do alone. It is intricate and complex in the way it gives color and depth to our lives. Communication is a process with no beginning and no end. We are in the *middle* of it as we try to understand and influence our own behavior and that of others.

Figure 8-1 suggests the stages we go through as we proceed from an idea in our mind to the expression of it. Figure 8-2 follows the process from the point of view of the receiver of our expression. The models of communication suggested here are much simpler than reality. Each stage is influenced by and in turn influences every other stage, forming not a concrete series of steps so much as a continuous interaction of personalities and situations, within a cultural context.

Starting with an Idea

We have to begin somewhere, even if it is in the middle. We start with an idea. Sometimes we know where it comes from, but usually it's just there. Something occurs to us. It can be fleeting or so persistent that all we can do is ruminate. Someone may have attracted our attention, or, perhaps, we have given our imagination free reign and a creative thought has emerged. The idea—a series of mental images—begins to take shape in its color and form. It is modified by the *situation* of the time and place. The idea is associated with the multiple *needs* we experience. Various *words* or other symbols float to the surface to give our idea some recognition and substance. We are aroused by an event occurring within us and *intended actions* seem apparent. Almost immediately we expect *reactions* from those who may be affected by the implementation of our idea. The *roles* we play simultaneously or in sequence should be considered as we contemplate action. What conforms to one role may conflict with another. On the basis of our subjective *probabilities* of success for the

[1] Jack R. Gibb, "Defensive Communication," *Journal of Communication,* 11 (September 1961), p. 141.

figure 8-1   Communication Process Stages: Sender's Point of View

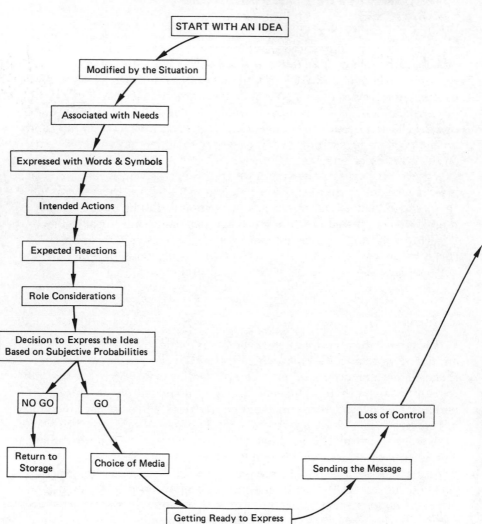

figure 8-2 Communication Process Stages: Receiver's Point of View

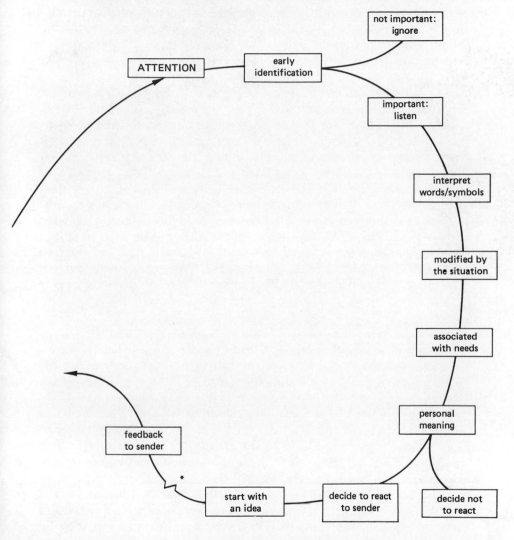

paths available to us, we make a decision to *go* or *not go* with an expression of our idea. If we express ourselves, we must decide which media best serve our needs. Do we speak it, write it, or use a token or symbol to indicate it? When we feel ready, we will use tongue, paper, picture, touch, or token to send our message on its way. And then we lose control as the message is taken by the receiver. *Interference* may prevent our idea from being transmitted. The *attention* of the receiver may not be gained. If our message does get through, it may be treated with *indifference*. The receiver may *listen poorly* or have *no reaction* at all. We learn it can be frustrating to attempt to communicate!

Our intended receiver has some of the same problems as the stages of communication continue to unfold. First, before anything else happens, we must have *attention!* That is a state of being that must occur in the *receiver* and is beyond our control. We can try to get it, but, ultimately it has to be given. The receiver tries to identify the nature of the incoming message and decides to either ignore it or listen to it. This listening may be of good or poor quality. The listener will interpret the words or symbols of the message according to the listener's past experiences, biases, misconceptions, and stereotypes—not the sender's. The listener's situation and needs will shape, modify, or distort the incoming message in unique ways to produce some personal meanings for the listener. The listener may or may not react. If the decision is to react, then the listener becomes a potential sender who starts with an idea. . . (and so it goes).

The Significance of the Situation

Communication is situational. Words, tokens, and events have meaning because of the situation in which they occur. That pitcher with the ball is a communicator. He stands there holding the symbol of the game. He turns it, rubs it, hides it, and grips it to throw in a manner unknown to the batter. A ball is a ball. Five ounces of rubber or cork, twine and horse hide. That's what it is, but it's more than that, too. The first ball pitched has a different feeling and significance attached to it than the last one of the game. If a pitch turns into the home run that wins the series, it is priceless to the fan who catches it. What happens to that ball has economic, social, and emotional significance that is different for the pitcher, batter, manager, fan, and the army of technicians who publicize and profit from it. What that ball really is, is defined in many ways by those who respond to it. "Baseball" is a word. It is an object, a medium of expression, a form of communication, which becomes a process of human exchange.

Definitions tend to be boring. Try this one:

Baseball: a game played with a ball, bat, and gloves between 2 teams of
9 players each on a large field centering upon 4 bases that form the cor-

ners of a square 90 feet on each side, each team having a turn at bat and in the field during each of the 9 innings that constitute a normal game, the winner being the team that scores the most runs.[2]

That definition does not begin to conjure up the roar of the crowd, the smell of beer, hot dogs, and popcorn, the hypnosis of the television, or the betting and endless discussions and arguments about who is the best or what would happen if . . . You have to be there to appreciate the impact of the event. Words cannot adequately convey the nuances and subtleties that make the situation so meaningful.

The ball is a symbol, as are words. It has a meaning which depends heavily upon the situation. For each of us, the words and other symbols we use to communicate thoughts and feelings have meanings unique to us. Each of us is in our own situation. You have to be there to appreciate its significance. Only one person knows one's own situation. Others can surmise, and we hope they will try to understand. But personal situations are unique in their origins and influence.

Successful communication between two people depends upon the transmission of ideas as represented by words or other symbols *agreed upon and understood by both.* Understanding the meaning of words and other symbols depends upon knowing the situation in which these words and symbols are used. How do we begin to understand the situation in which these words and symbols are used? How do we begin to understand the situation unique to another person? How can we know the special pressures, needs, roles, and desires of the person with whom we wish to communicate? How do we empathize, "wear the shoes," or "get inside the skin" of another person? Our discussion in Chapter 7, on achieving greater sensitivity to individuals, suggested a number of obstacles to understanding, as well as methods of enhancing our understanding. Reducing our defensiveness, understanding our own biases, and careful specific listening can be good beginnings.

Keeping in mind that a person's situation is a mixture of needs, role expectations, and cultural pressures, we might ask ourselves the following questions to help focus on the total situation of a person to whom we wish to communicate.

This person is in the middle of a stream of events. What are they?
What deadlines or time pressures are being faced?
What distractions are being experienced?
Is my presence seen as an intrusion?
What is the relationship between us, as that person sees it?
What roles are being played now by each of us?
What does that person "need" to see or hear now?

[2] Definition from *Webster's Third New International Dictionary* (Springfield, Mass.: Merriam, 1971).

What are some special concerns that may be felt?
Are technical or human considerations more important?
What biases or blind spots are present?
What words are being used? What is their meaning to that person?
Do the verbal and nonverbal messages seem consistent?
How consistent has this person's behavior been in the past?
What can I do now that will be helpful to this person?

These are general questions. However, even if we had only partial answers they would help us understand and predict that person's future behavior. Each of us, as we begin the communication process, could think of other more specific questions. When we concentrate our thoughts on someone else's situation, we are less likely to be preoccupied with our concerns and may, therefore, be more open to what the person is trying to tell us. As a test of our understanding of that person's situation and their reaction to it, we might make short-range predictions and then see how accurate they are. For example, we might wonder: how will that person react to my suggestion, or offer of help, or request for help? Then we can proceed with our offers or requests and compare our predictions with what actually happens. We can use the scientific method of observation discussed in Chapter 1.

LISTENING FOR MEANING

Can you imagine two excellent listeners engaged in conversation? You can be sure it would not be an unbroken silence. Listening is an *active* skill. It requires intense concentration and much energy. The good listener pays *attention* and gives steady and reliable feedback to the speaker. The good listener attends to what the speaker is saying, what is not being said, and what the speaker wants to say but has difficulty articulating. The good listener tires more quickly than the speaker. You can be worn out with five minutes of this "unnatural" kind of activity!

How nice to be listened to. How hard to listen. If you have agreed with these two statements, you are quite typical in your humanness. We are attracted to the person who really listens to us, who seems interested in what we say and what we mean by what we say. We are drawn to the excellent listener as the moth to a light. We feel important because someone is listening to *us*. We feel respected by the listener. We feel a self-esteem because the listener seems to value us enough to want to know our thoughts, feelings, inclinations, and desires. How nice to be listened to. How tiresome to listen.

Obstacles to Listening

At work or play, we have worries, concerns, and interests with which we are understandably preoccupied. It could be our production record, financial concerns, worries about children, frustration in marriage, or an exciting idea or project in which we are totally absorbed. It can be a running stream of ideas and images which carries us along to the solution of a problem or a resolution of a conflict. Sometimes, it's more like a whirlpool in which we seem to just go round and round. We may suddenly remember an event or a person from years ago, and it seems to have no connection with anything else we were thinking about. It can be a nagging doubt or fear which makes it extremely difficult to concentrate on what we're trying to do at that moment. Lost in thought, we may or may not notice that someone is trying to talk to us. To listen means to abruptly shut off this background mental noise and "tune in" to the speaker; we may do this momentarily, then find ourselves back in that ongoing stream of consciousness. We half-listen. Because of the speed of the mind in flitting from one thing to another, we are able to dip in and out of the speaker's message and still follow the gist of it. Or do we? Our internal mental preoccupation with personal concerns acts like static on the radio, which obliterates part of the message and may distort the intended meaning. It's static which interferes with listening, but the speaker may not know it is happening.

Lack of interest in the speaker or the message, combined with an ongoing preoccupation with personal concerns, creates an effective obstacle to the listening process. Let us look more specifically at some of the internal conditions which keep us from being effective listeners:

1. Self-centeredness
2. Reluctance to become involved with others
3. Fear of having to change opinions
4. Desire to avoid the embarrassment of asking for clarification
5. Satisfaction with external appearances
6. Premature judgments of meaning
7. Semantic confusion

Self-centeredness. Self-involvement may be a way of life for some and for others only a temporary condition. The self-involved person may simply have never grown up. As children, we look to others for sources of personal gratification: "What will they do for us?" As mature adults, some of our finest moments come when we feel needed and can be helpful to others. Part of our definition of the professional person, in Chapter 7, was that the concerns of the client, or other person, were paramount. The self-centered person is more likely to demand that others listen, than to consent to listen to others. The salesperson who desperately needs a sale may not listen to the needs of the prospective customer. The manager whose primary concern is looking good in the eyes of superiors may not listen well to the needs and desires of the subordinates. Parents whose self-esteem depends upon their childrens' superior accomplishments may not listen to what the children feel their desires or talents may be. The physician who wants her daughter to go to medical school may be insensitive to the daughter's needs and capacities. The sales manager who wants his son to become a top salesperson may not listen to the son's protest that he wants to become a teacher. If, in any relationship, our needs, desires, and interests are paramount, we will be more inclined to tell or demand than to listen and accept.

Reluctance to Become Involved. Fear of risk inhibits listening. Self-involvement is one thing. To be involved with another is something else! To be drawn in or engrossed in a relationship can be a beautiful or dreadful experience. Since we cannot always be certain which it will be, involvement includes an element of risk. Listening means we are absorbed in the ideas, feelings, and intent of another person. This can mean feeling obligated and entangled in their life. To listen means to take the risk of getting involved with someone. The reluctance to become involved is one of the most common obstacles to listening. Why don't we want to become involved? There are many reasons:

1. Involvement provokes an uncertain reaction
2. Our self-image may be threatened
3. The freedom to become involved includes the freedom to fail
4. Involvement takes energy

If we take the initiative, moving toward someone to become involved in the listening process, there is always the risk that we may be rejected. Not everyone wants the close encounter called listening. They may not want to be known. With the uncertainty of reaction when we move towards others, it is understandable that reluctance to get involved becomes almost a national characteristic. Almost daily, newspapers carry accounts of bystanders who do not come to the aid of someone in distress. "I didn't want to get involved" is the frequent response. True, the witness to an accident or crime may face the inconvenience of testifying or the pressure of a television interview. We may avoid involvement with individuals in need because our own feelings will be aroused, and for some that will be uncomfortable. Close relationships are unpredictable. We can't control how that other person will feel or react to us! If loss of control frightens us, we will tend to avoid becoming a listener, for listening *is* an involvement with someone.

The image we have of ourselves is a mix between how we feel about ourselves *and* how others react to us. If we offer our interest and friendship and it is rejected, we may feel inferior and inadequate. This threat to our self-image may be enough to keep us from that personal involvement called "listening." It is true that keeping our distance will minimize the threat of discomfort, but at the same time it will prevent all the positive, human, loving consequences of involvement. But involvement with certain individuals can do much to increase our sense of self-worth and esteem. Many of us find strength and courage in seeking the help of a professional counselor. It is not the specific content of the conversation that leads to improved mental health or security as it is the deeply involved and trusting relationship which develops. To be listened to feels good; to be ignored, hurts. If someone appreciates our desire to listen, it makes us feel needed and trusted; if our desire to listen is seen as nosey interference, it can hurt. Needing to protect our self-image can become a defense mechanism preventing good listening.

Involvement is an act of freedom and responsibility. No one can involve us but ourselves. We freely become involved or are not involved at all. If we do become involved in a listening conversation, and it turns out badly, we can blame no one but ourselves for becoming involved in the first place. The freedom of choice includes the possibility of succeeding or failing. In this sense, freedom can be frightening. Listening can be frightening because we become responsible for the consequences of our choice. Indifference may be chosen over involvement precisely because it is an avoidance of responsibility. The free act of involvement and the distinct possibility of failure combine to make listening a form of human exchange with risks which some may wish to avoid.

At the end of a long, stressful, tiring day, you may not want to get involved in any further human exchange. But, if your day has been filled with irksome details and without human companionship, you may very much want to get involved. If these two sentences describe the day of two people living together, there may not be much good listening going on. The one who doesn't want to get involved will see the involvement need of the other as an invasion, an assault or, perhaps, just an annoyance. As stated before, it requires energy to get involved and to listen. It may not seem worth it. If an individual frequently is faced with a number of inner conflicts of values, interest, or feelings, so much energy may be used in trying to resolve these conflicts that little is left over for human involvement. Listening is hard work; sometimes we may not be up to it!

Fear of Change. If we really listen to someone, we may learn something. Learning means that it may be necessary to question the opinions we have and the ways in which we do things. This can be unsettling. So, often, we argue not to learn something but to try to change someone else's point of view. Occasionally, a point of honor is involved. We argue not to learn the truth but to win a kind of win-lose game. If "I'm right and you are wrong" is an attitude two or more people have as they enter a conversation, listening is unlikely. There is a kind of comfort in knowing that "My mind is made up!" Change can be exciting, but status quo, quite comforting. Why listen to someone else if we already know "What's what"?

Fear of Asking Questions.   Is it *embarrassing to ask?* Have you ever had a question you wanted to ask during a lecture or committee meeting, but didn't? Has someone ever told a joke you didn't get, but you laughed anyway? When everyone else seems to understand the point or the joke, we may be reluctant to ask for clarification. We hesitate to say, "I don't understand what you are saying. Would you explain?" This understandable reluctance to be embarrassed can become an obstacle to listening if we let it interfere with attempts to understand. If a point being made by the speaker is unclear, but we hesitate to ask for clarification, we may be so distracted by our sense of ignorance and reluctance to reveal that ignorance that we cease listening. The secure person will say, "I don't understand what you just said. Will you help me see it more clearly?" The insecure person will grin, nod, fidget, and pretend to understand but will also be creating an internal barrier to further listening.

Satisfaction with External Appearances.   We make a statement and see our conversation partner nod. If we're satisfied with that sign of understanding, we will fail to listen more intently to see if understanding does prevail. People do nod even though they do not understand. Statements are made that only begin to express how an individual thinks or feels. We can be satisfied that all has been said that needs to be said, or we can ask for more detail and listen for the clarification. Being satisfied with the brief, surface statement is characteristic of the poor listener. The good listener will probe and question and ask for more information, will ask for examples of the point the speaker is making, will want to know the meanings of the key words or phrases used by the speaker. Good listening means looking beyond the literal meanings of what is being said to see if additional information is being suggested. Rarely does a person express all that is thought or felt in the first sentence—or even two or three. If we interrupt after the first sentence, being satisfied that we know what the speaker intends, we may qualify as a very poor listener, indeed.

Premature Judgment.   This is a sure way of missing the full meaning of what is said. How often have you been interrupted by someone "listening" to you with their helpful completion of your sentence, restating it in a way you never intended? "Oh, I know what you mean," may be a clear signal that you are not being listened to. Uncertainty is unpleasant for most of us, and we tend to try to make things seem certain, even if they're not, to reduce the discomfort. Gross generalizations about people are made because that is easier than coping with the intricacies of individual differences. It is easier to generalize, for example, by describing a person as "dominant" than to realize that a specific person may be dominant only in certain situations, such as where a few people are involved, when they are of the opposite sex, when money is not involved, and when levels of education are the same; the same person may not be dominant in larger groups, where financial considerations are involved, or when a professionally trained specialist is present. Choosing the simple over the more complex, we may, at the same time, be choosing fantasy for reality. What is simple is not necessarily more clear. Life is complex. People are complex. We do not contribute to understanding by labeling people. Prejudice is fostered when we are satisfied with superficial appearances and engage in name-calling. Listening is fostered when we set aside quick judgments and over-simplified labels to attempt to understand the person who is trying to tell us something.

Semantic Confusion. Semantics is a study of the differing *connotations* of words that may have similar *denotative* meanings. The denotation of a word refers to the dictionary definition. It is what the word points to or explains. For example, "mother" is a female parent. But "Mother" suggests, implies, or represents emotional tones and implications, too. The connotation of "Mother" creates images that depend largely upon our experiences with our own mother. To different persons, "Mother" may mean, guilt, love, comfort, fear, threat, understanding, annihilation, or security. Again, the denotation of words can be looked up. The connotation must be understood through capable listening. Words are signs on paper or sounds in the air. We give meaning to words, and the meanings we give may differ from those given by others with whom we communicate. "It's all a question of semantics" is something we say when we think we are only dickering with words. But dickering with words may start wars or prevent them. Words and their different meanings can raise or lower morale, bring people together or blow them apart, enhance or inhibit understanding, and help or hinder human growth. Words and their meanings contribute to or detract from the human growth possible through social interaction. Let the statement, "It's all a question of semantics" instead alert us to the real world of people reacting to words whose meanings depend upon the *individual* in a certain *situation* at a certain *time*.

Improving the Listening Process

Communication is the transfer of knowledge and understanding from one person to another. Figures 8-1 and 8-2 illustrate how an idea, once expressed, goes through a stage where the sender loses control of the message and is dependent upon what the listener decides to do with it. The listener decides whether the sender's message should be ignored or not, gives meaning to the message, and is motivated accordingly. The listener is much more in charge of a conversation than the speaker. Listening is an active skill which grows stronger through exercise or atrophies through disuse. Good listening requires an active interest in the speaker and the message. An active interest cannot be pretended. It cannot be demanded. Genuine and sincere interest in what someone is saying, or trying to say, is an issue of self-motivation. We can exhort, *"Listen!"* but that does not make a person listen. Each of us is in charge of our own listening.

What can we do to become more effective listeners?:

1. Develop a willingness to listen
2. Listen longer
3. Listen more often
4. Listen with respect
5. Listen with feedback
6. Listen without premature evaluation and judgment
7. Use silence for thoughtful listening
8. Listen analytically
9. Listen without defensiveness
10. Listen with a minimum of biases and stereotypes
11. Listen to the nonverbal signals and look for inconsistencies

Willingness to Listen.   This is a matter of self-motivation. By definition, willingness cannot be faked. We can lean forward, open our eyes wide, put a smile on our face, and attempt a note of eagerness in our plea, "Tell me about it," but listening is a matter of comprehending the meanings being expressed by the other person, and comprehension cannot be faked. A well-known book on personnel-selection interviewing suggests the forward-leaning posture and smiling countenance as a way of convincing the speaker that you are interested in listening. At best it is a stratagem designed to make the speaker think you are listening. But, to emphasize again, such an effort on the part of the "listener" to appear to be listening can be so distracting that actual listening is inhibited! Willingness is an attitude. An attitude cannot be directly observed by others but can be directly experienced by the one possessing it. Willingness to listen is an inner condition. It is the degree of willingness experienced by the listener which determines whether the rest of the suggestions for more effective listening will be helpful or not.

Listening Longer.   This is one of the simplest and most basic rules of more effective listening. This means that we give the other person enough time to express views and feelings more fully before we interrupt with our own ideas. Isn't it irritating when someone breaks into the middle of our sentence when we are trying to say something? The good listener remembers how it feels to be interrupted and, perhaps, finds it easier to allow the speaker to take a little more time to find the words and illustrations to express the special meanings and nuances necessary to convey *both* information and understanding. But what do we do with the interminable speaker who seems to talk endlessly without conveying meaningful information? To simply listen longer can only prolong our own considerable agony. Can't we do something to help the speaker say it, get on with it, or come to the point? Point 5, "Listen with feedback," will provide some helpful suggestions.

Listening More Often. This is another way of saying that listening is a skill which must be practiced like any other skill. Listening may be practiced anywhere, anytime, without any special equipment or physical facility. All it takes is the attitude of readiness. There are a number of situations in which we deliberately can practice listening. Some of the more obvious times and places, of course, are close to home. The adage, "Children should be seen but not heard" sounds antiquated, but it reflects the lives of some modern parents, too. Telling, explaining, persuading, cajoling, demanding, and threatening may be more familiar parental activities than listening, helping, and supporting. "Why won't Johnnie clean up his room?" "Why won't Janie get off this boy craze and pay attention to her school work as she used to?" "Why does my child have to dress like a slob?" "What's gotten into these kids now-a-days, anyway?!" Much of the mystery may forever elude us, but some may become more understandable if we listen to what they say, even if we don't like what we hear.

Spouse-to-spouse listening is another opportunity for practice. Needing to tell, to explain, to control, and to persuade can lead both members of a marriage to feel emphatically, "I'm right and you're wrong. I'm good and you're bad. I'm OK and you're not OK.[3] Things would be better in our marriage if only you would change, and here's what I think you should do!" What an opportunity to practice listening in order to understand! If the husband and wife are competing with each other or are engaged in a power struggle to determine who really is head of the household, this conflict will make it difficult for either to listen to the other. The same situation may exist in an organizational setting where boss and subordinate find the power struggle too intense to allow listening. "I wonder what would motivate my employees to work harder and more conscientiously" is a question which logically could be followed by, "Have you asked them?" Strange how often the answer is "No."

---

[3] Transactional Analysis is one approach to understanding the interactions between people. For a discussion of TA concepts applied to organizations, see: Dorothy Jongeward, *Everybody Wins: Transactional Analysis Applied to Organizations* (Reading, Mass.: Addison-Wesley, 1973).

Listening to the parking-lot attendant may create a level of interest and intimacy which makes your car slightly special and worthy of a little more care in its handling. Listening to the receptionist may help connect you to the company grapevine and all the useful information transmitted by it. Listening to the news commentator may alert you to the inconsistencies and absolute lack of logic being expressed. Listen more often! It's a skill that can add to our knowledge, our ability to predict human behavior, and the ultimate control over our lives, which we discussed in Chapter 1.

Listening with Respect. This is more of an attitude than a technique. It suggests that we have a sense of regard, worth, and esteem for the speaker. That respect may come from our perception of the status, power, or position of the speaker, in which case it is a conditional respect. Or, respect may come from a belief that all humans are "endowed by their Creator with certain inalienable rights," one of which is the right to be listened to. If our interest is in being professional in our dealings with others, then it would be consistent to search actively for qualities in the speaker we might respect. Certainly a feeling of respect for the speaker will give added impact to our assertive listening.

Listening with Feedback. The speaker will have a better idea of how well the message is being understood if you do this. Feedback is necessary for effective learning. We need to see, or feel, or realize the effect of our efforts in order to modify those efforts toward greater effectiveness. The good listener will interrupt the speaker to attempt clarification of what the speaker intends. Ordinarily, this will not be considered rude. However, to interrupt in order to change the subject, or talk about what you want to talk about, may be quite upsetting to the speaker and result in a communication breakdown. There are four types of feedback, some more helpful than others.

Perhaps the most common and least effective form of feedback is for the listener to say, "I know what you mean." The speaker reacts to this kind of feedback by saying, "*Do* you know what I mean?" In either case, false assumptions of understanding easily may occur. We may think we understand when in fact, we don't. We may not understand but be unwilling to indicate this to the speaker. This first type of feedback may be entirely nonverbal, as with a nod of the head. Nodding our head rapidly up and down is feedback to the speaker that we understand. In fact, we may be nodding only to indicate that we want the speaker to get on with it and tell us the message.

A second form of listening feedback is to put into your own words what you think the speaker means. This can be done in the form of a memo sent to the manager of your department indicating your understanding of what is expected of you. Repeating to the speaker the exact words used in the message may not indicate that the listener does understand. In fact, it may be perceived as a taunt: a poll-parrot.

A third and much more effective form of feedback is to form an example of how you would intend to use the idea you have just heard. We may be able to repeat the speaker's idea in our own words even if we do not have a full understanding of it, but it is more difficult to give an example if we do not understand. Giving examples, illustrations, and anecdotes reflecting the use or application of the speaker's ideas is more helpful feedback.

The fourth, and ultimately the best form of feedback, is to carry out the action requested by the speaker. We communicate in order to change behavior, either immediately or later. For the speaker, whether teacher, coach, or manager, to see the student, player, or subordinate carry out the intended actions is a reassuring and usually gratifying form of feedback. This fourth type of feedback may take a long time. It may be years before we see whether or not the student's behavior reflects what was listened to in the classroom. At the time, the teacher may simply say, "Are there any questions?," and hearing none may blissfully assume understanding and move on to another subject. We wonder how often these false assumptions of understanding permeate all our organizations from the home and classroom to businesses, nonprofit groups, and political bodies?

Listening without Premature Evaluation. This is sound advice, but not for the person whose mind is made up and does not want to be bothered by facts. Preevaluation or prejudice means forming conclusions and making decisions prior to gaining specific knowledge that would have a bearing on the decisions or conclusions made. A judgment can be so final! We began this volume with a scene from a court of law, in which we were being asked to tell the truth, the whole truth, and nothing but the truth. Do we ever know the whole truth about much of anything? Probably not. Especially where humans are involved. Listening is that assertive procedure which allows us to conduct a scientific investigation of the facts before we make a judgment or come to a conclusion. The scientist delays judgment until the data are collected and analyzed. The nonscientist may make a judgment and then listen for those facts which seem to support that initial judgment, while excluding or not listening to facts contrary to the judgment. Good listening is scientific with delayed judgment. The human tendency is to search for the easy, early answer. The professional, scientific human being recognizes that there are two, three, or more sides to an issue and listens long enough without jumping to a conclusion so that the final conclusion reached is based on the most reliable and valid information available.

Listening Analytically. Here is another way of describing the scientific method of inquiry introduced in Chapter 1. Analysis is "a detailed examination of anything complex made in order to understand its nature or to determine its essential features . . ." (*Webster's Third New International Dictionary*). The analytic listener begins to form hypotheses while the speaker talks. "What are the issues, the intent, the logic, the contradictions, the claims without support?" are some of the questions the analytic listener may mentally formulate during a presentation. In the personnel-selection interview, the listener may compare the job requirements with the evidence of past work experience being expressed by the candidate for the job. Following the scientific spirit, the listener will think, "If the speaker means what is being said, then the underlying values must be thus and so." And if this is the case, later statements on another subject should follow a predictable pattern. Continued listening then has as its aim the testing of such hypotheses. Do the later facts support the hypotheses or fail to support them? We are thus engaged in analytic listening.

Listening without Defensiveness. This is a super human task. Defensiveness makes up a large part of our daily patterns of interaction. We want to defend our self-image against attack. We want to defend ourselves against awareness of needs and motives we find unacceptable. We need to defend our status positions and protect our sources of power and influence over others. Yet, defensiveness tends to blind us to others and what they are trying to express. To the extent that two people in a conversation both think, "I'm right and you're wrong. I'm good and you're bad," basic interpersonal conflict will prevent much listening. While defensiveness is common and seems to be part of normal living, we may not be aware of what it is we are defending. If the speaker mentions something with which you basically disagree, you may not only disagree, but think you must disprove the point in order to preserve your honor, your status, your adequacy as a man or woman, or to save face in your social situation. But are these important issues of status, adequacy, or face saving really under attack just because someone has a point of view different than yours? Does our sense of adequacy as a person depend upon *always* being right and "winning" the argument? If a disagreement over a point of opinion threatens our basic sense of adequacy, then our inner conviction of adequacy may be very weak, indeed. Perhaps, we need to build this sense of adequacy through competence and earned achievement rather than through "winning" debates of questionable importance.

Listening with a Minimum of Biases and Stereotypes. This, too, is a larger-than-life task, for it demands that we understand fully those familial, social, and cultural influences which have shaped our lives. Chapters 2, 3, and 4 helped provide that background of information and understanding of our many selves which could help us grow in our listening capacity. We need to minimize the effect of those learned biases and stereotypes which distort our listening perception. It is doubtful that we can ever completely rid ourselves of these mental distortions. It will help if we can identify when and how we allow ourselves to be swayed by our background. The accuracy with which we respond to a unique human, within the present time and situation, depends upon our own relative freedom from bias. The effective listener is aware of when past experiences enter into the present listening efforts to alter, detract from, or add to the intended meanings of the speaker. Humans seem to be introspective creatures. It is critical that we use our best and most scientific introspection as we attempt to understand the meanings intended by those to whom we listen.

Listening in Silence. This may seem to contradict the suggestion of listening with feedback. Silence may be used in the active sense. If a silence occurs in an interchange, we can reflect on what the speaker has said, on our reaction to it; on what seems to have been left unsaid; on what we know for sure versus what we infer; on what may be causing the present silence and how we and the speaker seem to be reacting to it. A prolonged silence (more than 4 or 5 seconds) makes some individuals uneasy, so uneasy that things may often be said that are neither relevant nor logical. "Meaningless" chatter often is used to fill the emotional void of silence. Silence may, sometimes, mean disapproval or rejection. Depending upon the relationship, silence may also convey warm acceptance. A popular notion is that we have the capacity to listen and understand information several times faster than we can speak. Most of us have had the experience of listening to a speaker and tuning in and out, taking mental side trips, reflecting on the connections between what we are hearing and what we have heard or read before, and still follow the message. This mental agility may be used to advantage during the listening process. We may use silence to give the speaker more time to convey the message; we may analyze the content and method of delivery; we may reflect on our rising or lowering defensiveness and ponder the effects of our cultural heritage on our present behavior. We may even use silence to savor and enjoy the sensations and feelings we are experiencing as we compliment the good speaker by being a respectful listener.

Listening to the Nonverbal Signals and Looking for Inconsistencies. We cannot *not* communicate. Our presence, our posture, gestures, clothing, facial expressions, physical distance, groans, sighs, or other vocal but nonverbal signals all communicate something to those in our presence. Nonverbal communication cannot only be listened to, it can be seen, sensed through touch, smell, sounds, the timing and sequence of actions, and the setting in which it takes place. We may avoid talking, but we cannot avoid communicating by our behavior. Nonverbal communication frequently conflicts with and contradicts verbal communication. We may more often believe the nonverbal message when it conflicts with a verbal one. Our red face may be more believable than our denial of embarrassment. Our shaking hand may reveal the tension we say we are not experiencing. The too quick smile and its quick disappearance does not seem consistent with our statement of how pleased we are to be in the presence of another. Much information is now available concerning the extent of human communication without words.[4]

Two conclusions should occur to us as we think about nonverbal communication: nonverbal communication is a powerful addition to that repertoire of word-symbols we use to convey understanding and exercise influence; nonverbal communication often contradicts our verbal messages and, without realizing it, reveals a truer account of our intentions. "Show and tell" combines the verbal and nonverbal languages; actions sometimes speak so loudly we cannot hear what is said.

Just as words have only the meanings we give them, actions, too, are personal. We use words to convey the meanings we associate with them, not the meanings printed in the dictionary. Oh, sure, sometimes when we argue over the meaning of a word, we turn to a dictionary and scan the multiple denotations to find the one closest to what we meant. In the same way, our gestures and body movements convey personal messages—personal in that they reflect our unique experiences in our family, work, and social groups. Drumming fingers may suggest impatience for many, but not for all. Arms folded may suggest a closed mind or a determined opinion, but for others it may be simply a means of changing posture or relaxing. "Listening" to nonverbal signals requires the same open-minded curiosity and delayed judgment necessary when listening to words. Individuals communicate with a set of words and nonverbal signals from their own "private" dictionaries—"private" in the sense that words and actions come from our lifetimes of unique experiences.

INTIMACY AND ALIENATION

Of the many dilemmas in human relationships, perhaps the greatest is the dilemma of needing to be close to others but fearing to get too close. As we consider the problems, principles, and opportunities involved in understanding and influencing human behavior, we face the conflicting conditions of intimacy and alienation. Intimacy is that closeness of relationship based on a depth of knowledge and understanding which leads not only to friendships or unusual ties of love but also to the security and serenity of trusting how another will act. Alienation is a feeling of

---

[4] Marianne LaFrance and Clara Mayo, *Moving Bodies: Nonverbal Communication in Social Relationships* (Monterey, Calif: Brooks/Cole, 1978).

separateness or isolation, which can make life meaningless and without direction. It has its ultimate expression in the act of suicide.[5] But alienation can also be considered a chronic condition of withdrawal from life, of self-defeating or self-destructive activities which lead to a living death. Survival, perhaps, but not aliveness. An "alien" is someone foreign to the land. The alienated person does not feel at home. Does not feel a connectedness with family, the work situation, or life itself. Does not *feel* in the normal, healthy sense. Many talk about our society as being alienated: alienated from the ecological demands and requirements of our planet Earth; full of individuals alienated from the institutions of their society; and run by businesses and governments alienated from each other. Youth feels alienated from their elders and the "Establishment."

Employment, for many, heightens the sense of alienation. Work specialization—which involves assigning individuals a small part of the overall task of producing products and services—was designed to increase efficiency but often produces alienation, too. The efforts of many highly trained specialists are necessary for the design, parts manufacture, assembly, delivery, and sales of a radio, for example. Soldering one connection in the radio on the assembly line may be the single function of a worker, who repeats this endlessly. While some skill training is necessary, such a worker can be replaced easily; that worker may fail to see much meaning in the task or sense any personal importance while doing it.[6] White-collar workers, technicians, managers, and even some who work in professions may face a similar routine, limited in scope and meaning. The very size of business and government organizations with huge numbers of employees makes it difficult to avoid feeling lost or unimportant. The solution to these feelings of insignificance lies not in returning to the pre-Industrial Revolution style of life but in making personal choices and in reorganizing the work itself.

For many who are employed, but by no means all, the work itself is not sufficiently challenging, mentally. There may not be the opportunity to use one's skills and experience; new learning may be limited; the work may lack variety and responsibility; arbitrary decisions regarding the work may be made without consulting the employee; creativity may not only be discouraged but forbidden. Results? Boredom replaces interest. Lethargy stifles initiative. Passivity discourages assertiveness.

---

[5] The sociologist Emile Durkheim thought that one factor contributing to suicide was an unresolvable discrepancy between one's aspirations in life and the means and opportunities of achieving them. See: Emile Durkheim, *Suicide: A Study in Sociology* (New York: Free Press, 1951).

[6] For a discussion on meaningless, alienation, and the individual's ability to cope, see Eric Klinger, *Meaning and Void: Inner Experience and the Incentives in People's Lives* (Minneapolis: University of Minneapolis, 1977).

Reorganizing the work and work situation may increase a sense of identification and involvement, especially if it is possible to work on or complete the "whole" job. Assembling an entire radio seems to be more satisfying than putting together only a part. Being part of a project team, following the process from problem identification to solution to implementation, is usually more satisfying than working blindly on only one step of the process. Seeing the larger meaning of what we do may decrease the sense of alienation. Being able to participate in decisions affecting our work may decrease the sense of alienation. Receiving feedback on the effect of our work, its efficiency and its worth, may further decrease the feeling of alienation. Being assigned to work which fits our interests and aptitudes will encourage involvement and identification with the product or service being offered. But with all these structural and process changes, the individual still retains the basic choice of responding to the situation with involvement or with alienation.

To feel needed, to see the direct connection between one's efforts and some result which seems necessary and important, and to feel a sense of belonging and closeness, are still matters of personal choice, even in our automated, large-scale, fast-moving society. Human exchange, in its richness and depth, is a matter of personal choice. With courage we can move *toward* others and exchange values, beliefs, and feelings. With fear we may move *away* from others into a life of routine, meaninglessness, and void. The choice is an important one. But there are risks involved.

Risk and Growth Through Intimacy

We have seen how reluctance to become involved can be an obstacle to effective listening. The fear of involvement and intimacy deprives us of the basic human need for inclusion. These fears become profoundly self-defeating in our quest to understand, predict, and influence human behavior. Communication is a process of human exchange. We cannot communicate in a void. Without the human exchange of values, of consideration and respect, of care, concern, and affection, much is lost. Without extensive emotional and spiritual exchange between individuals who work or live together, it is difficult if not impossible to achieve that level of understanding necessary for prediction and coordination of efforts.

The risk of involvement and intimacy may seem obvious; what may be less obvious is the risk of *not* becoming involved. Intimate involvement with others allows specific, direct, and detailed feedback which may enhance our humanness. The professional counselor provides positive, caring feedback to clients who are made more aware of the consequences of their behavior. This is a growth experience. Without the intimate help from caring friends, we are likely to continue making the same individual and group mistakes which historians faithfully report. In management, child rearing, friendships, and in all human contacts, the ability of the participants to become involved is necessary for the achievement of mutual self-fulfillment. In a therapeutic conversation, it is not so much the specific content which helps lead the patient to improved mental health as the fact that an experience of personal involvement—with the therapist—has become possible. It is the counselor's sense of self-worth and lack of fear of emotional involvement that encourages the client to experiment with health-inducing involvement.

Managers may avoid becoming too close to their subordinates for fear they may take advantage of that closeness to ask for special considerations. The manager may fear that the subordinate will not attempt to reach expected work standards if a close friendship is developed. "Familiarity breeds contempt" is a creed believed by many who are convinced that social and emotional distance between managers and subordinates is essential to maintain the integrity of the work relationship. However, the manager who is not close may fail to understand the needs and motivations of the subordinates and find it difficult to predict their work behavior. This dilemma may be resolved by recognizing there are at least two problems: one is determining the appropriate depth of the involvement; the other is holding subordinates accountable to work standards. Managers who feel secure in their self-confidence and are not frightened by involvement often find they can be self-disciplined enough to maintain high standards and hold their subordinates strictly accountable to those standards.

Eric Fromm, in his classic book *The Art of Loving*, discusses the importance of loving ourselves as a precondition to loving others. Love includes the concepts of caring, of being concerned for the welfare of others, feeling respect for them, maintaining a sense of responsibility *to* them, and desiring to know them better. Parents who love in this full sense will be quick to help their children realize the consequences of their behavior: their children will be held accountable to certain standards of behavior precisely because the parents experience a loving, caring concern for their continued growth. Parents who experience self-doubt, low self-worth, guilt or an excessive and inappropriate need to be liked by their children at all times may well hesitate to discipline them. Such parents may learn to be afraid of their children and emotionally withdraw from them, eventually becoming indifferent to and alienated from them. These emotionally abandoned children have a higher probability of becoming emotionally deprived adults because of their relatively low ability to cope with the complexities and demands of social life.

The Costs and Benefits of Self-disclosure

Self-disclosure is that process of making yourself known to others. It may be deliberate or unwitting. There may be things about ourselves that we do not want others to know, but which we reveal unintentionally. For example, our nervousness before making a speech or giving a report may be something we wish to hide; but our trembling hands and cracking voice manifest our nervousness anyway. By the time we reach adulthood, we acquire skills in masking our feelings and concealing our motives. But, we don't always succeed. Our attempts to maintain a "poker face" may conceal our true feelings, but others are likely to sense that we are covering up *something*. We succeed in masking the truth about ourselves, but others perceive us as being deceitful. The lowering of trust in these relationships is just one of the costs.

Another cost of dissembling or hiding under a false appearance is that the energy and concentration necessary interferes with our ability accurately to perceive and understand others. Covering our face to hide feelings prevents us from seeing how others are reacting. An even more insidious cost of hiding from others is that we increasingly hide from ourselves. Pretending to others easily leads to pretending to ourselves. Knowing less and less of the truth about ourselves cripples our ability to understand, predict, and influence the behavior of others.

The person who finds it hard to practice self-disclosure is much more likely to experience poor mental health. Low self-disclosers are more likely to experience inner stress associated with heart attacks and other physical breakdowns. How can we calculate these costs, as well as the cost of loneliness, which inevitably accompanies low self-disclosure? They are high.

Deliberately, assertively, and consistently disclosing our self—what we feel and believe, what we value, and how we are responding to others—is the strategy of living which most directly leads to the primary aim discussed in this book: understanding, predicting, and influencing human behavior. The high self-discloser more accurately perceives his or her many selves, the sociocultural situation in which human events take place, and the many ways others respond. The high self-discloser will more often be perceived as authentic and will thereby be more trusted. Others are more likely to reveal more of their true selves in the presence of a high self-discloser. And because the high self-discloser has less to hide, feelings of security and serenity will prevail.

Self-disclosure is a risky choice. There is some probability that those to whom we reveal ourselves will reject us, condemn us, and use that knowledge against us. Many of us have the underlying fear that if others knew our true selves they wouldn't like us as much. But the probabilities are in our favor if we choose to be authentic and live with integrity. As two people learn more about each other, the probabilities are high that the relationship will become more positive.

COMMUNICATION AND HUMAN GROWTH

Three of our most basic human needs are inclusion, affection, and control. We need to be included as a valued member of a group or, at least, one personal relationship. We need to give and receive love and affection. And we need that sense of control which comes when we are able to influence others and be influenced by them for mutual gain. Communication is that people process by which we satisfy these basic needs. Communication is the exchange of information *and* understanding that makes it possible for humans to help or hurt each other. It may be that both our greatest strength and weakness is this capacity to choose.

SUMMARY

That process of human exchange we call communication gives us the cloak of culture, which we never remove. It shapes our identity and motivates us. It is the process of exchange which gives us the choice of self-enhancing or self-defeating reactions. It is the exchange of information and understanding which allows us to predict and influence our own behavior and that of others. Words and events have meaning because of the situation in which they occur, and listening is that active communication skill that allows us to reach for an understanding of what others mean by what they say and do.

Listening is that empathic process that allows us to enter partially the personal world of others and see it as they do; it is a way of showing our regard and respect for them. It is an involvement with others that includes both risks and benefits. It is a human dilemma that we both need to be close to others yet fear getting too close. How we individually resolve that dilemma largely determines our personal rate of growth or decay.

QUESTIONS FOR REVIEW AND DISCUSSION:

1. Our ability to communicate with others depends upon our awareness of their situation. What can we do to become more sensitive to the other person's total situation.?

2.   Why is psychological, emotional, and spiritual involvement with others potentially so frightening?

3.   Good listening is an attitude as well as a technique. Discuss.

4.   We communicate verbally and non-verbally. Give an example of how nonverbal communication may have a greater impact than verbal communication.

5.   It is said that we cannot not communicate. Give an example and discuss the implications.

Index